Western Rationality
and the
Angel of Dreams

Western Rationality and the Angel of Dreams

Self, Psyche, Dreaming

Murray L. Wax

ROWMAN & LITTLEFIELD PUBLISHERS, INC.
Lanham • Boulder • New York • Oxford

ROWMAN & LITTLEFIELD PUBLISHERS, INC.

Published in the United States of America
by Rowman & Littlefield Publishers, Inc.
4720 Boston Way, Lanham, Maryland 20706

12 Hid's Copse Road
Cumnor Hill, Oxford OX2 9JJ, England

British Library Cataloguing in Publication Information Available

Library of Congress Cataloging-in-Publication Data
Wax, Murray Lionel, 1922–
    Western rationality and the angel of dreams : self, psyche,
dreaming / Murray L. Wax.
        p.   cm.
    Includes bibliographical references and index.
    ISBN 0–8476–9374–0 (alk. paper). — ISBN 0–8476–9375–9 (pbk. :
alk. paper)
    1. Dreams.   2. Dream interpretation.   3. Freud, Sigmund,
1856–1939.   I. Title.
BF1078.W38   1999
154.6'—dc21   99–10344
                                                                   CIP

Printed in the United States of America

♾ ™The paper used in this publication meets the minimum requirements of
American National Standard for Information Sciences—Permanence of Paper
for Printed Library Materials, ANSI Z39.48–1992.

Contents

v

Acknowledgments

For assistance with German: Erika Bourguignon, Ph.D., and Elizabeth W. Trahan, Ph.D.

For assistance with French: Valerie Agosta, Ph.D.

For critical and imaginative readings of the text: Joan Cassell, Ph.D., and Roy M. Mendelsohn, M.D.

For advice and encouragement: Jonathan A. Cohen, M.D., and Patrick J. Mahony, Ph.D.

For guidance toward sociological and practical realities, my life long friend: Leo J. Shapiro, Ph.D.

Portions of chapter 4 were published in "Interpreting Dreams: Joseph, Freud, and the Judaic Tradition," *Journal of Psychology and Judaism* 22, no. 1 (Spring 1998):21–32. Portions of chapter 6 were published in "Who Are the *Irma*s: What Are Their Narratives?" *Journal of the American Academy of Psychoanalysis* 24, no. 2 (Summer 1996):293–320.

Western Rationality

The reason why dreamers can't understand what their dreams mean, and why we have such difficulty in constructing adequate accounts of what they might have meant, is that they didn't mean anything.
—David Foulkes, *Dreaming: A Cognitive-Psychological Analysis,* 1985

And the Angel of Dreams

Let us learn to dream, gentlemen, and then we may perhaps find the truth.
—Friedrich Kekulé, 1890, who revolutionized organic chemistry by his discovery in a dream of the structure of the benzene molecule

Introduction

Nine Theses on Dreaming

When I came to the restudy of dreams, I began with two salient texts: Freud's *Fragment of the Analysis of a Case of Hysteria,* the case of "Dora"; and chapter 2 of *The Interpretation of Dreams,* "the analysis of a specimen dream: 'Irma's Injection.'" I did not just reread these texts with a critical eye but listened with "the third ear" (to use the happy phrase of Theodor Reik). The interpretive process was intensified because I was assigning these materials in a university class in comparative social psychology, where I was conversing with bright and skeptical undergraduates.

My understanding was helped by the ability to confront the texts in the original German; this was hardly essential, but Freud's texts evoked images from the Yiddish of my childhood, so that I could sense nuances not apparent to Anglophones confined to the "authorized" (Strachey) translations. Facing a class of students, I was encouraged to reflect deeply on the texts, and, as I did so, I was appalled at Freud's treatment of "Dora": not only at his lack of insight but at a clinical posture that was remarkably unsympathetic and doctrinaire. This was especially apparent in his misinterpretations of the two dreams she had brought to their work. Then, when I turned to his own dream of "Irma's Injection," I realized that he had also missed its most significant aspects.

When I turned for assistance to the English translations and interpretations, I was appalled. As a radical innovator, Freud's missteps could be understood; however enlightened in some characteristics, he was a product of a particular time and place. Nevertheless, the dynamic of scientific and scholarly disciplines is that the missteps of one generation are noted and corrected by the subsequent. Instead, I found cultic worship. The first edition of *Die Traumdeutung* (*The Interpretation of Dreams*) appeared

1

in 1900, and the book subsequently went through many editions with re-
visions and commentaries. None mentioned the absences in Freud's interpretation of "the specimen dream" of "Irma's Injection." The first edition of the case of "Dora" was published in 1905, and it too went through
multiple republications. The 1963 preface by Philip Rieff to the authorized English edition is replete with such comments as "[Freud's] mind
moved with breathtaking speed and accuracy." Peter Brooks (1993) com-
pares Freud to Sherlock Holmes (further praise—past and present—
is cited in chapter 7 on "Dora"). In countering this reverence with a thoroughly researched restudy of the case, Patrick J. Mahony, a trained and
experienced psychoanalyst, found it appropriate to introduce his text
with the epigraph: "Cowardice puts on prudence as a ready mask.
Courage simply is—and does not like being worn."

Freud had died in 1939, but only with the comments of Erik H. Erikson in a 1954 essay (earlier a lecture to his colleagues) was the gateway
opened to a reinterpretation of "Irma's Injection." A few years later, Erikson opened the door to critical reevaluation of the case of "Dora." Erikson was now of great stature within both the psychoanalytic profession
and the larger intellectual world. As a former resident of Vienna, analyzed by Anna Freud, Erikson had abundant credentials. Moreover, he
could speak from an intimate knowledge of the Freud family and its milieu, as well as his cross-cultural researches among children and adolescents. Retrospectively, one is glad that someone of his status could begin
the process of clarification and reinterpretation. The tempered nature of
his criticisms and revelations is revealing. The familiarity with the history
of the psychoanalytic movement would have informed him that, no matter how illustrious the credentials, no matter how close to Freud and his
family, a thinker (such as Ferenczi, Rank, Reich, Adler, Stekel, Jung)
would be disciplined or ostracized if he were regarded as departing from
what had become dogma.

Erikson's shaded comments confirmed my own interpretations of the
dreams of Freud and Dora. Of course, I also consulted the secondary literatures, which were abundant. As Erikson commented, analysts knew
these materials by heart; many were driven to comment, but until recently—and then only with a minority—their efforts lacked the critical
insight that one would have expected from within a community of psy-
choanalytically trained scholars. It was the disproportion between what I
was perceiving in the dreams (and texts) and what was stated in much psychoanalytic literature (as recently as the 1998 collection edited by Matthis
and Szecsödy) that then led toward the writing of this book.

Once embarked on this project, I found that I had to rethink the entire argument. I was assisted considerably by the interdisciplinary breadth
and depth of my university training, the variety of my subsequent re-

searches, and the colleagueship of Joan Cassell and Roy M. Mendelsohn, as well as correspondence with Jonathan A. Cohen.

For those readers who wish to begin the book by viewing the underlying logic of my argument, I outline its theses as follows.

First, dreaming is universal in history and among all the peoples of the world. To explain or understand so universal a phenomenon, we must view it within the context of human life as it has evolved. Human beings live a group life and so reproduce themselves. It is therefore a cardinal error to attempt to understand dreaming as if it were simply and solely the physiological activity of an isolated sleeping individual, rather than a participant in group life.

Second, although human beings have their rational moments, human group life is not merely the association of an aggregate of rational or cognitive instruments—"wet computers," in the jargon of artificial intelligence. If one regards dreaming as the activity of "a mind" viewed as a cognitive instrument, one would logically then conclude—as do prominent investigators—that dreams are meaningless, being the equivalent of random noise in the nervous system. Dreaming can only be appreciated and understood when viewed in relationship to the range of activities of psyche-and-soma (mind-and-body), which include the aesthetic, visionary, ritual, and ceremonial aspects of group living. Dreams are most akin to the plastic and narrative arts.

Third, it is plausible that other animal species experience dreams. However, when we discuss and interpret human dreams, we are dealing with phenomena narrated in *language*. Human group life is based on natural language, which has the potentiality for complex intercommunication beyond bodily gesture and response.

Fourth, within a domestic nucleus—a "primary group"—children acquire language, and, as they do so, they also develop (human) *selves*. So viewed, the *self* is a social product, and not simply a physiological mechanism. The self emerges from a *mirroring* process, but the mirroring is social, not simply ocular (the physical reflection of an animal form).

Fifth, the dream can only appear because major functions of the self have been suspended or diminished. A similar suspension may occur under a variety of other circumstances, such as prolonged meditation. Because the mnemonic capacities of *the self* are diminished in dreaming, amnesia for dreams is typical, unless the dream is translated into speech or other deliberate countermeasures are adopted (e.g., recording the dream with pen and paper).

Sixth, "altered states of consciousness," or states of "flow," or intoxication, are labels for other instances in which functions of *the self* are suspended or minimized. These range from total involvement in a creative performance to erotic, drug-induced, sadomasochistic, tranquilized, or hypnotized states by techniques such as repetitive chanting, drumming, and dancing. Theories of dreaming must be sensitive to that parallel context.

Seventh, *free association* that is truly "free" (i.e., in an atmosphere of trust, frankness, emotional openness) will bypass some of the control of the self. If the dream is there reinvoked, its significances may become transparent, but this is no more an interpretation or translation than is a response to an aesthetic object: painting, dance, poem, musical composition.

Eighth, group life presumes emotional intercommunication on levels beyond the operations of the self systems of the participants. Because dreams can point to distortion and miscommunication, their appearance may be welcomed and their roles appreciated, as in many small communities, especially of non-Western peoples. However, even in communities of trust—and particularly in situations of mistrust—there can also be *mis*interpretation of dreams. Ritual and clinical encounters offer testimony of both processes.

Finally, emotional development is cumulative and hierarchical, proceeding on the basis of earlier experiences. This is manifest in the process of understanding the significances of a dream, as each character in the dream theater may embody several others, and each symbolic object may have a range of meanings.

The range of these theses is grand, but the book is modest in size; in trying to encompass that range, it is necessarily uneven, somewhat disjointed. I elaborate where I can, and where I cannot, then I must elide. While my background is interdisciplinary, my abilities and experiences are finite.

PART ONE
SELF, PSYCHE, DREAMING

Chapter 1

Evolutionary and Cross-Cultural Perspectives on Dreaming and Social Life

Harmony and Attunement: Psychic Mechanisms

White man got no dreaming,
Him go 'nother way.
White man, him go different,
Him got road belong himself.

> (Australian Aborigine explaining *the dreaming* to Stanner, 1956)

Returning from fieldwork among small exotic groups, anthropologists have stories: narratives of being swept into vibrant and dense emotional life; acquiring relatives and friends, rivals and enemies; being subjected to potent states of love, hate, fear, anxiety, security, and trust. Living in these small groups is not paradisiacal, but it is quintessentially human.

Far from being effortless, group living requires psychic and emotional labor—not only working and sharing, giving and receiving, but treating one's fellows with consideration and concern, even under severe provocation. Failure—or the threat of failure—to be regarded as a respected member of the group provides an inner discipline. Individuals may be targeted as witches, sorcerers, or other malign influences, who then may suffer ostracism, punishment, or death (a dramatic illustration is described in Briggs 1970).

To maintain harmony and cohesion, to ease the cooperation of men with men, women with women, people with people, small groups rely on a handful of interpersonal devices. Not all groups use all devices, but each relies on some. The universal is dreaming, about which much more will be said in this book. Frequent is the reciting of dreams to intimates, leading to discussions of their portent and meaning. Also frequent is the

7

seeking of visions; the search may be incumbent upon all young males or all members of the group or the special requirement of those who would heal the afflicted or provide guidance in states of group crisis. Additionally, there are the trance, ritual, ceremonial, and the narration of myth, to be discussed later.

Dreaming as a Social Event?

The milk tree is the place of all mothers of the lineage . . . where our ancestress slept when she was initiated. "Initiate" means the dancing of women around and around the milk tree where the novice sleeps. One ancestress after another slept there down to our grandmother and our mother and ourselves the children. That is the place of our tribal custom: where we began, even men just the same, for men are circumcised under a milk tree. (Ndembu ritual specialist talking to Victor Turner 1958/1967:21)

Informing the dreamer as to the events and intercourse by which the group was conceived, dreams orient to the emotional reality that is encountered daily. As sources of knowledge and guidance, dreams are above and beyond—superior to—what is experienced and learned in mundane activities. While Western scientists think of dreams as arising from the nervous system of the dreamer, these small groups regard them as messages through the dreamer, and possibly about him or her, from the significant beings of the world (deities, in Western parlance). A troubled person—or a person in transition from one status to another—will deliberately seek for the guidance of a dream or vision, although counsel may also emerge without conscious seeking. In the Hebrew Bible are several incidents of visionary experiences—nocturnal messages not always labeled as dreams.[1]

Considering these phenomena seriously, rather than dismissing them as reflecting collective ignorance or psychopathology, one realizes that the significance—and meaning—of dreams must be sought not in the private but in the social and interpersonal realms. This seems a profound paradox—certainly within the biomedical paradigm—since dreams are private affairs, occurring on an inner screen when the person is withdrawn from social intercourse, the body not under voluntary control. Augmenting the paradox is the powerful intellectual tradition that is skeptical about the possibility of dreams having either function or meaning. Its contemporary representatives think of dreams as random activity of the nervous system, like an engine idling. In contrast, there are the mystics of the counterculture who hope through dreams to gain access to a superior reality. Both parties—skeptics and mystics—unite in viewing dreams from an individualistic perspective. Nevertheless, both skeptics and mystics are misoriented (or drastically incomplete) in their views because they have been approaching dreams from the traditional Western view of the isolated and autonomous individual.

In its approach to morality, knowing, and dreaming, Western intellectual thought has been dominated by an ontology in which only the individual is real, and society secondary, even artificial. Hobbes, Rousseau, Leibnitz, Locke, and numerous others wrote as if organized society were the problematic, while the individual could be taken for granted. So, too, Freud, who developed a marvelous—and murderous—myth to account for the existence of society, and an equally violent myth to account for the development of the child into a socialized being governed by internalized moral law.

The fact that an infant cannot survive without a mother, and the mother can scarcely survive without a supportive group, was strangely neglected in "social contract" theorizing, in which the philosopher inquired what would lead the isolated and seemingly self-sufficient males to enter into a social compact and form a society. Without mothering and group nurture, these males would never have come into existence. Hence, the individualistic focus is profoundly misleading about society, its elementary basis, and the role of dreaming.

At the most elementary level, dreaming makes sense, not as the "idling" of a nervous system whose operative function is temporarily suspended but as the activity of a social being in relationship to other social beings. However, my thesis is even more revolutionary: without the psychic processes of dreaming, human group life could not have evolved or been maintained. Seemingly, this thesis is unprovable—although common to traditionalized small groups, who like the Aborigine (Stanner), or the Ndembu (in the accounts of the Turners), or many others,[2] think of their people and their world as having emerged in dreaming and dream time. To formulate this thesis explicitly is to expose the limitations of present discussion and so redirect inquiry.

How Is Group Life Possible?

The same condition that made possible the development of a new behavioral plateau, characterized by language and fully developed forms of cultural adaptation, was also that which enabled dreams, visions, and products of imaginative processes to be articulated, and thus to assume the form we find in *Homo sapiens*. (Hallowell 1966/1976:451)

Paleontologists debate about the (pre)historical appearance of the distinctively human: upright posture and bipedal gait; primacy of vision among sense modalities; opposable thumb; changing of habitats and diets; transformations of sexual periodicity, receptivity, and the birth process; adaptations to ecological niches that varied with major shifts of the Earth's climates. What they do not debate is that for countless millennia, hominids, human beings, lived in small groups. During those millennia, humans evolved intricate systems of cooperative activity, epitomized by spoken language and facilitated by its use in foreseeing and planning. What paleontologists (and animal behaviorists) also do not debate is that in complexity and intricacy, the cooperative activities of human groups far exceed those of other primates (and other mammals), and they are responsible for human evolutionary success—so far.

While the prehistoric groups are inaccessible, a number of traditionally organized small groups still remain. The issue is not whether these groups are touched or untouched by their contact with others and with civilized societies. Of course, they have been so influenced, adopting many items. Despite this contact, what has remained or endured for decades, even centuries, was the social dynamic of small-group existence, and this has been strikingly evident to anyone (e.g., a fieldworking anthropologist) who chose to share their lives.

Especially to a person reared in a modern urban environment, the dynamic of these small groups is overwhelming. By now, there are many accounts from cultural anthropologists of such immersion: the richness and emotional density of interaction; the passions of love and hate, friendship and enmity, trust and mistrust, cooperation and rivalry; the sense of us versus them. These are accompanied, intensified, moderated by continual and pervasive ceremonial and ritual, singing, dancing, drumming, narrating of myth.

If the life of a small group is oriented at one pole about securing food, safety, and shelter, it is oriented at the other pole about motherhood, infants and children, their nurturance, care, enjoyment, and socialization. To be successful, these processes require long-term cooperative effort on the part of beings who are emotionally bonded. The imagery of mother-and-child predominates and reminds us that without maternal bonding—and the joy of play—neither mother nor other adults would devote themselves to the demands and frustrations of child care. The mass media remind us daily of the consequences of the failure—or misfitting—of bonding: the abuse, torture, abandonment or murder of infants.

Given the divisiveness of human relations, the anger, hatred, envy that are the counterparts of love, cherishing, and concern, we need to ask how group bonding is sustained. This book is oriented about these issues, offering a multifold response. Each individual handles some of these problems via the work of dreams. Beyond this, and equally universal within these small groups, are the use and positive valuation of dream sharing, vision seeking, and states of trance, within settings of ritual and ceremony.

Life within these small groups does not proceed smoothly. People quarrel, fall ill, are injured; children die; hunters return empty-handed; gardeners find little to harvest. None of these events is considered the result of chance. Nor is illness or injury to be explained physiologically or biomedically, as simply an arbitrary event in the life of the affected person. In the intricate fabric of living, illness signifies a rent, and its repair requires conjoint efforts of human and nonhuman beings. As a sensitive fieldworker recounted of the traditional Mohave:

> The Mohave believe that all illnesses were foreordained, established, and experienced at the time of creation. The event of Creation included (in principle) at least one concrete case of every illness and at least one actual cure of that illness. . . . The Creation *myth* is not a finished product [but] reports simply those portions of the myth that had been revealed in dreams up to that time. Thus, when firearms were introduced and caused bullet wounds, a shaman promptly dreamed of having witnessed the portion of the Creation that pertained to the primordial, prototypical, and precedent-setting bullet wound and its cure. (Devereux 1966/1980: 280–281)

Emotional Attunement and Self-Regulation

Among the most amazing abilities of *Homo sapiens* is the performing of tasks requiring intricate cooperative efforts by intelligent, relatively autonomous beings. At the modern technological extreme these would include the journeys to and from the moon, the building of bridges and skyscrapers, and the interconnecting of the world through computer networks. At the technologically primitive and most elementary, these would include cooperative efforts in hunting and trading and, most important of all, in human reproduction: prenatal care, assistance during delivery, sharing of the nurture of the infant. Ultimately, each of these cooperative human activities is premised on—and exemplified by—the prolonged process of infant care and child rearing, by which the child is socialized and encultured, while its presence is appreciated, valued, enjoyed. These nurturant, educational and disciplinary processes required not only the development of language but of other profound social mechanisms and strategies. Our contemporary public attention can be easily distracted by examples of asocial and antisocial activities, which we perceive and label as pathological. Too easily, we forget the fantastic demands of our communal interdependent living, premised on emotional attunement, on the one hand, and self-regulation, on the other.

Freud was among those who recognized these demands, in his eloquent *Das Unbehagen in der Kultur* (*Civilization and Its Discontents*, 1930), but his biologically driven focus was on the control of instinctually rooted impulse, neglecting the positive counterpart, the enabling of cooperative activities based on emotional attunement among intelligent yet relatively autonomous group members.

While that set of requirements is most obvious among the small bands in which human beings lived for millennia, they are nonetheless present in modern urban environments, although in such radically different format that even social scientists are apt to misperceive them. Whatever the locus, the emotional burdens of intensive, intimate, prolonged human interaction are handled by dreaming, social ritual, and erotic relationships. Within the small bands of gatherer-hunters, interpersonal (emotional) attunement was facilitated by myths and rituals ("religion") and by the public recitation of dreams. The dreams of the individual did not have to be translated ("interpreted") in order to communicate ("unconsciously") to fellow members.

Within a common cultural-linguistic community, dreams establish communion, speaking most directly within an intimate relationship. With the transition to urbanized mass societies, dreams and other earlier psychic mechanisms (e.g., much ritual) have lost these potentialities. (Note that in the contemporary world of objectified impersonalized communication via computer network, insults and aggression emerge so easily and quickly that Internet and E-mail novices have to be cautioned; the limiting mechanisms of small groups cannot emerge within this space.)

The ability of dreams to provide emotional communication was *re*discovered by Freud as he instituted the intimate clinical procedure of psychoanalysis, although his insight was limited by his biomedical bent. Seemingly, the clinical attunement can be discussed and taught, but it is nonetheless as subject to the vagaries of that intimate interaction as ordinary speech with our fellows. As participants in a speech community, we comprehend—and miscomprehend—each other, but "machine translation" (i.e., a "scientistic" procedure) is essentially impossible.

Disenchanting the Dream

A central meaning of The Dreaming *is* that of a sacred, heroic time long, long ago when man and nature came to be as they are; but neither "time" nor "history" as we understand them is involved in this meaning. (Stanner, 1956:51, writing of Australian Aborigines)

A century ago, Sigmund Freud claimed to have discovered "the secret of dreams." Writing to his close friend, he judged the discovery to be of a magnitude so great that he could fantasize a marble tablet being erected in his honor. Freud's claim to eminence was startling. Throughout the ages, countless numbers had believed that they understood the "secret of dreams." Freud's claim could be novel only within the demythologized worldview of biomedicine, where neither dreams, love, sex, nor the interior of the body could hold secrets.

It was not just that Freud had (re)discovered their secret but that he had disenchanted dreams by situating their formation and interpreting them within a biomedically inspired paradigm. As a physician trained in neurology at a leading medical institution, he claimed authority for his strategy.

Freud's *Interpretation of Dreams* (1900) has gone in and out of intellectual favor—saluted as one of the great books of the century, derided by others as delusion and possibly a cocaine-based phantasm. Regardless of the eloquence of Freud's argument and the artfulness of his examples, regardless also of a hundred years of subsequent psychoanalytic practice, influential figures of contemporary neuroscience maintain that dreams are meaningless, simply manifestations of the random activities of a nervous system at rest. In dramatic contrast to this biomedical skepticism, the mystics of counterculture view dreams as pathways to "altered states of consciousness."

In this state of scientific—and unscientific—disagreement, few appeal to anthropological evidence or an evolutionary logic. By consensus of the peoples studied, the ayes should win the dispute: almost everywhere and every time, people have maintained that dreams have significant meaning and furnish guidance. And given the universality of dreaming, it would be a paradox of major proportions were dreaming to lack significant function or functions. The key question for evolutionary theory is then not whether dreams have functions but rather where should we look to find this function (or set of functions).

With the discovery of rapid eye movement (REM) stages of sleep, as indicating dreaming, it has become possible to disrupt dreaming systematically. When that is done, individuals lose their normal equilibrium and exhibit psychotic symptoms. The laboratory investigation confirms folk wisdom that dreaming is necessary for the stable functioning of the dreamer.[3]

This psychophysiological—and social—fact should instruct that dreams have a distinct function not reducible to some other or translatable as text. Accordingly, each of the foregoing views—skeptic or mystic—is inadequate. Metaphorically, each is akin to the view that poetry, dance, or ritual either is meaningless or has a simple translatable meaning (i.e., is a statement in an exotic language then equivalent to an interpretation). In our modern objectified milieu, that view often seems natural but is basically misdirective. The person who awakes from sleep in a state of sexual arousal is manifesting the psyche's having been preoccupied with erotic imagery, and an interpretation or translation would be impertinent (although the puritanical have preferred to attribute the arousal to the mechanical effect of the bladder, as though a full bladder automatically engenders arousal rather than a need to void).

Freud and Psychodynamic Theories

> Great discovery is the realization of something obvious; a presence staring us in the face, waiting until we open our eyes. (Polanyi 1946/1964:35)

Bold, ambitious, restless, confrontational, Freud investigated problematic facets of human existence and was moved to ask profound questions. By his findings, he dignified both psychopathology and its professional care. His writings are provocative, learned, and eloquent, yet they exhibit a man who was patriarchal, phallocentric, ruthless with friends, and demanding of disciples.

What is not commonly realized is the degree to which the stimulus to Freud's investigations derived from non-Western peoples. What Freud accomplished, or sought to accomplish, in each case was the domestication of an alien achievement into contemporary European biomedicine. Paradigmatically, in his early professional career, Freud sought to discover medical uses for coca. The irony was that this botanical had been productively used for centuries by the natives of highland South America, but in nineteenth-century Europe, its properties were little known. Likewise, Freud was among those who sought to use hypnotic trance as therapy in psychopathology. Again, the irony was that trance, and hypnotic trance, had been productively and therapeutically used for thousands of years by many of the peoples of the world. Finally, and with greatest success, he assimilated dream interpretation into biomedicine.

In the chapters devoted to Freud, I expose the blessings and the shortcomings of his remarkable endeavors. Concentrating on his interpreting of dreams, I show how his perspective—biomedical, Darwinian, phallocentric, authoritarian—led him to ignore significant meanings while imposing his own fantasies and theories. What was thus ignored has haunted the institutionalized profession—psychoanalysis—that he created, dominated, and controlled. Only gradually, painfully, and after severe internal dissension has psychoanalysis been liberating itself from that intellectual tyranny.

The crux of the problem lies in what orthodox Freudians consider Freud's very achievement: bringing dream interpretation within the paradigm of biomedicine. Where dreams had been considered messages from other beings (including the deity or deities) or meaningful in relationship to some canon, such as the Holy Scriptures, now dreams were interpreted individualistically within the clinical context according to Darwinian impulse: sexuality or aggression. Freud could make sense of the emergence of a dream only by contending that each dream represented a "wish fulfillment"; that theoretical demand drastically restricted understanding, because it focused on the dream as a neurological phenomenon within the isolated individual. Thinking of sleep as the unproblematic essential, Freud argued that dreams protected sleep by offering hallucinatory gratification of the wishes emerging within the mind of the sleeper.

Because so much is now known of Freud and his patients, I can freely utilize his and their dreams to demonstrate significances, without violating privacies or confidentialities.

Dreams and the Irrational

When we assume that contemporary individuals in our society are able to recall and interpret dreams, we are postulating psychological capacities and an evolutionary level of communication and cultural adaptation that did not exist at the earliest levels of hominid evolution. The capacity for recalling, communicating and identifying "more or less coherent imaginary sequences during sleep" as a "dream" not only implies complex psychological functions, but a culturally defined attitude toward a particular kind of subjective experience. (Hallowell 1966/1976:452)

Given the skepticism with which contemporary scientists had approached dreams and magic, Freud could well feel that his presentation of the secret revealed to him merited a marble tablet.[4]

For he had domesticated (demythologized) dreams. He had not only situated them on a neurological template but related them to the sexual drive and the great process of Darwinian evolution. Moreover, the interpretive process was not a (hermeneutic) search for meaning (questionable to clinicians who were ideologically anti-Vitalist) but the recollection by the patient within a clinical situation. Within Freud's psychology, "repression" meant that the wishes latent within a neurotic symptom, or a dream, had once been present in the awareness of the actor. The work of the clinical process was to move the patient into recalling and recognizing wishes that had been repressed because of guilt or shame. No rabbits were being interpretively (magically) pulled out of psychic hats (as in the biblical tale of Joseph and the Egyptian pharaoh).

Interpreters and Interpretive Schemes

The biblical stories of Joseph—his dreams and the responses of his family; his interpretations of the dreams of others—remind us that not only is dream interpretation an ancient craft but that at certain levels of sensibility it makes intuitive sense. There is no tradition of skepticism about the contents of Genesis, chapters 37–41. Given the availability of the Bible and the widespread familiarity with the texts, I am able to use these materials as the basis for discussion, without having to supply the background that would be necessary were I to take case histories from the Sioux or the Ndembu.

The biblical materials allow us to perceive both this natural acceptance of dreams as meaningful and prognosticative, together with a tradition of skepticism about possible heretical guidance:

> For thus saith the Lord of hosts, the God of Israel: Let not your prophets that are in the midst of you, and your diviners, beguile you, neither harken ye to your dreams which ye cause to be dreamed. (Jer. 29:8–9; JPS)[5]

As evident in the narrative of Joseph in Egypt—just as in Freud's case of "Dora"—the interpreting of dreams may have profound moral implications.

Notes

1. For example, God's revelation to the young Samuel in I Samuel 3 is not presented as a dream. (Specifically, the revelation is from YHWH).

2. To list but a few, note the attitude toward dreams of the peoples described in Graham (1995), Hallowell (1966), Irwin (1994), Lincoln (1935), Ridington (1988), Smith (1998), Tedlock (1987), and Wallace (1958).

3. A brain-damaged veteran of the Israel Defense Forces, Y.H., exhibited almost no REM episodes in his sleep. Lavie (1996: chap. 12) reports no mental pathology. One might say that he did not dream, except that "he had been referred to the Technion Sleep Laboratory because he had been awakening in panic while shouting loudly" (142). The case has drawn much attention, as it seems to contradict the necessity of REM sleep and accompanying dreaming. But one is then left with the query about Y.H.'s panic and shouting.

4. "Glaubst Du eigentlich, dass an dem Hause dereinst auf einer Marmortafel zu lesen sein wirt: Hier enthüllte sich am 24. Juli 1895 dem Dr. Sigm. Freud das Geheimnis des Traumes" (from Freud's letter to Wilhelm Fliess, June 12, 1900, as reproduced in Freud 1960:237).

5. The canon of the books of the Bible varies among religious denominations, as does the exact text and its translation. In this book, I cite passages from several editions and indicate their source as follows: the Jewish Publication Society (JPS); the Jerusalem Bible (JB), authorized by the Roman Catholic Church; and that of Rabbi Raphael Samson Hirsch (RSH). In chapter 4, dealing with the biblical Joseph, I rely mostly on RSH.

Chapter 2

Theoretical Perspectives on the Socialized Self

Imaginary Gardens with Real Toads[1]

When detached from the rest of our existence, dreaming becomes perplexing and problematic within an age of "*behavioral* science." Distinct from overt behavior, dreaming occurs on a private screen inaccessible to anyone other than the sleeper; nevertheless, dreams are a phenomenon known to all human beings. The dream is uniquely ours, yet within its dramatic actions we are but one of its characters, and the process unwinds beyond our control.

In this chapter, I approach dreams in a fashion parallel to the dream process itself, seeming to be concentrating on other problematics: the notion of *the self;* the possibility of multiple personality (as in psychic disorder or "possession-trance") or of multiple (or "dissociated") selves. The very notion of the self is paradoxical, for not only is *the self* an ambiguous (polysemous and polyvalent) term with a cluster of meanings, but it is impossible to focus toward the most central meaning without becoming involved in both perceptual and definitional circularity and kindred conundrums—as David Hume noted several centuries ago.[2] Later in this work, these problems will surface and be further explored.

The act of dreaming invites the notion or possibility of multiple personality. When the dreamer is but one of the autonomous actors within the dream theater, what is the psychic source of the others? These characters can only be emerging from within the dreamer, yet each has its own dynamic. If this is so, then what of the unity of "the self"? Our latent (distinctly Euro-American) notions of the wholeness and integrity of the self then become of issue. Thus, by clarifying some of the conceptual muddles about the self, we may gain deeper insight into the nature of dreaming.

The Unitary Self?

Le coeur a ses raisons que la raison ne connait pas (Pascal, *Pensées,* 277)

Within Western philosophical literature there is no simple consensus about the self. Plato (via Socrates) described a tripartite self whose proper ordering required study and discipline. The dominant figures of "modern" European philosophy (Descartes, Locke, Kant) imagined a self that was unitary and perduring. Descartes has been the exemplary case, in his famous argument that he could doubt the truth of everything, except that he himself was a doubting being; and, as a doubting—or thinking—being, he (Descartes) must therefore exist (*cogito, ergo sum* = I think, therefore I am). The world as stable and fathomable is thus grounded on a self that in its doubting (or thinking) is necessarily unified and enduring. The tradition exemplified by the Cartesian logic underlies the clinical skepticism of the reality of "multiple personality."

In many cultures, neither the self nor the body perdures in our modern fashion. For example, in the ritual stories and folk tales of the Plains Indians, the actors may move back and forth among a variety of animal shapes, each possessing distinct potencies and limitations. A young man may encounter an attractive young woman who transmutes into a buffalo heifer; he may have competitive encounters with her buffalo kin, and his victories may then eventuate not only in his marriage to the shape-shifting heroine, but in his having the (magical) power to kill members of the herd when they are needed for consumption by his human kin. It is also noteworthy that in these societies, an individual would then change his name, in accordance with accomplishment of various deeds.

Again, there is a rich literature on the differences between Euro-American and other societies in their conceptions of self, but at this point it would be appropriate to review a particular tradition of conceptual analysis of the self, its origin and development.

The Tradition of American Pragmatism

From within the rich tradition of early twentieth-century Pragmatism, I have singled out three figures who wrote insightfully about *the self:* Charles Horton Cooley, George Herbert Mead, and in consonance Harry Stack Sullivan. Since few psychodynamic thinkers recognize this tradition, the following will supply a useful corrective to contemporary theories of the self.[3]

Charles Horton Cooley (1864–1929)

> Each to each a looking-glass
> Reflects the other that doth pass.

The systems of modern philosophy (Continental Rationalism, British Empiricism, Kantianism) had assumed an ego that was seemingly independent of the social world. I have cited Descartes but could as well have cited Berkeley or Kant. In several influential contemporary psychologies (behaviorism, or neuroanatomy) a similar view is implicit. In contradistinction, Cooley brought the observation that the self was a social product. (Here, he cites both James Mark Baldwin [1861–1934] and William James [1842–1910], referring specifically to the latter's "admirable discussion of the self.")

Rejecting the Cartesian tradition, Cooley saw *self*-consciousness and "*social* consciousness" as correlative: "we can hardly think of ourselves excepting with reference to a social group of some sort, or of the group except with reference to ourselves" (1909/1962:5). Although he was disputing a philosophical and psychological tradition, he found confirmation of his views in the writings of poets and dramatists (among others, he cited Shakespeare, Montaigne, Goethe, and George Eliot). In particular, these observers had noted that a person tends to accept the view of himself held by those he respects. So Cooley became famous for introducing the notion of "the reflected or looking-glass self" (1902/1964:184):

> "I," then, is not all of the mind, but a peculiarly central, vigorous, and well-knit portion of it, not separate from the rest but gradually merging into it, and yet having a certain practical distinctness. . . . It may be thought of under the analogy of a central colored area on a lighted wall . . . [or] be compared to the nucleus of a living cell, not altogether separate from the surrounding matter, out of which indeed it is formed, but more active and definitely organized. (Cooley 1902/1964:182)
>
> A self-idea of this sort seems to have three principal elements: the imagination of our appearance to the other person; the imagination of his judgment of that appearance, and some sort of self-feeling, such as pride or mortification. . . . The thing that moves us to pride or shame is not the mere mechanical reflection of ourselves, but an imputed sentiment, the imagined effect of this reflection upon another's mind. (Cooley 1902/1964:182, 184)
>
> The self may be regarded as a sort of citadel of the mind, fortified without and containing selected treasures within . . . what we love intensely or for a long time we are likely to bring within the citadel, and to assert as part of ourself. (Cooley 1902/1964:188)

Informally, Cooley had been observing children, and thereby he was led not only to confirm the vision of the nature of the self but in connection with its development to introduce the notion of *the primary group:* "characterized by intimate face-to-face association and cooperation . . . fundamental in forming the social nature and ideals of the individual. . . . Human nature is not something existing separately in the individual, but a *group nature or primary phase of society*" (1909/1962: Chap. 3). The small groups discussed in the previous chapter are exemplary of the primary group.

Although learned in the scholarship of his age, Cooley was not a systematic thinker, neither as social psychologist nor philosopher. Nevertheless, within social psychology he was an influential ancestor.

George Herbert Mead (1863–1931)[4]

The opposition of "the individual" versus "society" had been a staple of philosophical and political discussion for centuries. Like Baldwin and Cooley, Mead argued that this polarity was conceptually confused: the self was a social product. Without society, as manifested in a nurturing, facilitative family, no self would emerge. More specifically, the family must employ language, and language is intrinsically a social phenomenon.

Mead perceived that an utterance is heard and interpreted by the speaker in a process akin to the response of the auditor. Human language is far more than parroting or expressing emotion. It requires that the speaker also assume the position of the listener. In addressing children, parents encourage them not merely to react but to respond vocally (or symbolically). In that auditory process, the child finds herself addressing not merely her parents but herself. Via language the child begins to address herself as do her parents. It is not merely that the child babbles or parrots. Children come to talk, and in the talking they assume the voice or voices of their parents, thereby bringing into their "play" the drama of their life with their elders. In this dramatic process, via language, the child begins to adopt the voice and thereby the perspective of the parent in regarding herself. This process results in the creating of a *self* within the developing child.

Although my summary is faithful, it makes Mead easier to comprehend, because I have rephrased his ideas in a more contemporary language. Writing at the turn of the century within an academic environment of animal-based, behavioristic, "stimulus-response" psychologies,[5] Mead echoed their vocabularies but challenged their postulates by insisting on a social world and social objects, including the constructing of the human self:

> [T]hat the human animal can stimulate himself as he stimulates others and can respond to his stimulations as he responds to the stimulation of others,

places in his conduct the form of a social object. . . . Any gesture by which the individual can himself be affected as others are affected, and which therefore tends to call out in him a response as it would call out in another, will serve as a mechanism for the construction of a self. (Mead 1912:405)

Mead's use of *gesture* indicates that his analysis would apply equally to a familial environment employing a sign language.

Before explicating Mead's system, I note that it is consonant with the later developments associated with Jean Piaget, Lev Vygotsky, and Noam Chomsky.

Mead perceived that this analysis required supplementation. For it could as plausibly lead to the emergence within the child of *selves* rather than a stable integrated self. Each familial drama, each set of interactions with each facilitating elder would lead the child toward a different view (or views) of "self," and indeed the self of the young child is labile. Mead spoke here of the child "taking the role of the other"; and since there are a number of significant "others"—and since each of the others may themselves fluctuate in orientation toward the child—then the young child would then either have a self that fluctuated or might as plausibly develop a multiplicity of selves:

> We can carry on a whole series of different relationships to different people. We are one thing to one man and another thing to another. . . . We divide ourselves up to all sorts of different selves with reference to our acquaintances. . . . There are all sorts of different selves answering to all sorts of different social reactions. . . . A multiple personality is in a certain sense normal. (Mead 1934:142)

In deciphering today what Mead meant by "taking the role of the other," there is a certain ambiguity (Cook 1993: Chap. 6) as well as a natural tendency to read modern psychodynamic notions of "internalizing" the significant others (Freudian "objects"[6]) in the creating of a self. In his social-psychological moments, Mead prefigures the psychodynamic internalizing. However, in his more behavioristic moments Mead may have been following the epistemic logic of persons such as the prominent linguist Leonard Bloomfield (1933), for whom words were to be regarded as stimuli.[7] Postulating that a word was a psychological stimulus, Mead was noting that, for human discourse to occur, that stimulus must be identical for speaker and auditor. The range of meaning in Mead's phrase "taking the role of the other" is a historical conundrum that need not be deciphered in this essay, but it should be noted.

Implicit in Mead's view of society was a reasonably stable and untraumatic social environment. So situated, a competent, developing child would construct a "generalized other" that integrated the perspectives of relevant persons toward him- or herself. As such a generalized other was constructed, the child's sense of self would become more coherent, and his or her conduct would become stabilized.

The stable self enables complex, planful, long-range actions. Here, Mead moved to the analogy of a game, such as baseball, where the expert player takes into account the likely behaviors of a coordinated group of actors, including the likely consequences of the actor's alternative behaviors, so shaping the player's actions: The fielder pursuing a ball must anticipate not only the path of the ball but the behaviors of teammates and (if they are present) base runners. Such envisioning must include their likely responses to his or her alternatives in handling and redirecting of the ball, when caught. An equally complex example—not employed by Mead—would be poker, in which, within a social and rule-bound matrix, each player joins with others, while attempting to confuse, deceive, and manipulate them. To accomplish this social feat the player skillfully must take the perspectives of others toward her own performance.

Mead's analysis moved toward a summary employing the correlative notions of I and me: the "me" being the grammatical and social object, what the actor perceives of him- or herself and his or her conduct; the "I" referring to the actor as acting, only known after the fact of the action, when perceived as a "me." Thus, within the Meadian system, the person of the actor is psychically, grammatically, syntactically other than the self. In trying to make sense of this configuration, commentators attribute "impulse" to the active I, but this is a distorting simplification. The "I" is the person as actor; the "Me" is the person as perceived by him- or herself. We may think of how we listen to ourselves speaking, and as a monitoring listener we may then become aware of an inaccuracy, a mispronunciation, or (other) parapraxis on the part of the speaker; or of some unanticipated feeling, revelation, or insight; or we may realize that the speaker is not truly addressing the listeners who actually are present.

As presented by Mead, the self is not only social but active and interactive. As compared with the notion of the self within the writings of some classical philosophers (e.g., Descartes), the self is not simply an observer and thinker but an agent active in the world. Moreover, the agent's activity involves others; indeed, one may argue that implicit in Mead's vision of its origin is the notion that the self emerges as a response to the challenges of human social existence.

Additionally, one may add that the self is temporally situated. Via the self, the individual is able to project the possibility of acting in different ways and so to anticipate the differential consequences. Yet, because the self has been formed in past interaction, the individual who is thus constructing possible actions is also embedded in the matrix of the past judgments of influential others. Mead is clear about the forward projection and not so clear about the influence of the past.

Mead's disciples have noted that while he was surely influenced by his studies in neo-Hegelian philosophy (under Royce at Harvard and under Wundt, Dilthey, Ebbinghaus, and others in Leipzig and Berlin), also formative was his early experience as a land surveyor for railroad companies. Throughout Mead's writings is an image not of the detached, closeted, "philosophical" observer but of the inquiring agent addressing questions to nature, questions whose answers will determine subsequent social activities, such as where railroad lines should be laid out. He hoped to create a social psychology that would be faithful to the human ability to generate complex social interactions, such as the constructing of a bridge, building, or railroad line. Together with John Dewey, William James, and Charles Pierce, Mead was one of the creators of American Pragmatism, with its implicit vision of the actor as social participant, rather than detached and isolated. In like manner, these pragmatists approached society with an inquiring intelligence, analyzing its problems so that solutions might be constructed. Mead himself was active in such reform efforts as the settlement house movement spearheaded by Jane Addams.

For the purposes of thematic discussion of the self, I want to highlight several implications of Mead's analysis: (1) What initially develops is not a unified self, but a system that has the potential for becoming integrated. (2) The human actor is not transparent to him- or herself but becomes aware retrospectively (retroactively). What is observed is the "me"; what is elusive is the "I." (3) Memory becomes not a detached and impartial record but a psychic activity that is ancillary to action:

> [M]emory images derived from past responses of others to similar stimuli tend to flow into our responses to our own conduct. . . . [W]e may think of the imagery as consisting of sensuous contents derived from past experience of others' responses, which merge with and fill out the present stimulus. (Cook 1993:88–89)

Memory is not then written on the mind as chalk on a blackboard but is at the service of the self engaged in the constructing of possible acts.[8]

Harry Stack Sullivan (1892–1949)[9]

> The self may be said to be made up of reflected appraisals. (Sullivan 1947:10)

If there were any influences from Cooley or Mead on Sullivan, these would have been indirect.[10] Nevertheless, it was as if Sullivan translated their schema from the arena of language and cognition into that of affect, and from the arena of the normal to the pathological, so that the several views complement each other. By speaking of "the self system" or "the self dynamism" rather than "the self," Sullivan's phrasing emphasized processual qualities akin to those of Mead and Cooley. Where the two parties most differ is in emotional ambience.

Sullivan perceived a self emerging as a defensive mechanism within a milieu that provokes anxiety within the child. His philosophical predecessors had been more positive, seeing the self emerging from the growth and potential of the child within the family. For Sullivan, the infant and mother were linked empathetically, and her disapproval elicited anxiety. The *self dynamism* is built from this experience of approbation and disapproval:

> As [the self dynamism] develops, it becomes more and more related to a microscope in its function. Since the approbation of the important person is very valuable, since disapprobation denies satisfaction and gives anxiety, the self becomes extremely important. It permits a minute focus on those performances of the child which are the cause of approbation and disapprobation, but, very much like a microscope, it interferes with noticing the rest of the world. (Sullivan 1947:9–10)

With this view of the self dynamism, a notion of *dissociation* is immediate (see Mitchell 1993: chap. 4). The actor is inattentive to events—within or without—that are not within the purview of "the microscope."

> From the time that the self-system begins to emerge, three aspects of the personality can be readily distinguished: first, the waking and thoroughly active self; second, the part of the personality not readily accessible to awareness— the rest of the personality, which in another context can be considered as the whole personality with the self as the eccentric part; and finally, the period spent in sleep, in which the self is relatively dormant and many things are done which cannot be done when the self is functioning actively. (Sullivan 1956:4)

Perhaps because Sullivan did not directly study childhood, his portrait of the emergence of the self dynamism has significant deficiencies (Guntrip 1971: chap. 4). Clinically, Sullivan was gifted at working with schizophrenics, and his vision of the self system does provide insight into their attempted resolution of profound psychic disturbances. But his vision of how the self system is formed and how it might become inadequate does not deal with what interactional processes might give rise to a multiplicity of selves (or "self systems"?).

> The self-system, unlike any of the other dynamisms posited to organize knowledge about interpersonal relations, is extraordinarily resistant to

change by experience. This can be expressed in the theorem that *the self-system from its nature—its communal environmental factors, organization, and functional activity—tends to escape influence by experience which is incongruous with its current organization and functional activity* [Sullivan's emphases]. . . . The self-system is derived wholly from the interpersonal aspects of the necessary environment of the human being; it is organized because of the extremely unpalatable, extremely uncomfortable experience of anxiety; and it is organized in such a way as to avoid or minimize existent or foreseen anxiety. (Sullivan 1953:190)

At this point Sullivan has fallen into the trap that awaits psychodynamic clinicians, who daily confront the pathological.[11] He makes it seem as if the emergence of the self is geared to a pathological relationship between mother and child. To the contrary, the growing child has the potential to walk, talk, and develop a self system. These do not emerge in response to maternal anxieties, although they can be hindered or inhibited by environmental or developmental trauma. If one follows Mead, the emergence of the self is no more pathological than the emergence of walking or talking. Each of these may be shaped and distorted by a troubled parental relationship.

While Sullivan's description of the self system left ample room for a discussion of dreaming, including the function of dreaming for the person, and the clinical usage of dreams, Sullivan himself had little interest in them.

[Perhaps] his overriding concern with the treatment of schizophrenia turned him away from a free-associational approach to nightly dream phantoms and toward real talk about real problems in living. . . . The subtleties of the dreaming mind were not for him. . . . [even though] he acknowledged that dreams (and myths) represented "a relatively valid parataxic operation for the relatively insoluble problems of living." (Lippmann 1996:146–7)[12]

Clearly, Sullivan was no Freudian, but his theories echo those of Freud insofar as he believed that the root of schizophrenic processes is the conflict that develops when the self system is not able to encompass biologically rooted desires:

The schizophrenic patient is often a person who has in the past persistently shown the dynamism which we call dissociation as a means of resolving the conflict between powerful needs and the restrictions which the self imposes upon satisfaction of these needs. That is, people who have dissociated anything as powerful as lust, for example, are in great danger of schizophrenic collapse. (Sullivan 1956:6)

Today in the United States, the problematic for the self-system is more likely to be trauma and abuse:

> Experienced clinicians know that dissociative patients are often in trance; they have learned, or taught themselves, to use trance long before they entered the therapist's office. In fact, being in trance, involuntarily, is one of the defining features of dissociative disorder. (Hegeman 1997:154)

We will be discussing trance further in the next chapter.

Some Implications of the Foregoing

Self and Psyche

> Mead recognizes the temporal structure of self-reflection. In self-reflection the actor does not turn back upon himself in a frozen present—as in a mirror—but reflects upon the future possibilities in the present conditions, which issue from the past. Selfhood does not consist in immobilely remaining identical with oneself; rather, it is the continuously active, reconstructive processing of occurrences and the planning of actions. (Joas 1985:192)

Following the views of the pragmatic trio—Cooley, Mead, and Sullivan—the self and the psyche are not coterminous. Of the entire machinery or apparatus of body-and-spirit (soma-and-psyche), the self is an active emergent, a system that by intense awareness, focusing, and organizing then enables minute observation and control. But the notion of awareness—attention to a class of phenomena—implies the possibility and necessity of unawareness and inattention. Sullivan spoke of "selective inattention" (as Freud of "suppression" and "repression"). It would follow that what the individual apprehended was composite. As viewed in simplistic bipolar fashion, there were materials within awareness, available to be used by the self dynamism, and materials that were not within the purview of the self system.

Other writers have proposed different conceptualizations of the self, associated with alternative conceptual-theoretical systems and different natural languages.[13] Some writers view the self as reflexive but not socially, interpersonally reflexive. Referencing James Mark Baldwin, Jacques Lacan (1949) stated that the presence of an emerging self is made evident in such phenomena as an infant's response to his or her image in a mirror.[14] This illustrative basis to the self would have been rejected by Cooley, Mead, Sullivan. Daniel Stern (1985) cites Baldwin and Cooley in his initial pages and devotes his book to the infant's sense of self, but he does not deal with the role of language. On the basis of the animal's response to its image in a mirror, animal behaviorists have argued that other species besides *Homo sapiens* could be inferred to have "a self" (Parker, Mitchell, and Bocca 1994).

If one accepts Mead's analysis, then the self and language—linguistic discourse—are coterminous: one cannot have one without the other. To converse—as a human being rather than an expressive or parroting animal—one must have a self, able to take the role of the auditor. Thus, the process of acquiring the ability to converse (discourse) is concomitant with the process of constructing a self. Citing Foster (1992), Mitchell comments:

> Studies of bilingual patients suggest that, especially when one language is learned at a developmentally later point than an original language, the different languages reflect very different organizations of the self. . . . There are enormous differences in nuance, affective tone, and often access to memories, coded and filed in one rather than the other language. (Mitchell 1993: 105)

Several writers (e.g., Hacking 1995) have emphasized the role of the media in creating an "epidemic" of persons claiming multiple selves. In their view, the phenomenon has become lurid, frequently fraudulent or exhibitionistic, rather than psychopathological (and often tragic). By returning to observers and theorists of an earlier date, I hope to detach the argument from contemporary fashion and furor. My approach is rather to regard these phenomena as human potentials and social facts (*faites sociaux,* in the words of Durkheim and his school) that have manifested themselves throughout human history.

Dreaming

On the logic of Cooley, Mead, and Sullivan, the self is analytically distinct from the person, or the psyche taken as a whole. This fits with such commonplace experience as that one's conscious awareness may be directed on one set of problems while the person is ("mechanically") occupied with another set of tasks, or that events may then be "observed" for which, initially, one has no conscious memory. Dreaming then becomes an avenue whereby events apprehended by the psyche but not visible to the self dynamism are now incorporated and integrated. During (normal) sleep, the self dynamism is suspended, for (conscious, motivated) action does not occur. In this hiatus, the focusing of the self dynamism (Sullivan's metaphor of a microscope) becomes minimal, and other materials then intrude. With awakening, as the self becomes active, there may be the struggle to bring the dream within the ambience of language, but unless this effort is made, the dream vanishes. The dream is not repressed but rather remains dissociated from conscious awareness. We might well speak here of amnesia.

This does not mean that the self must be identical from situation to situation. Quite the contrary, Mead clearly noted an initial tendency for the self to be variable, or perhaps *flexible, labile,* or *unstable* are terms more precise for capturing his meaning. The self acquires stability only as the individual constructs "a generalized other," rather than framing the interaction so as to deal only with the other who is immediately opposite.

How, then, could one have a multiplicity of selves? Does the notion make sense? Certainly, it makes sense that the person would be sensitive to each distinct social situation, perhaps so sensitive as to appear to be a different type of actor in each different situation. That is not theoretically troublesome and fits with empirical observation. Especially in the urbanized milieu, many situations require of adult actors that they modify the person who is projected within a situation, whether in ceremonial or theatrical performance or role playing.[15] Moreover, confidence tricksters notoriously have had the ability to project images of selves of rectitude.

Notes

1. This heading is from the poem "Poetry" by Marianne Moore (1935). Intriguingly, it resonates with recollections of "Frau Emmy von N," one of Freud's early patients:

> Another memory was how, at nineteen, she lifted up a stone and found a dead toad under it, which made her lose her power of speech for hours afterward. . . . Once she said, when she had been walking with her husband in a park in St. Petersburg, the whole path leading to a pond had been covered with toads, so that they had to turn back. (Freud in Breuer and Freud, SE, II:55, 74)

2. For my part, when I enter most intimately into what I call *myself,* I always stumble on some particular perception or other . . . . I never can catch *myself* at any time without a perception, and never can observe anything but the perception. (Hume 1738, I, IV, vi)

> The senses in which the self is constitutive of but not an object in experience constitutes what [Todes 1967:166] terms 'epistemological schizophrenia' with respect to self-knowledge. For a radical dissociation seemingly exists between the self as knower and the self as known. (Roth 1996)

3. Galatzer-Levy and Cohler (*The Essential Other: A Developmental Psychology of the Self,* 1993) do not cite Cooley or Mead, and have but one minor reference to Sullivan. None of the contributors to *Pragmatism's Freud: The Moral Disposition of Psychoanalysis* (Smith and Kerrigan 1986) cite the three pragmatists (one minimally cites John Dewey), yet they fulsomely cite trendy French theorists Derrida,

Foucault, Lacan. No one mentions Sullivan, although the text was sponsored by the Washington School of Psychiatry, of which he was principal founder.

The only serious engagement with Cooley and Mead is by Levin (1992) and a short essay by Grolnick (1986). In reference to discussions of mutuality, Benjamin (1988) does note George Herbert Meade (!).

4. In addition to Mead's essays (Miller 1982; Reck 1964) and the posthumous *Mind, Self, and Society* (1934), I have relied on the following secondary literature: Aboulafia (1986); Blumer (1969); Joas (1985); Miller (1973). As a graduate student during the 1950s, I heard the expositions on Mead of Herbert Blumer. Mead's work became foundational to the Society for the Study of Symbolic Interaction.

5. In his autobiographical memoir, the influential behaviorist, J. B. Watson, wrote, "I took courses and seminars with Mead. I didn't understand him in the classroom, but for years Mead took a great interest in my animal experimentation, and many a Sunday he and I spent in the laboratory watching my rats and monkeys" (cited in Miller 1973:xxvii).

6. As Lacan was to rediscover decades after the work of Mead, *other* is more felicitous, more evocative, and phenomenologically more precise than *object,* the latter being an unfortunate heritage from the biodynamic phrasing of Freud's *Three Essays* (1905). One may note the discussions of "object," "object choice," and "object relationship" in the Freudian dictionary compiled by Laplanche and Pontalis (1967/1973).

It is a wry commentary that Lacan should derogate American contributions, which would include the brilliance and insight of its Pragmatist philosophers/social psychologists (Mead, Dewey, Pierce, James), while finding invaluable the conceptual discoveries of whose ancestry he was ignorant. So, his translator can inform the innocent reader that *objet petit a [autre]* was developed "out of the Freudian 'object' and Lacan's own exploitation of 'otherness'. . . but that Lacan insists that *objet petit a* should remain untranslated" (Sheridan in Lacan 1977:xi). "After his early period, Lacan used "other" more or less as a synonym for the ego as he conceived it" (Mahony 1998).

In his influential essays of the 1960–1970s, Heinz Kohut introduced the term *self-object,* which conceptually has a close kinship to Mead's notion of "taking the role of the other." Unfortunately, I cannot explicate here the similarities and differences to the pragmatic heritage.

7. Bloomfield's *Introduction to the Study of Language* appeared in 1914, and his magnum opus *Language* in 1933. His tenure at the University of Chicago (professor of Germanic philology) overlapped Mead's. As contrasted with, say, the systemic approach of de Saussure, Bloomfield whole-heartedly embraced a stimulus-response approach to language, and so there is a similarity with Mead worthy of notice. Nevertheless, the possibility of influence is not mentioned by Cook, Joas, or Miller.

8. Inversely, "Without memory, there is no self. Meaning in personal experience is composed of narratives" (Mitchell 1993:76).

9. In addition to Sullivan's lectures collected in such works as *Conceptions of Modern Psychiatry* (1947) and *Clinical Studies* (1956), I have relied on Chapman

(1976) and Mullahy (1970). During World War II, I attended Sullivan's lectures at the Washington School of Psychiatry.

10. In addition to the ideas of William Alanson White, Adolf Meyer, and Edward Kempf, Sullivan was influenced by the concepts of many psychiatrists and social scientists (some of whom are now little known) such as T. V. Moore, W. H. R. Rivers, William McDougal, David Levy, Edward Sapir, Charles H. Cooley, G. H. Mead, Bronislaw Malinowski, and others. However, the system of thought which Sullivan eventually matured by the early 1940's cannot be traced to any single predecessor or group of predecessors. (Chapman 1976:44)

Note also Mullahy 1970: Chap. 3.

11. In his 1968 lectures at the Washington School of Psychiatry, Guntrip was highly critical of Sullivan's conceptualization of the development of the self. He commented that Sullivan's was "not the basis for a whole person psychology. It only answers to what Winnicott would call 'a false self on a conformity basis' and offers us no help for a psychology of the true self." He also notes that Sullivan and Freud both use the idea of a microscope to stand for the psychic apparatus or the self (Guntrip 1971:75).

12. Lippmann is here comparing the views on dreams of Sullivan and Erich Fromm, "the two major architects of early interpersonal thinking" (1996:146).

13. Pontalis (1977/1981:126–47) notes that the anglophone notion of *the self* differs from the francophone *le soi*. He also deals with the emphasis on the self that may be found in writings of Harry Guntrip and others.

14. Reviewing Baldwin's influence on his friend, Pierre Janet, Ellenberger (1970:404) cites the following passage: "My sense of myself grows by imitation of you, and my sense of you grows in terms of my sense of myself. Both *Ego* and *Alter* are thus essentially social; each is a *Socius* and each is an imitative creation" (Baldwin 1895:334–8 as cited in Ellenberger 1970:404).

15. Riesman (1950) contrasted the "other-directed" person of the modern urbanized world with the "inner-directed" person of Reformation Protestantism and the "tradition-directed" person of earlier societies. Here he was elaborating a schema of Erich Fromm (1947).

Chapter 3

Losing or Multiplying the Self
via Dreams or Trance

Within the Western intellectual tradition, the normative actor is alert, individualized, autonomous—a product of a unified rational self. The states of sleep and dreaming are interesting because they might be facilitative to rational functioning. Trance and possession are abnormal, miraculous, or pathological.

The state of dreaming challenges the normative imagery on a deeper level, for it invites the notion or possibility of a multiple rather than a unitary personality. Within the dream, the dreamer is but one of the actors: actors who are unbidden and behave independently. What then of the unity of "the self"?[1] Our latent (distinctly Euro-American) notions of the wholeness and integrity of the self then become of issue, unless we begin to relate the self, not to a philosophical abstraction (in the spirit of Descartes), but to art: poetry, dance, fiction. For the better the artistic effort, the more the performer seems to penetrate into the psyche of another (or others). Moreover, while the actor likely does prepare in advance, the consummate performance occurs—or seems to occur—without deliberation, at an unconscious level.

From *The Iliad* and *Phaedrus,* from William Blake and W. A. Mozart, to the present day, many of the great artists have described or exhibited a dissociated consciousness. Socrates spoke of "possession by the Muses" without whose aid no poet can achieve greatness. Not only poets but other artists have testified that they were driven by beings or forces outside themselves (see Grosso 1997). In an intriguing parallel American Indian shamans often spoke of being pressured by deities into assuming that role.

To understand dreams better, we need then to juxtapose them to performance and the aesthetic, rather than follow Freud and juxtaposing to the neurotic or follow sleep researchers who think in terms of brain function. Ethnographic materials about possession, trance, and "multiple personality" enrich our reflections (Barrett 1997; Krippner 1997).

The Ethnographic Evidence

Culturally Specific Disorders

Is "multiple personality" a syndrome or "disorder" confined to the relatively recent Euro-American civilization, or is it more general, possibly universal among human societies past and present? Recent clinical discussions have focussed upon a few sensational cases of pathology: from Morton Prince's Christine Beauchamp; to Thigpen and Cleckley's "Eve" (1957); Schreiber's *Sybil* (1973); Chase's "Troops" (1987); Schoenewolf's *Jennifer* (1991), and so forth.

In contrast, seldom does the ethnographic literature report an event that is labeled by the observer as "multiple personality *disorder*."[2] Nevertheless, that literature does frequently report accounts of individuals becoming the passive host or vehicle of another being or person. The applicable concept then becomes not "multiple personality" but *possession* or "possession-trance," a compound term that Bourguignon uses to distinguish this ritual phenomenon from other forms of trance or "altered state of consciousness." Working as an anthropologist among the African/Catholic-influenced societies of Haiti, Bourguignon has distinguished conceptually among the various forms of trance and possession. Note the very title of one of her major essays, "Multiple Personality, Possession Trance, and the Psychic Unity of Mankind" (1989).

Ethnographic studies remind us that the biomedical concept of disease is peculiar to the recent Western world. While every known society has a conception of health, strength, vitality—as contrasted to weakness, illness, disability—the syndromes that are culturally noted and subjected to treatment (or ritual action) differ widely. Not only do cultures recognize disorders that we do not distinguish, but the reverse is also true. Kleinman (1987) has formalized this well-established ethnographic variability by introducing the notion of "culturally specific disorder."[3]

Horse and Rider in Caribbean Vodou

In the *vodou* rites characteristic of Haitian society, the votary may become "a horse" who is "ridden" (i.e., possessed or inhabited) by a deity, behaving according to that deity's (culturally defined) character. The onlookers respond directly to the inhabiting deity—known as a *lwa* (Brown 1991, whose usages I shall be following, except when quoting other texts; e.g., Deren [1951/1970] uses *loa*). After the deity departs, the human "horse" is amnesic for the occasion (see Brown; Deren; Métraux). Let us register the following instance.

The scene is Haiti during the 1940s. Sebastien, a young man, wishes to marry his common-law wife. He is a devout *serviteur* of the Mistress Erzulie (a major deity in the vodou pantheon), who had made it known that she will consent to the mortal marriage only if he undergoes a preliminary marriage with herself. The wedding with Erzulie is then scheduled for a Thursday, the day sacred to her, and the mortal wedding on Saturday.

Beautifully groomed, the human couple come to the decorated shrine. Led by the *père savane*, the congregants pray and sing. It is expected that Erzulie will inhabit the fiancée, but instead one of the women who was to be witness begins to sway, her eyes close, she falls backward, and Erzulie has appeared:

> The transformation was complete. Out of an insignificant young woman, the loa [deity] had created an irresistible coquette, who leaned languorously on the shoulders of two young men summoned to support her and to lead her to the room reserved for her use. There Erzulie performed her meticulous toilette with the finest soap, put powder and make-up on, combed her hair endlessly before arranging the golden combs and flowers in her black tresses under the veil of tulle which was held with a blue satin bow. Finally she appeared in her bridal dress, perfumed, shining with golden jewelry, a bouquet of flowers on one arm and a light-blue handkerchief in her hand, her long skirt often lifted to reveal the pink taffeta petticoat, and smiling in recognition of the flattering whispers: "Oh, what a beautiful lady is Mistress Erzulie!" Her eyes shone, her full, moist lips were parted slightly. All men belonged to her and she honored them all. . . . Erzulie did not remain long. She left as quietly as she arrived, and the young woman, returned to herself, looked with astonishment at the bridal gown which she still wore . . . The civil and Catholic wedding of Sebastien and his mortal bride took place the following Saturday. (Rigaud in Deren 1951/1970:264f.)

Although spiritual possession is scarcely unique within ethnographic and ethnohistorical accounts, what is particularly charming in this narrative is the unanticipated choice and the elegance of the performance. What is particularly dramatic is the arrival and departure of the deity, which in psychiatric language would be labeled as dissociation and amnesia. Yet, for Caribbean vodou, the narrative would be unexceptional.

In the course of her participation in the ceremonials, Maya Deren, the woman who came to study and film, herself succumbs to the process. She reports being mounted by Erzulie initially at a ceremonial and then subsequently at other occasions that she had planned to record:

> I had ordered a set of drums and arranged to have them baptized and "put to sleep" overnight with a special ceremony. I was very anxious to make a

wire recording of this infrequent ceremony. . . . When I regained consciousness, about four hours had passed, and I was informed that I was very
lucky since Erzulie herself had performed the complete drum ceremony.
(Deren 1951/1970:322–3)

Her report is not unusual. Most ethnographic observers indicate that
possession is not deliberately sought and is sometimes resisted. They also
reveal that the dancing and accompanying drumming—and the psychic
and physical fatigue so induced—can overwhelm the self. Deren describes
her initial experience of being mounted by Erzulie:

> Still looking out, I say to myself, also, "This is the moment you must make
> your decision." For I now know that today, the drums, the singing, the move-
> ments—these may catch me also. I do not wish that. There is both fear and
> embarrassment in the idea. . . . To run away would be cowardice. I could re-
> sist; but I must not escape. And I can resist best, I think to myself, if I put
> aside the fears and nervousness; if, instead of suspecting my vulnerability, I
> set myself in brazen competition with all this which would compel me to its
> authority. With this decision I feel a resurgence of strength, of the certainty
> of self, and of my proper identity. . . . My entire being focusses on one sin-
> gle thought: that I must endure. I cannot say, now why I did not stop; except
> that, beneath all this is always a sense of contract: whether in the end, one
> can be victor or victim, it is to be in the terms one has accepted. One can-
> not default. So focused was I, at that time, upon the effort to endure, that I
> did not even mark the moment when this ceased to be difficult. . . . I am
> caught in this cylinder, this well of sound. There is nothing anywhere except
> this. There is no way out. (Deren 1953/1970: chap. vii)[4]

Possession-Trance

To a naive outsider and to the popular media, the possession-trance together with the accompanying rituals of vodou may be spectacular:
bloody sacrifices that are only symbolized within the Eucharist of orthodox Christianity; drumming in driving pulses; ecstatic dancing. Nevertheless, the phenomena are scarcely unique, as the anthropological and
historical literatures contain accounts from numerous societies of individuals becoming possessed by some other being: an ancestor; a deity; a
spirit being, sometimes of animal origin. In some cases the individual directly manifests the possession, as by proclamations in an altered voice;
in other cases, the possession is diagnosed by a shaman, who attributes
problematic behaviors to an inhabiting spirit:

> Spoon . . . was suddenly sent for in great haste and told that his wife, who
> had attended a sabbath at such and such a spot, was taken with the madness

of the gods. He went as fast as he could to the place indicated, and found that his wife was really beside herself, and dancing like a person possessed. He had never before noticed in her the slightest sign of possession. The spirit began to speak, as soon as she was somewhat calmed down, and gave answers to the questions put to it: "I entered into this *ligodo,* i.e. into this body, this vessel, in such and such a manner. Her husband [Spoon] had gone to work in the gold mines. I entered into him while he was seated on a stone, and when he returned home I left him and entered into his wife." (Junod 1927/1962, II:487–8)[5]

Within the joint traditions of Judaism, Christianity, and Islam are numerous accounts of possession by spirits. The prophets of ancient Israel were regarded as speaking with the tongue of the Lord (YHWH), delivering his message. Jesus exorcised malevolent spirits from afflicted humans. In classical Greece, the oracle at Delphi was possessed by the spirit of the god Apollo. Kabbalistic Judaism knows of possession by a *dybbuk,* the spirit of someone deceased. During the ceremonials of some Christian denominations—frontier revivals at rural campgrounds; primitive Baptist congregations; charismatic Catholic communities—it was and is frequent for at least some participants to be seized with "the Holy Ghost" and thereupon engage in phenomena such as "speaking with tongues" and bodily paroxysm, becoming amnesic afterward. What should be emphasized about these cases is not merely an individual's being "possessed" (or "inhabited" by another being or spirit), but the even more significant fact that the audience accepted the display as veridical, neither fraudulent nor "psychopathological." I do not want to postulate a credulous audience that invariably accepted the claim of the presence of a foreign spirit or divinity within the human host, as there are accounts in which some or all of the native observers were dubious as to the actuality of "possession"; but this skepticism was a critique of the particular instance rather than of the phenomenon in general. With Durkheim and his school we may speak of "social facts" (*faites sociaux*), as contrasted to physiologically oriented investigators who seek to disenchant by demonstrating that the individual's nervous system does not contain an alien self.

Where possession differs from multiple personality is in the scene, the scenario, the nature of the personae who inhabit. In the contemporary "disorder" the "inhabitants" are other human "selves"—seemingly, aspects of the actor. Whereas in the anthropological and historical cases the inhabitants are clearly intruders or invaders, even if invited or solicited, in Western discourse the inhabitants would usually be considered "divinities" (benevolent or malevolent), but they might also be ancestral or nonhuman spirits. Moreover, in the typical anthropological account, the event is socially structured as ritual rather than as happenstance; and where it is considered as betokening "disorder," the disordering is envisioned as social and familial rather than individual and idiosyncratic. However, one must also note that in some minority of cases, possession by a vodou deity occurs outside of the formal ceremonial configuration; Métraux attributes these events to "fatigue" or shock, such as an automobile accident (1958:116). Within the milieu of Brazilian Umbanda, akin to Haitian vodou, are cases of individuals who are mounted by "disincarnate" spirits—of deceased persons who had led especially wicked lives (Bourguignon 1989 citing Pressel 1977).

The Self in Possession-Trance

The leading characteristic of possession-trance within vodou is *play* or *theater*. The person mounted—*montée,* usually female—is no longer "present" as an actor and so is not responsible for her (physical) actions, which are perceived by her confrères as the behavior of the lwa (deity). It is as if she is performing a totally absorbing role within a theatrical play, for what is performed by the actress cannot be considered as integral with her "real life." *Playing* Medea, the actress on the stage then deceives her stage partners, murders her rivals, and slaughters her own children. Nevertheless, once she leaves the stage no one presumes to bring her to judgment; rather, the critics will salute the veracity of her performance—how convincingly she played the role, how much terror and horror she provoked in her audience.

What is similar within vodou possession is the boundedness of the role. The behavior of the horse is specific to and limited by that particular ritual event:

> Almost every detail is specified for the aspects of the loa, and these serve both to identify him and to guide his ritual service. Postures, voice level, attitudes, epithets, expressions, etc., are formalized for each aspect. (Deren 1951/1970:95 footnote)

While any instance is thus bounded, its enactment does not even presage what might occur within the next ceremonial, except that there will be a presumption that the human horse is likely to be mounted by the same lwa, a presumption that may be strengthened by other ritual events (such as a ritual "marriage" to the lwa).

To be an adult within a social community is to be embedded in enduring relations with others, to have duties and responsibilities and be accorded privileges and intimacies that are long term. The framing of the vodou ceremonial provides the opportunity for a "time-out"—a shattering of that connectedness, a disruption that seemingly is both sought and resisted. The concentration on the rhythms of the dancing and the music, the fatigue and the monotony, the emphasis on the moment to moment, provides a psychic channel for disrupting the connections to daily existence. When possession does occur, then—to move into Sullivan's vocabulary—this brings "into play" aspects of the psyche that are not within the self-dynamism of the quotidian actor. ("The self must leave if the loa is to enter. . . . Never have I seen the face of such anguish, ordeal and blind terror as the moment when the loa comes. All this no man would ordinarily accept" [Deren 1970/1951:249].[6]) I note, for example, that possession, especially in the early stages, is often marked by aggressive and destructive behaviors.

As is evident from Campbell's preface to Deren's book, the Jungian vocabulary of archetypes seems applicable to the conduct of the person possessed by a lwa. Were this simply a release of repressed impulses (aggressive, erotic, malicious, sadistic, masochistic, etc.), one might expect conduct that was idiosyncratic and ungoverned, rather than conduct so stereotyped that the mounting deity is immediately identified.

Suspending the Dynamism of the Self Process

A "suspension of self" may at times be sought, actively, enthusiastically. The implication would be that maintaining the self is a burden—quintessentially human but nonetheless tiring (energy consuming?). Suspending the self is, characteristically, a phenomenon that may occur within either erotic or ritually religious situations.[7] Here in the realm presently labeled as "altered states of consciousness," it will be useful to distinguish states of trance from those of dissociated performance, whether within vodou possession or multiple personality. To the extent that the mnemonic system is associated with the self dynamism, amnesia—partially or entirely—for the experience would be a consequence.

For the amnesia that characterizes both multiple personality disorder (MPD) and spiritual possession, we have labels, *repression* and *dissociation*, and some psychodynamic insight.[8] In the case of the disorder, investigators attribute the amnesia to trauma and conflict, but even these explanations are inadequate, since, following Sullivan, the self-dynamism emerges precisely in order to handle anxiety and disapprobation.

If the self is situated in relationship to problems of emotional valence, it would follow that as the individual sheds those concerns, then the self-dynamism becomes minimal. We have already noted two exemplars: dreaming and the ceremonials of vodou. We may also add that in the scenarios (or charades) of "Bondage and Discipline" (S&M), the submissive surrenders volition, as in the configurations described by Murray (1996). As he notes, pain is not the goal but the pathway.[9]

Other pathways may be found in the well-known ritual techniques that push or pull the individual into totally concentrating on immediate sensual experience and surrendering any concern with actions, problems, desires. Bharati, trained in both European schools and Hindu ashrams,[10] explains:

> [T]hough meditation is a purely mental process it aims at eradicating mentation in the end: the mind experiences a complete catharsis, it gets emptied of all contents. [In his lectures, Bharati spoke of "zero state."] This is totally different from sleep, stupor, drowsiness, imbecility and certain drug-induced states, for there are all sorts of contents in these states, albeit misarranged, or pathologically distorted. Meditation leads to an emptiness of mind which, again, just cannot be described to anyone who has not gone through it. (Bharati 1961:125–6)
>
> What, then, is the final target of tantric *sadhana* and of the tantric life? It is the same as that of all Hindu and Buddhist religion, namely the freedom from the misery of attachment. . . . Following Professor M. Eliade, I used the term "enstasy" instead of ecstasy . . . . Enstasy, in all these traditions, is a non-discursive, quasi-permanent condition of the individual agent, and is highly euphoric. In Indian theological parlance—Hindu, Buddhist, and Jain—it is tantamount with supreme insight or wisdom, and all other knowledge attained by discursive processes is thought to be vastly inferior. (Bharati 1965:285–6)

Trauma and Self Instability

If the social environment is traumatically unstable as the child is beginning to speak and to construct a self, then one would expect an instability within the self system. The child would be unable to construct a "generalized other" (as conceptualized by G. H. Mead) and would suffer a pathological lack of psychic integration.

With trauma so severe as to inhibit or deconstruct the self,[11] the consequence might then be autism or catatonia, the failure to develop speech or the loss of that capacity, the inability to interact with others by taking their role, or the consequent inability to act in an active or planful fashion other than by responding to momentary stimuli. But, were one to follow Sullivan's lead, those queries become preliminary to another set of questions. For, if the self emerges to deal with the approbation and disapprobation of the mothering person, why or how should that process fail, even given the inflicting of trauma?

Clinically, there is consensus that early sexual trauma causes lesions in the self system, and the damage is more severe when the sexual attacks are performed by adults to whom the child is emotionally attached[12] (in relationship to sleep and dreaming, especially relevant are the essays of Deidre Barrett 1996a, 1997). Part of the problem in accepting the frangibility of the developing self is the implicit assumption of unified selves of the mother or other caretakers. Once we realize that they, too, may have complex selves—and dissociated behaviors—then (within the Mead-Sullivan tradition) it would naturally follow that their offspring would have to split psychically to cope and survive.

The discourse among cultural anthropologists has likewise been nuanced and complex. Most agree that the mechanisms of "altered states of consciousness"—trance states, dreams, ritually induced visions—constitute a vital resource that has been denigrated by modern bureaucratic society at great cost to the psychic well-being of its members. However, others argue that the elaborate forms of possession trance, as in vodou or santería, are symptoms, being responses to exploitation and oppression, the assaults of imperialism, and the invasion of the market economy. Feminists note a greater incidence of possession among women than men. A dissident few suggest that the small exotic societies, so often regarded as the milieu of "the noble savage," are instead subject to more severe pathology than Western observers—themselves deracinated and alienated—permitted themselves to see (Edgerton 1992).

In short, the current clinical interest in multiple personality disorder and dissociation has the potential of an increase in the understanding of the psyche and the self, but only providing that the inquiry moves beyond the cultural frontiers of modern Euro-America.

Other Psychodynamic Theories

Besides Sullivan, many psychodynamic theoreticians have developed conceptions of the self. The work of the British "Middle Group" of psychoanalysts of the past generation—Harry Guntrip, W. R. D. Fairbairn, Donald W. Winnicott, John D. Sutherland—has been greatly influential in reshaping the psychoanalytic domain. Also influential among analysts have been the arguments of Heinz Kohut about the self and the nature of "selfobjects" (the latter echoing the American Pragmatists). The rhetoric of Jacques Lacan has been divisive among French analysts (Anzieu 1986; Oliner 1988), but remains popular in the United States. In addition, there is the research of Daniel N. Stern, and the cross-cultural comparisons of Alan Roland. While the critical exposition of these therapists and researchers would distract from the present discussion, I will note a few of the observations of the British Middle group that I have found congenial. I begin with the views of Winnicott:

> "[W]e are poor indeed if we are only sane." In fact, he [Winnicott] found that there were individuals "so firmly anchored in objective reality that they are ill in the direction of being out of touch with the subjective world and

with the creative approach to fact." Such people need help because they feel estranged from dream, "because they have lost contact with infantile experience in the merged state. . . . At the theoretical start, the baby lives in a dream world while awake. What is there when he or she is awake becomes material for dreams." In the creative experience in the potential space, something of this sort of affairs reappears. This something is also related to the hallucinations of the schizoid or schizophrenic individual. (Davis and Wallbridge 1981:163, synthesizing several of Winnicott's essays)

Sutherland noted that therapeutic studies of mother and infant (by Winnicott) supported the clinical findings of Fairbairn, which contradicted Freud's emphasis on the dream as "wish fulfillment":

Fairbairn regards dreaming not as wish-fulfillment but as the spontaneous "imaginative" playing out of relations amongst [others]. The person, in short, emerges as a cast of characters, each related to a specific [other]. These systems of self-object relationships have constant dynamic effects on each other and are also in perceptual contact with the other world, so that when it presents a situation that fits what an inner split self is seeking, then the latter can become activated to the point of taking overall control of the self. (Sutherland 1989:169–70; Scharff 1994:346)

As thus expounded by Sutherland, there is an echo of Cooley and a marked parallelism to the views of Sullivan.

Concluding Remarks

The attention of biomedicine is also focused on the solitary body of the individual sick person because of Western society's powerful orientation to *individual* experience. That illness infiltrates and deeply affects social relations is a difficult understanding to advance in biomedicine. Population and community-based public health orientations run counter to the dominant biomedical orientation, which takes for its subject the isolated and isolatable organism. In contrast, African healing systems see illness as part of kinship networks and healing as kinship or community effort [citations omitted]. The foundation of biomedical psychiatry is also a single self in a single body. The presence of alternative selves or dissociated mental states, measured against this norm, is interpreted as pathology. Trance and possession, which are ubiquitous cross-cultural processes that serve social purposes and can be interpersonally useful, are invariably cast by biomedical nosologies as pathology. In contrast, the sociocentric orientation of various non-biomedical forms of healing will strike many people as a more adequate appreciation of the experiential phenomenology of suffering cross-culturally. (Kleinman 1995:36–37)

My conclusions range from the simply empirical to the intuitive and theoretical and, I fear, far outrun the preceding discussion. First, the challenges to the possibility of "multiple personality" are misdirected. Mutabilities—whether of self or personality—are well established not only by both clinical and comparative evidence but within common experience. What may be at issue is the amnesia, but even here the issue should not truly be the possibility but the degrees and actualities of remembering, forgetting, and distorting in specific cases. If we conceive of mnemonic systems as aspects of the psyche and the self, then memory and forgetting become far more complex functions (as neuroscientists have rediscovered). Moreover, since amnesia is clearly established for some trance states, even that issue is less fraught than claimed.

Second, with vodou and other trance states as examples, amnesias of this sort are not necessarily signs of psychopathology. We do not know enough about these psychic exercises, except that both the comparative and laboratory evidences agree that some trance or meditative states have marked therapeutic benefits. What is psychopathological—and sociopathological—is the Euro-American image of the alexithymic "rational man," detached from affect. In judging either of these polarities we must be careful to acknowledge that we are dealing with matters beyond simplistic notions of psychic health but are instead normative and aesthetic.

Third, it is important to distinguish the self system as but a part, unit, or function of the total psyche (and total person). The ideal self system is paradoxical: on the one hand, able to focus intently on tasks; on the other hand, able to allow the processing and apprehending of experiences that were selectively inattended, momentarily occurring outside of focused awareness. Likewise, the ideal self system would permit alterations of the persona to fit the requirements of the social and physical environment yet have the stability, integrity, and toughness to perdure in the face of a difficult and harsh world.

Fourth, using Sullivan's metaphor of the self system as a microscope that focuses awareness, we see that dreaming is then an activity that allows the expansion of the self by permitting the entrance of perceptions from outside conscious awareness, whether recent or infantile.

Fifth, the Freudian notion of *transference* here reappears as mutability of self, dependent upon the nature of the social interaction.

Sixth—and a point I have not elaborated here but do elsewhere in this book—precisely because dreaming introduces materials that have been selectively inattended, the regular narrating of dreams among an intimate group serves to enlarge the sphere of commonality and to permit an emotional attunement among its members. Thus, knowledge acquired through dreaming is considered to have a special ambiance or truth.

Notes

1. "The dream character, as an hallucinated projection of aspects of the self, can be seen as a prototype for the MPD [multiple personality disorder] alter" (Barrett 1995:61).

2. In a 1996 paper Littlewood purports to balance between the skepticism of biomedicine and the suspension of disbelief characteristic of cultural anthropology. His own stance is clear from the initial Scotus epigraph (*entia non sunt multiplicanda praeter necessitatem*) together with his handling of a psychiatric case: an immigrant from Dominica who had attempted to handle a personal dilemma by recourse to multiple personality disorder (MPD) (note 46, pp. 43–45).

3. Comparably, one may note with Merkur (1993:3) that "[t]he modern study of mysticism began in the late nineteenth century when medical psychologists noted that phenomena resembling those recorded of Christian mystics were being produced by inmates of mental asylums." As his initial epigraph, Merkur cites Elias Ashmole: "Incredulity is given to the world as punishment."

4. [O]ne of the central surrender lessons has to do with possession. Through ritual means, an attempt is made to pull the initiate over the edge and into the deep waters of trance. . . . No one easily gives up consciousness and the control associated with it. . . . In 1980 Alourdes described possession in this way: "When the spirit going to come in you head you feel very light, light like a piece of paper . . . very light in your head. You feel dizzy in your head. Then after, you pass out. But the spirit come, and he talk to people. . . . Then he leaves and . . . and you come from very, very far. But when the spirit in your body, in your head, you don't know nothing." (Brown 1991:352–3)

5. Henri A. Junod (1863–1904) was a Swiss missionary who lived and labored for decades among the BaThonga of Africa. His accounts of possession indicated that diagnoses may establish that several spirits (indeed as many as ten) may be inhabiting the afflicted. His *The Life of a South African tribe* (1927) would be quite independent of the recent U.S. disputes about possession and multiple personality disorder and dissociative identity disorder (MPD/DID).

6. Citing Scott Tucker, Murray (1996:84) writes:

Mystics develop reliable techniques for achieving ecstasy and getting out of the self. "Sexual passion often promises—and threatens—a loss of self. . . . We deliberately concentrate sensation in order to diffuse personality," (Tucker 1990:30) wrote. Indeed, increasing pain and mortification are among the most tried-and-true techniques in the history of religion, although "pain largely remains a mystery even to insiders. Among sane and experienced leatherfolk, pain is a path and not a destination." (Tucker 1987:44)

7. I put aside the suspending of self that occurs within the framework of an authoritarian movement; see Fromm 1941.

8. If dissociation is a sorting process, then the various psychic units or personalities that exist within the individual are *not* subject to "amnesia." In dissociation there is no forgetting, no loss of memory. To forget one has first to be aware of something and then lose awareness of that thing. That is not what occurs in dissociation. The various psychic units *never had knowledge* of the experiences assigned to the other units and so could not *forget* them. (Crabtree 1992:8 as cited in Braude 1996:48)

9. "'For me to transcend doing S&M doesn't happen with severe stimuli but with a steady building of the stimuli. If I can gently take a curve that brings me over my pain limit—a gentle, sloping curve, as opposed to a sharp spike, then I actually leave my body'" (anonymous woman in Brame, Brame, and Jacobs 1996:224).

10. Born Leopold Fischer in Vienna, Bharati early devoted himself to Indic Studies. After World War II, he moved to India, where he joined a monastic order and continued his scholarly studies, eventually becoming ordained in the Dasanami Order of Sannyasi monks. Later, he came to the United States and until his untimely death was professor of anthropology, Syracuse University.

11. From the voluminous literature of controversy, I cite Barrett ed. (1996b); Bremner and Marmer (1998); Cohen, Berzoff, and Elin (1995); Freyd (1996); Gartner (1997); Hunter (1990); Krippner and Powers (1997); Pendergast (1995); Young (1995).

12. When a child is subjected over time to a trauma like sexual abuse by a trusted parent, the enormity of the betrayal and the physical and psychological violation challenges the child's very basic and essential capacity to trust and, therefore, to depend. . . . The young child is forced to integrate irreconcilable emotional schemata. . . .

The nature of unconscious process, rather than being embedded in fossilized stone, emerges more fluidly out of the particular constellation of self and object-related experience. . . . Not *one* unconscious, not *the* unconscious, but *multiple levels* of consciousness and unconsciousness in an ongoing state of interactive articulation as past experience infuses the present and present experience evokes state-dependent memories of formative interactive representations. . . . Not an onion, which must be carefully peeled, not an archaeological site to be meticulously unearthed and reconstructed in its original form, but a child's kaleidoscope in which each glance through the pinhole of moment in time provides a unique view. (Davies 1997:53, 55)

Among many others confirming the relationship between dissociation and sexual abuse in childhood, note Cohen (1996).

Chapter 4

Joseph, Freud, and the Judaic Tradition

In the two great centers of Near Eastern civilization, Egypt and Mesopotamia, at either extremity of the Fertile Crescent, the science of dream interpretation was highly developed as a specialized skill, and a vast literature devoted to the subject came into being. One extant Egyptian papyrus, inscribed about 1300 B.C.E. and claiming to be a copy of an archetype at least five hundred years older, is actually a reference book of dream interpretations arranged systematically according to symbol and meaning. We are told, for example, that seeing a large cat in a dream is good, for it portends a large harvest. Looking into a deep well, on the other hand, is bad, for it is premonitory of incarceration. (Sarna 1966:213)

Masters of Dreams

In neither the Hebrew Bible nor the Talmud is there a status for the specialist in dream interpretation (a "paradigmatic oneirocritic" [Harris 1994]). Within the Pentateuch, the most eminent interpreter of dreams was Joseph, who was recognized by Egyptian royalty for this ability; yet even he is not biblically designated as "a dream interpreter." His brothers refer to him as the "master of dreams" (ba'al ha-halomot[1]), but this is derisive, not designative.

Just as the biblical Joseph achieved eminence by skill in interpreting dreams within an alien society, so too did Sigmund Freud, who identified himself with his Hebraic ancestor. From the Joseph narratives, we can acquire perspective on dreams, their cultural significance, and what is implied by the act of interpretation. Moreover, the Joseph narratives are easily available in the biblical text of Genesis, and since they reveal much about the usages of dreams and their interpretations, I am devoting this chapter to their discussion.

Joseph and His Brothers

Joseph was the child of Jacob and the most beloved of his wives, Rachel.
Among the numerous sons of Jacob (Israel), it was Joseph who was most
cherished: his favored status symbolized by the paternal gift of an elegant
coat (in the King James translation, "a coat of many colors").[2]

The grandeur of this gift intensified his brothers' hostility, which became even stronger when he publicly recited his dreams:

> And Joseph dreamed a dream, and he told it to his brethren; and they
> hated him yet the more. And he said unto them: "Hear, I pray you, this
> dream which I have dreamed: for, behold, we were binding sheaves in the
> field, and lo, my sheaf arose, and also stood upright; and behold your
> sheaves came round about, and bowed down to my sheaf." And his
> brethren said to him: "Shalt thou indeed reign over us? or shalt thou in-
> deed have dominion over us?" And they hated him yet the more for his
> dreams, and for his words.
>
> And he dreamed yet another dream, and told it to his brethren, and said:
> "Behold, I have dreamed yet a dream: and, behold, the sun and the moon
> and the eleven stars bowed down to me." And he told it to his father, and to
> his brethren; and his father rebuked him, and said unto him: 'What is this
> dream that thou hast dreamed? Shall I and thy mother and thy brethren in-
> deed come to bow down to thee to the earth?" (Genesis 37:5–10, JPS)

What is noteworthy about this text is not merely the recitation of
Joseph's dream but that his father and his brothers immediately understood the significance of the dream and that the biblical narrator could
assume that the audience, in turn, would understand the total situation:
the dreaming, its meaning, the response of Joseph's family. Or, to invert
the situation, the narrator does not pause to explain to a skeptical audience that dreams have a meaning. Indeed, the meaning of dreams is so
indubitable that they can serve as the impetus for action:

> And Joseph went after his brethren, and found them in Dotham. And they
> saw him afar off, and before he came near unto them, they conspired against
> him to slay him. And they said one to another: "Behold, the dreamer [*ba'al
> ha-halomot*] cometh. Come now therefore, and let us slay him, and cast him
> into one of these pits, and we will say: An evil beast hath devoured him; and
> we shall see what will become of his dreams." (Genesis 37:17b-20, JPS)

Within a small intimate community such as the biblical family of Jacob—
or the psychotherapeutic dyad—a dream can express a meaningful pre-
hension. Unconsciously, the individual may perceive characteristics or at-
titudes of intimate others, and so of their potential interaction, and this
may then be expressed in the form of a dream. The spoiled and arrogant

Joseph had intuited his potential dominance over his brothers (akin to that of his father, Jacob, vis-à-vis *his* brother, Esau, as well as his father-in-law, Laban). Jacob had skillfully practiced deception and theft. Aided by his mother, Jacob had deceived his father, Isaac, and cheated Esau of his birthright. Later, he and Laban had each deceived the other, although finally Jacob had achieved the upper hand, departing not only with Laban's daughters (and their handmaids), but with much of his sheep and cattle, and even his household gods.

The Interpreter in Prison

Sold by his brothers to traveling merchants, Joseph was conveyed to Egypt where his talents first brought rapid advancement, then confinement within a prison designed for servants of the elite, and next a role as assistant to the warden. Two inmates, formerly servants to the Egyptian monarch, were troubled by their dreams. When they indicated that they wished for the services of a specialist in interpretation, Joseph interpolated himself with the comment "Do not interpretations belong to God?"

> And the prince of the butlers told his dream to Joseph and said to him: In my dream, behold a vine was before me. And on the vine were three tendrils, and as it budded, the blossoms bloomed, and its clusters matured into grapes. And Pharaoh's cup was in my hand, and I took the grapes and pressed them into Pharaoh's cup and I gave the cup to Pharaoh.
>
> And Joseph said unto him: This is the interpretation of it: The three tendrils are three days. Within yet three days, Pharaoh will lift up thine head and restore thee to thy office, and thou shalt give Pharaoh's cup into his hand, like the previous manner when thou wast his butler. (Genesis 40:9–13, Hirsch trans.)

> When the prince of the bakers saw that he had interpreted well, he said to Joseph: I, too, was in my dream, and behold three baskets of superior appearance were on my head. And in the uppermost basket were all kinds of Pharaoh's food, baker's work, and the birds ate them out of the basket from on my head.
>
> And Joseph answered and said: This is the interpretation: the three baskets are three days. Within yet three days shall Pharaoh lift up thy head from off thee, and hang thee on a tree, and the birds shall eat thy flesh from off thee. (Genesis 40:16–19, Hirsch trans.)

The text gives no clues for Joseph's interpretation. If there were linguistic clues, they might have been present in the Egyptian language of the time (whose terms do occur within the text of Pharaoh's dream, to be discussed shortly). There is a macabre word play in the twin interpretations, where Joseph speaks of each prisoner having his head "lifted up": to the butler signifying release and royal favor, but to the baker his execution.

Assuming the basic logic of the biblical narrative, the dreams of the imprisoned baker and butler reveal that they have correctly intuited the judgments of their master, Pharaoh. In thus deciphering their dreams, Joseph (in his turn) is intuiting their unconscious knowledge. His attribution to God of the ability to interpret dreams was accurate, in the sense that the ability does not derive from rational planful intention. Within the prison, Joseph had become the assistant to its superintendent, and, in consequence, he was for a season the person who attended to the care of the imperial officers imprisoned by Pharaoh. Accordingly, he might well have acquired "unconscious" knowledge of these men, prior to interpreting their dreams.

Unconscious Attunement

Whether or not the adventures of Joseph are historically accurate, millions have read them and found them plausible. I am contending that his ability at interpreting the dreams of the butler and baker testifies to a series of unconscious attunements: theirs to Pharaoh; his to them. A cynical rejoinder would be that Joseph's interpretations proved accurately predictive because the three parties had each been privy to court gossip; surely that would have been a historical possibility. Nevertheless, the intriguing aspect is not the original Egyptian events, but the willingness of generations of biblical readers to accept the scenario of Joseph's interpretation de novo. To these readers (or auditors), the biblical tale meshed with reality.

Somewhat diffidently, field ethnographers have reported similar oneiric intercommunication. From her field experiences among the Barok of New Ireland, Marianne George (1995) reports a dream encounter with her native adopted sister, an elderly woman. The next morning, the woman's sons inquired whether she had understood the message so conveyed, and their queries were those of persons who had been witnesses to the dream scene.

The Interpreter in the Palace

Joseph's accuracy in interpreting the dreams of the butler and baker—and so forecasting their destinies—was to result in his coming to the attention of their master, the Egyptian pharaoh. The Bible (and Freud) attribute this to his skill in interpreting dreams, but beneath the manifest narrative is a subtext revealing Joseph's keen abilities in discerning hidden anxieties and ambitions. The opportunity developed because of a pair of dreams that in the biblical text are each reported twice: once, as experienced by Pharaoh; then, as he narrated them to Joseph. Intriguingly, there are minor differences between the two reports. Here are the pair of dreams as experienced:

> [Pharaoh dreamed:] behold he stood by the river considering it.
>
> And lo, there came up out of the river, seven cows, well favoured and healthy in flesh, and they went grazing in the meadow.
>
> And lo, seven other cows came up after them out of the river, ill favoured and leanfleshed, and they stood next to the cows upon the brink of the river.
>
> And the ill favoured and leanfleshed cows ate up the seven well favoured and fat cows and Pharaoh awoke.
>
> And he slept and dreamt a second time: And behold seven ears of corn came up on one stalk, healthy and good.
>
> And behold seven ears of corn, thin and blasted by the east wind, grew up after them.
>
> And the thin ears of corn swallowed up the seven healthy and full ears of corn. And Pharaoh awoke and lo! it was a dream.
>
> And it came to pass in the morning that his spirit was unquiet, and he sent and called all those versed in hieroglyphics in Egypt, and all the wise men thereof, and Pharaoh told them his dream, but there was none that could interpret them unto Pharaoh. (Genesis 41:1–8; Hirsch trans.)

The small familial group of Jacob required no specialist to interpret the dream of one of its members, whereas Pharaoh's household did include such specialists; however, these worthies could not supply a plausible interpretation (or, at least not one that Pharaoh accepted as accurate). Thereupon the Prince Butler recollected the interpretive foresight of Joseph, who was consequentially brought to the palace. Joseph disclaims any personal skill: the ability to interpret "is not in me; God will give Pharaoh an answer of peace." The monarch now recites the pair of dreams:

> And Pharaoh said unto Joseph: I have dreamt a dream and there is none that can interpret it, and I have heard say of thee that thou hearest a dream so that thou interpretest it.
>
> And Joseph answered saying: That is not up to me! May God answer Pharaoh with peace.
>
> And Pharaoh spake unto Joseph: In my dream, behold, I was standing upon the edge of the river.
>
> And behold, out of the river there came up seven cows, healthy of flesh and beautiful in form, and they grazed in the meadow.
>
> And behold, seven other cows came up after them, poor and very ill-favoured and lacking flesh, such as I never saw in the whole land of Egypt for ugliness.
>
> And the thin and bad cows ate up the first seven healthy cows.

And when they had come inside them, it could not be recognised that they had come inside them, their appearance was so bad as at the beginning. Then I woke up.

And I saw in my dream, and behold, seven ears came up on one stalk, full and good.

And behold, seven ears, hard, thin, blasted by the east wind, sprang up after them.

And the thin ears swallowed up the seven good ears. (Genesis 41:15–24a; Hirsch trans.)

We should note the minor differences between the two versions of Pharaoh's dreams—the first as experienced, the second as recited. In both versions, he stands by the river: in the experienced version, he is considering it; in the narrated version, he simply stands by its edge. In the experienced version, the second group of cows are "ill favoured and lean-fleshed"; in the narrated version, the second group of cows are not only lean but ugly, an ugliness intensified by their failure to benefit from incorporating the fat cows; the cannibalistic feast does not better their condition. Furthermore, and what is not apparent from the English translation, the descriptive language used by Pharaoh is far from that of a butcher examining a potential carcass; rather, it is aesthetic, especially in the narrated version, in which the first group of cows are beautifully formed, while the second group are needy, miserable, badly formed. In short, the dream contains a clue that the cattle are symbolic.

As additional background, "the river" can only be the Nile. Annually, that river waxed and waned, and the nutrient waters of its flood stage provided the basis for the harvest of grain and for the reed grass that nourished the cattle. The Egyptian pharaoh was identified with the Nile, and his imperial cult was divinely responsible for its flooding and the resultant fertility of the land. That religious role had its risk, as evident from a text dating with the reign of King Djoser (ca. twenty-eighth century B.C.E.):

I was in distress on the Great Throne, and those who are in the palace were in heart's affliction from a very great evil, since the Nile had not come in my time for a space of seven years. Grain was scant, fruits were dried up, and everything which they eat was short. (Pritchard 1955:31 as cited in Sarna 1966:219)

It is thus reasonable—but not obvious—to interpret the figure of the monarchical dreamer standing by the river, "considering it," as being anxiously concerned with whether the river will progress into its annual flood. Joseph's interpretation thus displaced from Pharaoh the responsibility for the forthcoming drought: the onus was on the one God, rather than on the divine pharaoh within the complex Egyptian pantheon. I might also remark that the cow represents milk, and within the pantheon her apotheosis was Hathor, a figure of fertility. Finally, the Hebraic *seven* signifies satiety or plenty (Katz 1963) but here provides the binary opposition.

Joseph, that alien of remarkable intuition, is willing to state publicly the meaning of Pharaoh's pair of dreams, as providing a divine rationale for a vast system of taxation, presented as a cautionary program of centralized storage of grain. It is reasonable to presume that such a program would have generated grave discontent among the agricultural populace, so that it was politically appropriate that its director be conspicuously alien and putatively of great psychic potency, gifted at discerning the plans of the deity (or deities). Joseph's interpretation not only had the merit of displacing responsibility for the coming drought from Pharaoh himself to a higher order of divinity—denoted by Joseph's reference to the one God—but also suggested displacing mundane responsibility from the monarch to a potential minister:

> And Joseph said unto Pharaoh: The dream of Pharaoh is one, what God is about to do He hath declared unto Pharaoh.
> The seven good cows are seven years, and the seven good ears are seven years; the dream is one.
> And the seven lean and bad cows that came up after them, are seven years, and the seven empty ears blasted by the east-wind shall be seven years of famine.
> That is the thing which I spake unto Pharaoh: What God is about to do He hath shown Pharaoh.
> See seven years are coming of great plenty throughout all the land of Egypt.
> And there will arise after them seven years of famine, and all the plenty will be forgotten in the land of Egypt, and the famine will ruin the land.
> And the plenty will not be known in the land by reason of that famine which followeth it will be very grievous. . . .
> So now let Pharaoh look for a man discreet and wise and set him over the land of Egypt.
> Let Pharaoh do this, appoint officers over the land and impose a fifth on the land of Egypt during the seven years of plenty. . . .
> And Pharaoh said unto his servitors: Can we find such a one as this, a man in whom the Spirit of God is?
> And Pharaoh said unto Joseph: Forasmuch as God hath let thee know all this, there is none as discreet and wise as thou art.
> Thou shalt be over my house . . . only by the throne will I be greater than thou. (Genesis 41:25–40)

No claims need be advanced for Joseph's abilities as a long-range climatological forecaster, except to guess that he perceived—and utilized—a deep insecurity and powerful ambition on the part of the imperial overlord. Finally, it should again be noted that for the biblical writers and their audience, it was conventional and responsible—unremarkable—for a ruler to give close attention to dreams and make their interpretation the basis for major policy.

Moral Ambiguities

The shrewdness of Joseph's responses to Pharaoh propelled him from the prison house to minister of state. They enabled the monarchy to institute a vast system of taxation under the aegis of an alien gifted with supermundane insight. Taking seriously a biblical account that exhibits familiarity with the Egyptian court and its customs, I would critically note the collusion between the Egyptian ruler and the Hebrew slave. Joseph provided Pharaoh with a divine rationale for increasing the power and wealth of the court, while simultaneously nominating himself to head what would be presented as a preventative program of grain storage but resulted in expropriation:

> And there was no bread in all the land; for the famine was very sore, so that the land of Egypt and the land of Canaan languished by reason of the famine. And Joseph gathered up all the money that was found in the land of Egypt and in the land of Canaan, for the corn which they bought; and Joseph brought the money into Pharaoh's house. And when the money was all spent in the land of Egypt and in the land of Canaan, all the Egyptians came unto Joseph, and said: "Give us bread; for why should we die in thy presence? for our money faileth." And Joseph said: "Give your cattle, and I will give you [bread] for your cattle, if money fail." And they brought their cattle unto Joseph. And Joseph gave them bread in exchange for the horses, and for the flocks, and for the herds, and for the asses; and he fed them with bread in exchange for all their cattle for that year. And when that year was ended, they came unto him the second year, and said unto him: "We will not hide from my lord, how that our money is all spent; and the herds of cattle are my lord's; there is nought left in the sight of my lord, but our bodies and our hands. Wherefore would we die before thine eyes, both we and our land? Buy us and our land for bread, and we and our land will be bondmen unto Pharaoh; and give us seed, that we may live and not die, and that the land be not desolate." So Joseph brought all the land of Egypt for Pharaoh; for the Egyptians sold every man his field, because the famine was sore upon them; and the land became Pharaoh's. And as for the people, he removed them city by city, from one end of the border of Egypt even to the other end thereof. (Genesis 47:13–21, JPS)

For both Hebrews and Christians, Joseph has epitomized piety accompanied and rewarded by divine blessings, including psychic gifts and foretelling. The period of drought and famine would surely have justified the instituting of a system of requisition and storage of grain, but not the consequent expropriation and serfdom. The actualities thus fulfilled Pharaoh's dream as narrated: the seven fat and well-favored cows are devoured by the seven lean and ugly ones, who do not benefit from their cannibalistic feast but remain before us as lean and ugly; so the people and land of Egypt are now in far worse condition than they were before the seven years of plenty. There is an even more profound psychic symbolism in Pharaoh's dream: when the evil feed on that which is good and healthy, they do not benefit (Mendelsohn, personal communication, 1996).

I do not insist on the truth of the biblical tale of Joseph in Egypt[3] but am only noting the moral weakness of its status as parable (see Sternberg 1987:428f). I am therefore troubled not only that Freud identified so with Joseph, but even more that subsequent commentators (e.g., Szaluta 1994; McGrath 1986) should have judged this identification uncritically and generally favorably.

Freud's Identification with Joseph

> It is striking that the name *Josef* plays so great a role in my dreams. . . . I, myself, am easily concealed behind the people of that name, since *Josef* was the name of a man famous in the Bible as an interpreter of dreams.[4] (see 1900/1965:522, footnote)

Sigmund Freud had been introduced to the Hebrew Bible when young, and the identifications between him and Joseph are strong and acknowledged. Both had fathers named Jacob, who married several women. Both Joseph and Sigmund were preferred to their siblings and favored by their father and their mother. Both made careers by their cleverness and wits within an alien milieu dominated by an institutionalized religion unsympathetic to their people. Both were interpreters of dreams—their own and others.' Freud spoke of *Die Traumdeutung* as an "Egyptian dream book" (letter to Fliess, August 6, 1889), while beginning chapter 2 of *The Interpretation of Dreams* by differentiating his interpretive approach from that of Joseph, which he labeled "symbolic," further commenting that "the artificial dreams constructed by imaginative writers" are designed for a symbolic interpretation. The argument need not be pressed: Freud was aware of the biblical Joseph and, although differentiating his interpretive mode from Joseph's, nonetheless identified with him (see Szaluta 1994:18–22; McGrath 1986: chap. 1).

What we perceive with both Joseph and Freud is how the interpreting of dreams can be used not to further the self-knowledge of the dreamer but to advance the career of the interpreter. Overall, Freud seems to have been a person of high ethical standards (Rieff 1959), however authoritarian, patriarchal, and intolerant. Nevertheless, there is a taint of moral weakness in Freud's attempt to deflect guilt from Fliess in the bungled operation on Emma Eckstein, and equally so in his misinterpretations of Dora's age and her dreams.

At times Freud spoke of himself as having the temperament of "a conquistador" rather than a therapist or scientist. Within fin-de-siècle Vienna, a Jew might have required the ruthlessness of a conquistador to forge a professional career and institute a novel discipline, but that orientation would betray the movement which he brought into being. A conquistador is a poor model for a therapist of the soul.

Within the Austro-Hungarian Empire, Roman Catholicism was the established religion. Protestants and Jews were the objects of official discrimination. Jews were also targets of an anti-Semitism widespread among the ethnic groups encompassed within the empire. In a sense the Hapsburg monarchs protected Jews from the worst of these antagonisms, so Jews had reason to be grateful to them. Freud himself admired the British government of that era and revered such antiroyalist heroes as Oliver Cromwell. But as a Viennese Jew, he had excellent reason to be suspicious of the ethnic populisms of the empire. One can understand his appreciation of the role played by Joseph in imperial Egypt.

Dreams within Hebrew Scripture

> The meaning [of a dream] should not be read into it from outside but must come out from the dream itself. Such an interpretation of a dream is a deep psychological task, just as the explanation of any symbol, the hermeneutical interpretation of any passage of Scripture should be *pithron*, getting at the sense from within outwards . . . . Just as at organic birth and at the unfolding of every bud, there is an inner point of force from which the whole development takes its course, so at every "closed" symbolism there is one kernel, one central idea which has only once to be grasped, for all the rest to be understood and follow naturally. (Hirsch 1867/1971:I, 567)

Except for the celebrated case of Joseph, the Hebrew Bible has only an occasional reference to dreams (dreams notably requiring interpretation are in Judges 7; Daniel 2, 4, 7; while dreams conveying explicit messages from God may be found in Genesis 20, 28, 31, I Kings 3f, and elsewhere). The traditional exegesis of the Book of Esther states that it was a dream of Mordecai that guided him in countering the plot of Haman to slaughter the Jews (Rappoport 1928/1966:III, chap. 20). But, as if to counter such favorable evaluations, a chapter in Ecclesiasticus (Ben Sirach) flatly declares, "Divination, auguries, and dreams are nonsense, like the delirious fantasies of a pregnant woman. Unless sent as emissaries from the Most High, do not give them a thought; for dreams have led many astray" (Ben Sirach 34:5–7 JB). Other scriptural passages are distrustful of the use of dreams within the context of divination.

The most fitting rejoinder is from Rabbi Hisda: "Each dream has meaning, except one which is stimulated by fasting. Furthermore, the dream which is not interpreted is like a letter which is not read" (Berakhoth 55a, as cited in Fromm 1951:127; Harris 1994:3f). However, Rabbi Bana'ah stated, "There were twenty-four interpreters of dreams in Jerusalem. 'Once I dreamt a dream and I went around to all of them and they all gave different interpretations, and all were fulfilled, thus confirming that which is said: All dreams follow the mouth' " (Harris 1994:5). The multiplicity of interpretations would likely displease someone seeking to bring the skill under the rubric of a biomedical science. The statement "All dreams follow the mouth" has puzzled commentators, who usually have taken it to imply that whatever is stated by the interpreter to be the meaning must, then, be a possible meaning. True, that inability to decide among conflicting possible interpretations might be congenial to a modern deconstructionist. However, another interpretation of that statement would refer to the discourse of dreamer and dream interpreter, especially if the former's utterances partake of "free association." This reading is in accord with the practices of the Yeshiva: "There the distinction between the meaning of a text and its interpretation is not drawn; the meaning is in the ongoing discourse motivated or sponsored by the text. 'The voices around the text are the voices in the text' " (Olson 1994:610).

Concluding Remarks

The biblical story of Joseph exemplifies several distinct orientations toward dreams and their interpretations. Joseph's adolescent dreams echo the visionary experiences of a Plains Indian undergoing the "Vision Quest." His dreams, and their visions, provide guidance to the self and one's intimates as to inner potentials (*virtues*)—in modern parlance, career guidelines. They help the individual to cultivate her- or himself and to sustain a genuine self in the face of adversity: for Joseph, exile, enslavement, imprisonment. The Plains Indian youth would have been guided toward such alternatives as varieties of warrior, hunter, medicineman, or transvestite (*berdache*). Likewise, the story of Joseph in Egypt exemplifies the role of dreams and their interpreting within a larger, urbanized milieu. Morally, emotionally, intellectually, Joseph fulfills the potential of his adolescent dreams, including the overweening pride, lack of feeling and decency manifested by his narrating the dreams to his family. The raw ambition of this over-indulged youth bears its fruit in the morally tainted interpretation of Pharoah's dreams. The dispassionate narrative is all the more startling because he is portrayed as favored of the Lord, who has granted him his interpretive gifts.

We have thus been exposed to the range of orientations toward dreams within ancient Judaism: from direct intuitive sense to interpretive wizardry in the service of imperial ambition, from divine message to heretical temptations. So, the interpreting of dreams furnishes both the possibilities of profound knowledge and equally of plausible misdirection, even corruption. Little wonder that the subsequent Judaic tradition conveys stern warnings about the possibilities of being misguided by the dreams of alleged prophets (Deuteronomy 13:1–3; Jeremiah 29:8–9; Zechariah 10:2):

> And the prophets thereof divine for money;
>> Yet will they lean upon the LORD, and say:
>> "Is not the LORD in the midst of us?
>> No evil shall come upon us"? . . . .
>> It hath been told thee, O man, what is good,
>> And what the LORD doth require of thee:
>> Only to do justly, and to love mercy, and to walk humbly with thy God.
> (Micah 3:11b-12; 6:8; JPS)

Despite the possibilities for misguidance sanctified by purported prophecy, the rabbis nevertheless encouraged the faithful to heed the meaning of their dreams, a theme to be explored further.

Notes

1. Strictly, "one who has wings ready for his movements at his disposal . . . so, one who has dreams at his disposal for his purposes, a master of dreams" (Hirsch 1971:I, 547, n. 19). Oppenheim (1956:236–7) speculates that this is a derisory reference to the Mesopotamian notion of "a dream god" (*ba'al halom*), the chief of demons.

2. The spare biblical Hebrew allows several different descriptions: "coat of many colours" (King James and Jewish Publication Society); "embroidered coat" (Hirsch); "coat with long sleeves" (Jerusalem Bible); "long sleeved robe" (Oxford Study Edition).

The garment was called *passim*, which can mean "pieces and clefts" (Rappoport 1966, II: 5). Joan Cassell suggests that it was sewn of bits of cloth of different colors in a decorative style that has been elaborated in a number of different cultures. H. Russell Bernard, however, reads the overall biblical account as indicating that Joseph was homosexual and that his clothing was indicative.

3. The Joseph story "fits quite well into the setting of new Kingdom Egypt from

1550 B.C., and especially well in the time of the late eighteenth and the early nineteenth dynasties (approximately 1400–1200). . . . There is no reason to doubt that a foreigner could have assumed such a high position under the pharaoh. The Egyptian documents which have been recovered show that such a thing was not without precedent. . . . The Joseph cycle stems from someone who knew Egyptian life and society very well indeed" (Harrelson 1964:69).

4. "Es wird aufgefallen sein, dass der Name Josef eine so grosse Rolle in meinen Träumen spielte . . . . Hinter den Personen, die so heissen, kann auch mein Ich im Traume besonders leicht verbergeben, deren Josef hiess auch der Bibel bekannte Traumdeuter" (Freud 1900:G.W. II–III, 488, f. 1).

PART TWO

INTERPRETING AND MISINTERPRETING DREAMS: FREUD BRINGS DREAMS INTO BIOMEDICINE

Chapter 5

Coca, Hypnotism, and the Return of the Primitive

As a young physician specializing in neurology, Freud (1856–1939) was moved to investigate the properties of coca, a botanical alien to European biomedicine, although used for centuries by the natives of highland South America (Byck 1974). Freud's endeavor is the template for this chapter.

While the episode was eventful in Freud's career—as revealed by his dreams and regrets ("The Botanical Monograph" in *The Interpretation of Dreams*)—his investigation was but one incident in a long history of exchange and acquisition between Europe and "the New World." The Spanish conquistadors had lusted for gold, but of far greater value in the long run was the wonderful array of plants that had been domesticated and cultivated by Native Americans. The listing is staggering, among the most prominent being maize ("sweet corn"), ("Irish") potatoes, tomatoes, beans (of several varieties), manioc, cocoa (chocolate), pumpkins, citrus, quinine, rubber, tobacco, and coca. Following European invasion, exploration, and trade, knowledge and usage of these invaluable plants spread throughout the world, rapidly in the case of potatoes, maize, and tobacco, slowly in the case of coca.

Whereas Native Americans had been innovative with plants, Europeans had been domesticating animals (cattle, sheep, swine, horses) and innovating in mechanical and engineering arts—especially those associated with warfare and navigation. These had provided the technical foundation for exploration, conquest, and overlordship of numerous of the peoples of the world. Europeans then could regard themselves as a superior species of humanity, bearing Christianity, classical scholarship, and Roman law. At the same time, they were—selectively and with bigotry—incorporating the achievements of other folk: gunpowder; the compass; the decimal-place system of representing numbers; the botanical achievements of Native

Americans. Within this ambience, Freud's nineteenth-century experiments with cocaine (the alkaloid derived from coca leaves) was hardly novel and rather belated.

Laboring in the plateaus of South America, Native Americans had chewed coca leaves as a means of dealing with fatigue, hunger, and bodily discomfort, so marshaling energies for further effort (Moser and Tayler 1967). On initial contact, the European religious labeled the plant as devilish, but when the conquerors observed that its usage enabled prolonged and heavy labor by the subject population, they modified their judgement.

Investigated and refined by nineteenth-century chemists, the botanical then acquired modest uses among Europeans and Euro-Americans: in Europe, as an ingredient in a beverage, Vin Mariani, which acquired repute because it sustained Pope Leo XIII; in the southern United States as the key ingredient in a pharmacists's "headache remedy" (Coca Cola), which alleviated the aches and pains of rural Georgians.

What Freud was attempting with cocaine was parallel to what had been happening within European civilization. He was studying the achievement of an exotic people to fit it within the weltanschauung and accepted institutions of his time and place, in this case, scientific biomedicine. And his labors were occurring within an ambivalent climate, where psychoactive botanicals (the derivatives of opium and hemp) were being used yet becoming tainted with anxiety. Conan Doyle, educated as a physician, portrayed his great detective as utilizing these drugs to alleviate boredom; but in a few decades, the United States was to enact legislation (the Harrison Act) making their possession a crime.

Freud's adventures with cocaine are well known. His work paved the way for the discovery of its uses as an ocular and oral anesthetic. He himself found the drug brightened his outlook and increased his capacity for work, so he recommended the drug to others. Among them, his friend and mentor, Ernst von Fleischl-Marxow, suffering intractable pain and already addicted to morphine, now on Freud's advice became addicted as well to cocaine. Freud then had reason to reproach himself for naive enthusiasm; he also reproached himself for not having had the determination and insight to discover cocaine's potential as a local anesthetic, especially for eye surgery.

The ambivalent response of Euro-America to coca is almost an omen of responses to Freud's psychoanalytic achievements: respect and anxiety, although legally more complex. On the one hand, coca became the source of a drug invaluable for medical and dental practice. On the other hand, coca became the source of a recreational drug, legally prohibited; and since it could be highly addictive, the prohibition has served to generate a large and profitable illicit market. Its original native use—as enabling prolonged and fatiguing labor—quite vanished from public discussion. Moreover, the legal prohibition and the mythic terror has discouraged thoughtful experimentation based on the native use, although there was a minor furor a generation ago, when Eastern European investigators announced that it was useful for assisting the enfeebled elderly in becoming active. Indicative of the sociolegal environment is the fact that the use of cocaine derivatives in dental surgery only began to be accepted and prevalent in the United States in the 1930s.

Strikingly parallel to Freud's labors with cocaine was his work with hypnotism and dreams. (One may also note Swales's [1983a, 1983b] hypothesis that the action of cocaine became a metaphor for Freud of the influence of sexual chemistry.)

Induced Trance-Hypnotism

Bearing in mind the caution that words such as *trance, possession, dissociation,* and *hypnotism* are of the modern West, the phenomena have been recognized and widespread among many societies, past and present (Bourguignon 1979). How widespread the knowledge was of trance states, and of the mechanisms of their induction, cannot be answered assuredly. All that can reliably be generalized is that every civilized society, and many noncivilized ones, has known how to induce trance through such devices as psychoactive drugs,[1] repetitive singing, drumming, and dancing. Likewise ubiquitous is the use of trance by a shaman (or medicine man or woman) in diagnosing and healing illness and remediating societal problems.

Hypnotism is but a variety of trance induced within a configuration of authority. In eighteenth-century Euro-America, hypnotism reemerged as theater and therapy, bordering on mysticism, charlatanry, and the perverse (Crabtree 1993). Explaining one puzzling phenomenon by reference to another, it was spoken of as "magnetism" or "animal magnetism," and indeed some practitioners used (metallic) magnets as stagecraft. The perverse connotations of hypnotism were graphically evident in the popular drama of "Trilby" (composed by George du Maurier, 1894): an innocent North European maiden falls under the mesmeric spell of Svengali, a Jewish montebank, who by hypnotic arts transforms her into a singer capable of fantastic *bel canto* feats, until the evil spell is lifted when he dies, whereupon her gift for singing vanishes.

Meanwhile, there were serious therapeutic uses of hypnotism. In late nineteenth-century Paris, Jean-Martin Charcot used hypnotism in medical exhibitions of "hysterics." Theatrical as were these performances at the Salpêtrière, there was an underlying investigative orientation. Liébault's hypnotic treatment of rural folk at Nancy was impressive (although he was derided by medical colleagues as quack and fool [Ellenberger 1970:86]). In this climate an eminent, conservative Viennese physician, Josef Breuer, experimented with hypnotism as a way of treating "Anna O.," a young woman afflicted with a variety of "hysterical" symptoms. Intelligent, determined, and educated, Anna (Bertha Pappenheim) responded to his humane intervention by constructively utilizing the trance, while rejecting the authoritarian component. An intense bond developed between Breuer and Anna.[2] Breuer's protégé, Sigmund Freud, was apprised of the work with Anna O. and thus was led to seek instruction in hypnotism as a way of treating the psychically disturbed. Freud then acquired a reputation among his Viennese clientele as a *magnétiseur*.

Like Breuer with Anna O., Freud found that his patients could not reliably be brought into hypnotic trance. Along with one of his patients, he visited the clinic at Nancy, but to no avail. Comparing his medical practice with that of Liébault, I would suggest that the simplest explanation for his failure as a hypnotist would be that he did not qualify as a figure of authority to his upper-class Viennese patients. Rather, as a young impecunious physician, he was regarded and treated as a family servant. Nevertheless, what he did discover was an indirect strategy for altering the patient's "state of consciousness"—namely, "free association" (*freien Einfall* or *freie Assoziation*, the twin labels he was to employ, beginning in his 1909 lectures at Clark University [Freud 1910]).

Dreams and Dream Interpreting

In the Native American context, there is no distinct separation between the world as dreamed and the world as lived. These are states integral to the unifying continuum of mythic description, narration, and enactment. . . . Among traditional Plains peoples, dreaming is given a strong ontological priority and is regarded as a primary source of knowledge. The visionary dream in Native American religion appropriates a wide spectrum of mental and emotional experiences. (Irwin 1994:18–19)

Requested by Freud to "free-associate," patients often provided dreams. His labors with their—and his own—dreams then led Freud "to discover the secret" of dreams. As in the case of New World botanicals, trance states and hypnotism, Freud was not *discovering* but *re*discovering, and the "rediscovery" should be viewed as paralleling the orientation of the European adventurers during the great voyages of exploration. They chronicled themselves as *discovering* lands and peoples, which they then claimed as possessions of their imperial sovereign. So, Freud *discovered* the secret of dreams and claimed the discovery as foundational to his new science—

psychoanalysis—by casting it within the framework (paradigm) of the biomedicine of his time.

But as with coca and trance, the European domestication transformed the original. Within small human groups, dreams were—and are—regarded not as physiological events but as messages to the group as a whole, the dreamer being the messenger. In traditional Native American groups, dreams were messages from nonhuman beings—deities—establishing relationships, instructing, mentoring, diagnosing, forecasting. Even in the Vision Quest, in which the young man sought relationship and guidance toward his future, that future was framed in relationship to this small group.

The individualistic approach adopted by Freud resulted in a major distortion of his interpretive and therapeutic efforts with "Dora" (see chapter 7). Throughout the case, Freud focused on her problems in psychosexual development. He regarded her as the "subject" of his biomedical practice, rather than as a collaborator in growth, so although he noted her dreams, he was incapable of reading their messages. He minimized the negative roles of the adults in the two families and ignored her communications to himself.

Free Association and the Self

Free Association (Method or Rule of): Method according to which voice must be given to all thoughts without exception which enter the mind. (LaPlanche and Pontalis 1973:169)

Freud's great clinical discovery was free association. He presented it as normative, required of anyone coming for therapy. He and his followers spoke of it as inducing regression, meaning that the person thereby moves into a childlike state (with easier access to early memories). But, viewed detachedly, and from the perspective of the theoreticians of chapter 2, free association is the shedding of the defensive orientation that normally guards the self (or self system). To speak freely, uncritically, "thoughtlessly" revealing every idea that enters awareness, is indeed to play the role of the young child; but this means that the person forgoes the social strategies of ordinary civil discourse. The rule then may be experienced as threatening, especially to patients who have experienced abuse and are anxious about lowering their defenses to persons in authority.

Insofar as free association means that any topic may be discussed—discussed, not enacted—it is a remarkably liberating invitation. Insofar as mutual trust develops within the analytic dyad, both parties can access feelings and memories inhibited in normal discourse (Mendelsohn, personal communication). On the other hand, the more that free association is presented as rule and requirement, the more authoritarian becomes the shape of the dyadic interaction.[3] One of the tragedies of the psychoanalytic movement has been its refusal to recognize the bivalent aspects of free association: a liberating potential versus a destructively authoritarian relationship.[4]

In a notable instance centering about his own symptomatic conduct, Freud himself experienced the hazard of "the fundamental rule", and he refused to furnish free associations to Carl Jung, remarking that to do so would threaten his own position of authority.[5]

Specifically with regard to dreams, free association by the dreamer greatly enriches the text of the dream. An experienced analyst, familiar with a particular patient, can often understand much of the meaning of a dream without associations (see Mendelsohn 1990), but associations enrich the text and extend the range of meanings. They also pave the way for empathic attunement within the dyad and for emotional release by the analysand.

Of Time and the Dream

Most of the peoples of the world—but by no means all of them—have regarded dreams as portents, indicating a potential future. Their views would then be akin to those of George Herbert Mead, oriented toward how human beings construct their acts in relationship to their fellows.

Rather than continue with further abstractions, I invite the reader to examine some concrete instances of interpretation and misinterpretation in the following two chapters.

Notes

1. Richard Yarnell, ethnobotanist, said that he had been able to locate the sites of ancient American Indian pueblos by noting the presence of datura trees. Datura is the source of a potent hallucinogenic. Yarnell speculated that the datura blossom is the inspiration for what in the tourist trade is called the "squash blossom" design in southwestern jewelry.

2. After sundry misadventures in sanitaria, Bertha Pappenheim had a distinguished career as a pioneer in social welfare programs in Germany (Rosenbaum 1984).

3. "[E]ven here, in a paper on transference, Freud is stating that free association is *the* psychoanalytic rule. In the Standard Edition, it is translated as the 'fundamental' rule, and specified as 'whatever comes into one's head must be re-

ported without criticizing it.' This is quite a different translation with a good deal more of a guilt-provoking ring" (Ellman 1991:49, n. 13).

4. Anton O. Kris is untraditional:

A central feature of my views is that the analyst has no rights of authority within the method of free association. . . . [T]he analyst assists the patient in the task of free association without interfering with the patient's exclusive right and responsibility to make decisions for himself . . . I am in disagreement with the tradition in regard to the role of the analyst, as it derives from the earlier model of the physician. . . . To the extent that the analyst directs the patient to address his free associations to the analyst as expert, he assumes unwarranted and unnecessary authority. He is neither Joseph, plenipotentiary, nor wise and selfless sibyl. (1982:22–23)

5. Freud had a dream—I would not think it right to air the problem it involved. I interpreted as best I could, but added that a great deal more could be said about it if he would supply me with some additional details from his private life. Freud's response to these words was a curious look—a look of utmost suspicion. Then, he said, "But I cannot risk my authority." At that moment he lost it altogether. That sentence burned itself into my memory; and in it the end of our relationship was already foreshadowed. (Quotation from Carl Jung's autobiography [1963:158] in Rosenzweig 1992:66–67.)

Chapter 6

Who Are the *Irmas*?

What Are Their Narratives?

> [D]reams poems and novels either have no meaning or several meanings.
> . . . once one has recognized, detected or decided that they have meaning,
> they become open to interpretation, and characteristically several not mu-
> tually exclusive interpretations can be made of them. Characteristically, too,
> exegesis of these interpretations takes up more space and uses more words,
> than does the dream, poem or even the novel itself . . . . It takes Dennis Ward
> thirteen pages to answer the question, 'What did the sonnet "The Wind-
> hover" mean to Gerard Manley Hopkins?', i.e. just under a page to a line.
> (Rycroft 1979:162–3)

Akin to poetry or drama, but rather less tidy, a dream has significance
and meanings (not just a meaning); and these emerge from the narratives in which the dreamer is emotionally embedded. In this chapter I am
going to illustrate and embody this thesis by a discussion of Freud's
dream of "Irma's Injection," my goal being not to arrive at *the* interpretation of that famous dream but rather to take scholarly advantage of a
configuration where so much of such intimacy has become known. I do,
of course, reflect on the significances of "Irma's Injection" to that historical dreamer, an interpretive exercise I find tantalizing; however, that
exercise is instrumental rather than the end goal.

An intriguing complexity is that Freud used this dream as key illustration for his innovative theory as to the *interpreting* of a dream, a theory foundational to psychoanalysis. Thus, my discussion of "Irma's Injection" becomes counterpointed not only to his interpretation but also
to his theoretical argument. Freud's biomedical orientation led him to
overlook the hermeneutic quality of his clinical practice. While he emphasized self-awareness, he would have been uncomfortable about fully

69

recognizing the role of the dream interpreter/analyst (as would his followers, including Didier Anziev, a student of Freud's dreams[1]).

Wishes as Freudian Horses

For Freud, dreams were to be understood as wish fulfillments, and the goal of his interpretive process was to discern the generative wish. Freud also thought of dreams as if they were miniature neurotic symptoms, which likewise were to be understood in terms of wishes, forbidden wishes. He was comfortable with assigning a generative role to wishes because (within his psychophysiological parallelism) they could be considered as the psychic manifestations of neurological energies. Nevertheless, within the interactive process of the consulting room, the wishes of (adult) analysands were rarely manifested physiologically. What was presented by the analysand were words and gestures that provided Freud with the basis for "interpretation."

Interpretation connotes language and a process of translation. Indeed, Freud approached a dream as if it were—in more recent discourse—a text. The analyst then deciphered that text—"the manifest dream"—as if it were a coded message, engraved within the Egyptian hieroglyphics that so fascinated Freud and that employed the joint resources of imagery and sound. The process of interpretation was complete when the generative wish had been discerned and related to the dream text.

Freud did not recognize the methodological implications of what was occurring within the process of interpretation—namely, that this was a hermeneutic rather than an analytic (biomedical) enterprise. Examined closely, the process was a situating of the analysand within an historical narrative, or sequence of narratives (Wax 1995). Clinically, Freud was dealing with neurotic symptoms as if each crystallized or embodied a concealed ("unconscious" or "repressed") narrative; and if the symptom were to be relieved, then the narrative had to be recovered (i.e., brought into awareness). If a dream were a symptom or akin to a symptom, then it too embodied a concealed narrative. Bringing the repressed wish into consciousness was the constructing of a narrative.

Other, later analysts (e.g., Reiser 1990) thought of the process of interpreting a dream as of formally discerning a set of basic themes (in a spirit akin to Lévi-Strauss's work with myth). However, because narratives are not sought, the formalizing forecloses vision. Likewise, there is impatience and misunderstanding of dreams in the comment of a celebrated clinician-theorist:

We know too well that patients learn to exploit our interest in dreams by telling us in profuse nocturnal productions what they should struggle and tell us in straight words . . . even a periodic emphasis on dreams today is wasteful and may even be deleterious to therapy[!]. (Erikson 1954:6)

Who Is "*Irma*"?

With the abundant (and in some views even overabundant) literature about this and other dreams of Freud, and with the successive unfoldings and revelations about his life, one would think that—at least within the psychoanalytic literature—there would be basic agreement about the dream: its central characters, the nature of their actions, and thereby the meaning(s) or significance. Yet at the most fundamental level there are disagreements, the more startling because they are implicit, rarely being noted, and yet occurring among serious scholars who are analytically sophisticated. In the course of this chapter I shall explicate, but here I want simply to note disagreements about the identity or identities of the central character, "Irma" herself. Equally, if not more significant, is the lack of attention to the "minor characters" in the dream theater and to the complexities of the presence of the dreamer her- or himself. Here there is no disagreement but simply an absence.

Logically, two positions are possible: (1) there is one correct interpretation of this (and any other) dream, which then implies that alternate interpretations are simply in error; or (2) this dream (like other dreams) has a variety of meanings, from which it would follow that the several different interpretations each have plausible validity or significance. Throughout, I will be maintaining the latter position, noting that this posture respects the interpretive ability of the various students of this dream.

The Secret of the Marble Tablet

> Here, on July 24, 1895
> the secret of the dream
> revealed itself to Dr Sigm. Freud.

In a letter (June 12, 1900) to his intimate friend, Wilhelm Fliess, Freud fantasizes that, some day, a marble tablet might so be dedicated (Masson 1985:417).

The phrasing of the tablet is significant. Freud does not declare a great discovery but rather speaks of the secret as revealing (disclosing) itself.

That secret (as he was well aware) had been revealed and known long before, as evident in the words of Sophocles' Jocasta to a husband anxious about a prophecy that he will marry his mother:

> . . . have no fear of marriage with your mother.
> Many men before this time have dreamt that they
> Have shared their mother's bed. (lines 945–8, Arnott trans.)[2]

In the judgment of an experienced psychoanalytic anthropologist: "the dreams one encounters in Greek tragedy are authentically dreamlike: the dream Aischylos devised for *his* Klyteimestra could have been dreamed by her, had she been a real person, though it could probably *not* have been dreamed by the Sophoklean Klyteimestra" (Devereux 1976:ix).[3] For this to have been the case, these dramatists must have had a deep intuitive knowledge of the meanings of dreams; moreover, their audiences must have participated in this knowledge, so that they did not reject nor find implausible the characters who narrated dreams on the tragic stage.

Not just the tragedians of classical Greece, but throughout recorded history most of the peoples of the world have held that dreams had meanings and significances:

> The Hurons believe that our souls have other desires, which are, as it were, inborn and concealed. . . . our soul makes these natural desires known by means of dreams, which are its language. Accordingly, when these desires are accomplished, it is satisfied; but, on the contrary, if it be not granted what it desires, it becomes angry, and not only does not give its body the good and the happiness that it wished to procure for it, but often it also revolts against the body, causing various diseases and even death.[4] (Rageneau 1649, as cited in Wallace 1958:236)

The ethnographic literature contains numerous accounts of the respect other peoples have accorded dreams (e.g., George 1995; Graham 1995; Irwin 1994; O'Flaherty 1984; Ridington 1988; Smith 1998; Tedlock 1987; Wautischer 1994).[5] Here what I wish to establish is that what was unusual and dramatic about Freud's work, as published in his epochal *The Interpretation of Dreams* (*Die Traumdeutung*, 1900), was the casting of the revealed secret within the language and conventions of nineteenth-century biomedicine, thus making it reputable, if not respectable. He could contrast his own data and theories with the speculations in the "dream books" sold to "the credulous public." But, for that legitimation, a price was paid.

Trained in comparative neurology, Freud theorized about the psyche (*die Seele*) on the basis of his model of the nervous system of a primate (mammal) within a Darwinian world. The primate is animated by biological impulses, primary being sexuality, the drive to reproduce the species. Units of energy flow—or are impeded or fixated—within the channels of the nervous system. Freud imposed this organic metaphor on the empirical data that were being yielded by his novel clinical experiences with "hysterics"—and with himself. Especially when modulated with themes from classical antiquity (Virgil, Sophocles), the result was novel, even extraordinary, yet creditable within the biological sciences—and the intellectual community—of the time. This is not to say that it was necessarily convincing, but rather that *The Interpretation of Dreams* would be accorded a serious hearing (Kiell 1988). One should add these materials in turn were being integrated by a Viennese Jew, classically educated at an elite *Gymnasium*. At that time and place, when this combination of talents and approaches was brought to bear on understanding the dream, the result was revolutionary. Freud's investigations transformed the thinking of the literate world of the twentieth century (see Nelson 1957), and his vision of a marble tablet was by no means inappropriate.

Interpreting and Misinterpreting "Irma"

> In successfully identifying and understanding what someone else is doing we always move toward placing a particular episode in the context of a set of narrative histories, histories both of the individuals concerned and of the settings in which they act and suffer. (MacIntyre 1984:211)

Using his dreams as a basic guide, Freud began a process of self-analysis in 1895. When he then decided to present to the world his discovery of the secret of dreams, his text needed illustrations and examples, and these were most easily to be found in his own dreams. Besides, he commented, were he to use the dreams of his patients, critics might dismiss the argument on the ground that the dreams were those of neurotics (and he would have risked the violation of confidentiality). In any case, the first edition of *Die Traumdeutung* (1900) relied exclusively on his dreams. To the dream texts he furnished both "free associations" and background materials ("the day's residues")—personal, familial, professional—presenting the reader with an extraordinary personal document. Gradually, the book acquired a wide readership, and Freud attracted disciples, whereupon its later editions now included the dreams of others: colleagues, disciples, analysands. In consequence, the clarity of this epochal work was obscured by the variety of materials offered in illustration and confirmation of the scientific claims.

An American disciple, A. A. Brill, translated the book as *The Interpretation of Dreams* (1913). Later, the book underwent a retranslation by James Strachey and a second publication in 1931. Both English translations continue to circulate. I mention this because most of the American discussions of Freud's dreams have been focused on the English text of Strachey's "authorized translation"; yet the very notion of the dream as a message in hieroglyphics should have made analysts wary of such a procedure.[7]

Freud's psychoanalytic writings became foundational in the training programs of psychoanalytic institutes,[8] and *The Interpretation of Dreams* also enjoyed a wide circulation among intellectuals globally. "Irma's Injection" truly became "The Specimen Dream" of psychoanalysis; or, more faithful to the German text and its status among knowledgeable readers, "The Exemplary Dream" in the sense that Freudians now presented its interpreting as an exemplar for clinician-readers, for prospective analysands, and for students of myth and literature.

To the clinically sophisticated, Freud's dreams—together with his commentaries and free associations—revealed much about his family, his friends, and his person. So intimate were these revelations that for the first half of this century, the more discreet analysts preferred to allude to these levels of meaning rather than discuss them frankly, even within the technical literature. Note Rycroft's delicate reference (1979: chap. 1) to Freud's discussion of the Irma dream: "[I]t is the omissions that strike one."

A Model Dream: Irma's Injection

> *"Flectere si nequeo Superos, Acheronta movebo*—If I cannot bend the higher powers, I will move the infernal regions" [epigraph to *The Interpretation of Dreams*]. . . Juno unleashes on Aeneas the Fury Allecto, whose hair is twined with writhing serpents. She is one of the infernal powers that Aeneas thought he would be able to keep at a distance even though he went to look at them at close quarters. . . . The message is clear: no one can go down into the underworld of the mind without setting hidden forces in motion. (Anzieu 1975/1986:177–8)

> [The epigraph] tersely summarizes his fundamental thesis that wishes, rejected by the 'higher moral authorities' resort to 'the mental underworld (the unconscious)' to secure their aim. But the truculent tone of the verse, spoken by an infuriated Juno after her fellow Olympians have frustrated her wishes, suggests more than this. (Gay 1988:105)[9]

Chapter 2 of *The Interpretation of Dreams* is titled "The Method of Interpreting a Dream" and subtitled "The Analysis of a Model Dream" (*"Die Methode der Traumdeutung: Die Analyse eines Traummusters"*). The chapter is devoted to the analysis of what Freud dreamed in the early morning hours of July 24, 1895, which he recorded under the title "Irma's Injection." Let us examine the dream:

A great hall—many guests, whom we are receiving—Among these is *Irma,* whom I immediately draw to the side, as though to respond to her letter, and to reproach her for not having accepted the "solution." I say to her, "If you [*du*] still have pains, then this is truly your own fault." She answers, "If you [*du*] could only know what sorts of pains I have in my throat, stomach, and belly, I cannot catch my breath." I am appalled and look at her. She seems pale and bloated; I reflect that I must have been overlooking something organic. I take her to the window and peer into her throat. She resists somewhat, as do women unwilling to expose the wearing of dentures, and I think to myself, there is no need for her to behave so. The mouth then does open properly, and I find on the right a large (white) spot [*Fleck*] and—elsewhere—extensive gray-white scabs upon odd curly (conch-shaped) structures, seemingly patterned upon the turbinal bones of the nose. Immediately I call Dr. M. who repeats the examination and corroborates. . . . Dr. M. appears quite different than usual; he is beardless, very pale, and limps. . . . My friend Otto now is standing next to her, and friend Leopold is percussing her through her bodice, saying, "She has a dullness on the left; also points to the left shoulder where the skin has been infiltrated (which, in spite of the clothing, I can feel, as well)." . . . M says: No doubt it is an infection, but no need to worry; dysentery will follow and the poison eliminated. . . . We know directly the source of the infection. When she was not feeling well, not long before, friend Otto had given her an injection of a preparation of propyls . . . propyls, proprionic acid, trimethylamin (whose formula I see in heavy typeface) . . . One should not casually administer such injections. . . . Likely, the syringe [*Spritze*] had not been clean, either. (Freud 1900/1948, II:111–2)

In *The Interpretation of Dreams,* Freud argues that each dream has a single meaning—namely, a wish,[11]—and he does locate such a wish in his explication of this dream. After providing considerable personal and professional background, together with "free associations" to the elements of the dream, he states that the wish has to do with his treatment of a patient, whom we now know to be Anna Lichtheim (née Hammerschlag), whose father (Samuel) had been Freud's tutor in Hebraic matters and who herself was a friend of the family.

Recently widowed, Anna was not doing well, and her family had not viewed his treatment with approval. On the previous evening, Sigmund had encountered a junior colleague, Oscar Rie, M.D., who had been staying with Anna's family at their country resort. When Sigmund inquired about Anna's condition, Oscar responded, "Better, but not really well" ("Es geht ihr besser, aber nicht ganz gut"). Sensing this as a reproach, Sigmund was angered, and to justify himself he had devoted the evening to writing her case history.

As he then regards the dream of the following morning, Freud interprets it as declaring—in numerous and not consistent formats—that he be in no way judged responsible for the persistence of Anna's continued discomfort: the cause was organic; his colleagues were incompetent in their diagnoses and unworthy as critics of his efforts; the disorder would cure itself; and the true cause was an unsanitary injection of improper materials by one of these incompetent colleagues. Such an interpretation of the dream would seem reasonable. It is especially convincing to a reader because in contemplating the (manifest) dream, the awakened Freud has immediately identified the "Irma" of his dream with Anna Hammerschlag-Lichtheim, just as he has identified the dream's "Otto" with friend and colleague, Dr. Rie (who may then have been emotionally involved with Anna), and just as he has identified the other actors of that dream theater with specific people in his waking life. (In their learned discussion of "Freud's women," e.g., Appignanesi and Forrester [1992b:125] flatly state, "Irma herself is Anna Hammerschlag-Lichtheim.")

Yet, Freud's own interpretation is far from being the only possible reading of the dream.[12] Indeed, from a psychodynamic point of view that level of interpretation is superficial: he would not have had to dream to confront that level of significance—namely, the defensive notion that he was not responsible for Anna's continued problems (Sloane 1979/1990: chap. 5). To proceed we require further background.

Disciples and Exponents

As the veil of discretion was lifted within the psychoanalytic literature and more was revealed about Freud's personal life, many discussions of Freud's dreams, including "Irma's Injection," now appeared. Within the scholarly milieu, the capstone would have been Anzieu's encyclopedic review (1975/1986) of the published dreams in relationship to Freud's life and career. Anzieu proceeded dialectically, moving back and forth between Freud's increasing comprehension of his personal development and the consequential leaps of psychoanalytic theorizing. So, each dream (of Freud's middle years) was fitted into the great adventure, whereby Freud's increasing knowledge of his inner life provided the basis for such theoretical formulations as the primal scene, the castration complex, the Oedipus complex, and so forth. Freud's dreams were thus clues to a personal narrative, epitomizing the developmental narrative that was to become the foundation of psychoanalytic theory.

The thoroughness of Anzieu's work is of great help, but his reverence toward Freud—the discoverer of psychoanalysis—does noticeably affect his understanding of the dreams. Moreover, Anzieu relied on a thematic analysis that occasionally proved procrustean, as he insisted on fitting the elements of a dream into the theme or pattern that he came to feel was dominant. This was aggravated by Anzieu's psychoanalytic orthodoxy: the dreams reported by Freud were to be understood as successive steps in the progress of scientific discovery. In a more detached stance, a student of the dreams might have noted how Freud relied on his understanding of his dreams to develop psychoanalytic theory, and the student might have questioned whether or how each dream did so lead. Anzieu's stance is more fraught, for he clearly embraces the classically orthodox theory and so perceives Freud as discovering—through his own and his patients' dreams—the impact of "the primal scene" or "castration anxiety."

Thus, Anzieu is betrayed by his own discipleship. For what paradoxically thus emerges is that Freud's dreams not only reflected his personal life history and its crises, but—of equal if not greater significance—were also a wondrously creative guide, which thus would illustrate that dreams may have a potential role far beyond simplistic "wish fulfillment" and far beyond their status as mimicry of neurotic symptoms.[13] Indirectly and directly, Freud's dreams guided him through the labyrinth of clinical encounters (and personal anguish) and toward the formulation of psychoanalysis.[14]

I am thus reminded of the belief prevalent among numerous peoples that myths and dreams are the fundamental sources of knowledge: "The Dunne-za ["Beaver Indians"] assume that events can take place only after people have known and experienced them in myths, dreams and visions" (Ridington 1988:xi; much more detail appears in the ethnographic literature; see, e.g., Smith 1998; Tedlock 1987).

Freud's Erotic Impulses

Although the interpreting of this dream is presented as exemplary, and Freud frequently relates dreams to erotic impulses, no such interpretation was offered in the book.[15] Nevertheless, to anyone with insight, sexual desires and meanings are rife. Irma and Freud address each other not on professional distance but with the familiar *du*. Against her reluctance, Freud pressures her to open her mouth. In a familiar psychoanalytic duo, the oral and vaginal cavities are interchangeable, and the white fleck could be understood as semen. Anna was recently widowed. Freud had been corresponding with Fliess about the biochemistry of reproduction, and trimethylamin—written in heavy typeface at the conclusion of the (published) dream—was one of the compounds specifically mentioned. Finally, while *die Spritze* can be colloquial for "hypodermic syringe," it has the vulgar meaning of "squirter" (Erikson 1954), and in this context one could easily perceive a fantasied scenario of sexual relations. A decade later, Freud was taxed by his disciple, Karl Abraham, with having omitted this (erotic) interpretation:

> I should like to know whether the incomplete interpretation of the ["Irma's Injection"] dream is intentional. I find that trimethylamin leads to the most important part, to sexual allusions, which become more distinct in the last lines. . . .

Whereupon Freud responded:

> Sexual megalomania is hidden behind it, the three women Mathilde, Sophie and Anna are my daughters' three godmothers, and I have them all! There would be one simple therapy for widowhood, of course. All sorts of intimate things, naturally. (correspondence of January 1908 in Abraham and Freud 1965:18–20)

Putting aside the question of how these other two women (Mathilde and Sophie) are present in the dream (1900/1965:142–3), what is peculiarly startling is not the revelation that Freud might have had erotic desires toward his patients, as well as toward women other than his spouse, and that these desires surfaced within a dream, but that he should here have recognized a dual level of meaning of the dream, while elsewhere contending that in interpreting a dream the analyst sought a single motivating wish.

Fateful Consequences of Sexual Relations

> The furies who desire the death of that child as the price to be paid for the misdeeds of the father will not get the better of him. (Anzieu 1975/1986: 139)

The levels of interpreting this dream extend considerably further.[16] We know that at the date of the dream, Martha Freud was pregnant with their sixth child. His associations reveal that the previous pregnancies had not been easy for her.[17] Other evidence would indicate that financial responsibilities were severe, while his clinical practice was slow in building. And so, in all, he might not have been eager for another child and might indeed have regretted having initiated an act of intercourse (with a resisting spouse?) that resulted in conception (that unclean squirter) and wished that "dysentery would follow and the poison eliminated"![18] Given his friend Fliess's numerical speculations about male and female periodicities, there is even the possibility that Freud had timed that act of intercourse, believing there was then no risk of conception.[19] A further resonance to the dream is that Oscar Rie was physician to Freud's family, and his presence on the evening in question may have been to examine the pregnant Martha.

The child born (December 3, 1895) of this pregnancy was Anna, and it has been revealed that the child was not cherished by her mother.[20]

> [Martha] had borne the pregnancy ill. Unlike her older children—Mathilde, Martin, Oliver, Ernst, and Sophie—Anna was not breastfed. And within a few months of her birth her mother went away on her first holiday without the children. (Sayers 1991:146)

As if in compensation for the continued maternal neglect, Sigmund cultivated a particularly close relationship with this daughter. Ultimately, Anna was to become his psychoanalytic heir; he also "analyzed" her.[21]

Thus, Freud's free associations furnished with the dream and later in the book, together with his correspondence, reveal that *Irma* was a compound figure, condensed from a number of women in Freud's fantasy life, not just Anna Hammerschlag-Lichtheim but also Sophie Schwab-Panath and Mathilde Breuer—and most signally his wife, Martha; additionally, his eldest daughter (another Mathilde) and the children being examined in the Kassowitz Clinic (see note 11). (By 1908 and the correspondence with Abraham, daughter Anna was in her teens, while the three women [of the letter to Abraham] were cast as protective godmothers.) Nevertheless, we now perceive still a third level of meaning to this example.

The Moral Failures of a Friend

There are other levels of meaning, having to do with Freud's relationship with the Berlin physician Wilhelm Fliess (married to the sister of the wife of medical colleague Oscar Rie). Freud had recommended to Emma Eckstein, a patient and a disciple, that she undergo a nasal operation advocated by Fliess. Not only was the operation dubious, but Fliess had bungled (February 1895) by leaving gauze in the wound. Worse yet, Fliess had not admitted culpability, although his error had been gross: for the gauze left in the wound had provoked infection (see letters of March and April 1895 in Masson 1985). Instead of acknowledging his surgical error, Fliess had cast aspersions on those who had examined the ailing Eckstein and uncovered the cause. Since Eckstein was a patient and disciple of Freud's, she might well have been present in his life and his psyche during July (Schur 1966) and so might have appeared in his dream in the disguised form of Irma. Although *The Interpretation of Dreams* contains passages that allude favorably to Fliess, nevertheless, within a year or so, that intimate friendship had come to an end. Fliess could then have been one of the figures condensed into "Dr. M.," who is depicted as incompetent (but whom the awakened Freud had identified as his mentor, Josef Breuer, to whom the case history of Anna Hammerschlag-Lichtheim was being addressed). If Fliess were one of the persons fused into Dr. M., then the dream would then have been forecasting that the friendship could not survive the combination of professional error and moral failure (i.e., unwillingness to accept responsibility). This identification becomes plausible because a number of analysts and scholars have then identified Irma with Emma Eckstein, while others have regarded her as a fusion of Emma with Anna Hammerschlag-Lichtheim.

Earlier I referred to simplistic approaches to Freud's dreams by authors who presumably were analytically sophisticated. Indeed, a minor motive for this chapter is to direct attention to the situation. In particular, I note that the index to the otherwise comprehensive book by Decker (1991) has the entry "Irma (Emma Eckstein)." A parallel but inverse citation may be found in the index to Roazan (1971): "Eckstein, Emma ('Irma')." In contrast, Hughes (1994:127f.) writes as if Irma were unquestionably Anna Hammerschlag; Glenn (1993:13), as if she were unquestionably Emma Eckstein. Yet Freud himself stated that *Irma* was a "collective image," condensed from many women.

The Feminized Persona of the Dreamer

Finally, to keep in bounds this interpretive discussion, there is the fact that Sigmund himself had aches and pains involving his shoulder (and nose, as well as anxieties about his heart) and so resonated empathically with the suffering *Irma*.

> When the dreamer says that he can *"feel"* the infiltrated portion of skin on the (patient's) left shoulder, he means to convey (as Freud states in his associations) that he can *feel this on his own body*. . . . The dreamer, becoming again a doctor in the consenting community of doctors, thus at the same time turns into his and their *patient*. (Erikson 1954:33)

Erikson did not pursue this theme or ask *whose* patient Freud had become. However, Gilman (1993:103) does continue that theme:

> [T]he true sexual anxiety in this case was Freud's in his intense relationship with Fliess. In his exchange with Abraham he stands as the "doctor" curing these female patients; in his dream, he is the feminized patient as well.

This theme is confirmed in Freud's free associations, in which he fantasizes going to Berlin for medical treatment from his friend. But, if this friend had exhibited his lack of professional and moral reliability—in the case of Emma Eckstein—would an ailing Sigmund have journeyed to Berlin to consult him? Thus, the dream could be taken as revealing that a dramatic transition was occurring within Freud's emotional life.

The Self of the Dreamer

"Je suis un autre"
"On me pense"
                (Rimbaud [Rycroft 1979:67])

I have directed attention to the identity of *Irma*, but even more significant are the various ways in which Sigmund Freud is present within his own dream: he is the physician who hears a complaining Irma and then overcomes her reluctance to be examined; he is the femininized patient who is experiencing aches and pains and so is himself being examined by several physicians; he is the male who possesses and erotically penetrates a (fused) bevy of women; he is a member of the company of physicians who are speculating about the diagnosis and prognosis ("*We* know directly the source of the infection"); finally, he is a person being emphatically confronted (heavy typeface) with the technical symbolic formula of a chemical active in human sexuality[22]:

> Dreaming and waking imaginative activity resemble one another in that they both create "novel results" (Darwin's phrase) by uniting, condensing, and fusing images and ideas already present in the mind, in that they do so independently of the will and in that their meaning, when they can be seen to have one, is always multiple and manifold. Furthermore, the self or agent that creates them is not the "I" or Ego that opposes itself to the rest of the universe but some wider, less personal self to which the "I" has to abandon itself, in the case of waking imaginative activity by attainment of that receptive state of mind which Keats called Negative Capability. (Rycroft 1979:167)

A Child among Pregnant Women

> The proto-group that embraced the infant Sigismund [Sigmund] consisted of three families, headed respectively by the locksmith [landlord], Jacob [father], and Emanuel [son of Jacob and first wife, Sally]. . . . We should therefore expect notions of unity and of the triad to play some part in Freud's self-analysis; they do, appearing in the formula of trimethylamin that occurs at the end of the dream about Irma's Injection. (Anzieu 1985:13)

One further speculation is appropriate, for as Freud noted, at one point every dream is anchored in earliest history. If "Irma's Injection" is oriented about sexual relations, pregnancy, and a wished-for miscarriage, then it would indeed resonate with the experiences of Sigmund as the firstborn of Amalia (Jacob's third wife). Having been delivered May 6, 1856, Sigmund would surely have had powerful feelings about his mother's immediate next pregnancy and the birth of brother Julius in 1857 (exact date unknown), followed by the death of that baby some seven months later (see Erikson 1954:40). He would also have had reasons to speculate about reproductive anatomies (especially bodily cavities) and the activities that had resulted in pregnancies. We in turn can speculate that "trimethylamin" in emphatic typeface might be a tribute to the theories and understandings that were early formulated by Sigmund, while *Irma*—at a primitive level—might then include Amalia. Within the natal family, sister Anna was born December 31, 1858, and Sigmund never liked her (Anzieu 1986: chap. 1).[23] Additionally, from the pregnancy of Maria Freud (wife of half-brother Emanuel) was born Berta, February 22, 1859.

Freud mentions that as a child he was cared for by a nanny, Monika Zajic, who was allowed such latitude that she brought the Jewish boy to Catholic services. Considering the humble circumstances of the family of Jakob Freud, and the love of Amalia for her firstborn son, the hiring of a nanny would testify to Amalia's preoccupation with successive pregnancies and nursing of children; while in like manner, her "sister"-in-law Maria would have been preoccupied with John, Pauline, and Berta.

The Unmodeled Implications of a Model Dream

> The fellow [i.e., myself, Sigmund Freud] is actually somewhat more complicated: your description doesn't tally with the fact that I have had my splitting headaches and attacks of fatigue like anyone else, that I was a passionate smoker (I wish I still were), that I ascribe to the cigar the greatest share of my self-control and tenacity in work, that despite my much vaunted frugality I have sacrificed a great deal for my collection of Greek, Roman and Egyptian antiquities, have actually read more archaeology than psychology. (Freud's response to the biographical study of Stefan Zweig, cited in Schur 1972:9)

Confronting this breadth of detail about the possible relationships between the dream of "Irma's Injection" and the life of Sigmund Freud, one is awed at the wondrous intricacy. The dream can be woven into a number of stories, a filigree whose strands join soreness and perplexities. Evidently, a dream cannot be understood apart from the biography of the dreamer, and the more one knows of the biographical narratives, the richer the interconnections that may be perceived.

Freud was aware of feeling (unjustly) reproached by Oscar Rie, his junior colleague, and he regarded the dream as a response. Indeed, dealing with self-reproach may be an underlying theme of the dream: reproach for his sexual conduct with Martha; reproach for his errors with other patients; and, most primitive, reproach for the death wishes of the young boy directed toward his (younger) siblings.

As contrasted with the intricacies of the interrelationship between this apparently simple dream and the complexities of Freud's personal and professional life, what is especially significant about the structure of *The Interpretation of Dreams* is its theoretical imbalance. To employ a style of discourse foreign to Freud, what he did was to underplay the hermeneutical problem and his contribution toward systematizing its resolution; instead, he directed the reader's attention to a problem that, because it was phrased in bioenergetic terms, was not only unsolvable then but, likely, is essentially unsolvable.

Freud explains how a dream can be interpreted, which requires the free associations of the dreamer together with the sensitivity of the analyst to the psychic mechanisms used by our unconscious. The notion of dividing the dream into small segments and inviting the dreamer to provide (uncensored, nonrational) associations to each was innovative and has had remarkable consequences in psychotherapy. Also remarkable was Freud's attempt at formalizing the workings of the unconscious ("primary process"), so coining or invigorating a pregnant vocabulary, including (in its English version) *condensation, displacement of accent, symbolism, regression,* and *repression.*

Freud thus makes the interpreting of a dream seem simple and straightforward: an uncomplicated—appropriately (biomedically) clinical— procedure. Despite the fact that it requires an entire chapter (twenty-seven pages in English) to provide not only the text of "Irma's Injection" but background, free associations, and discussion—and that the additionally relevant materials presented by Schur, Erikson, Anzieu, and others would multiply that text exceedingly—Freud can happily conclude that the meaning of the model dream, or any dream, is the fulfillment of a wish. So, he minimizes the hermeneutical difficulties and his interpretive achievements (and failures), and the clinical and scientific problem of inferring the meanings of a given dream.[24]

The original edition of *The Interpretation of Dreams* dealt exclusively with Freud's own dreams, and these materials must have been carefully chosen and edited. Additionally, we have the materials in his letters to Fliess and his brief response to the query by Abraham. Beyond that, we are speculating, in the sense that we do not have the response of the dreamer Freud to the suggestions of an interconnection between the materials of the dream (e.g., turbinal bones of Irma's nose) and the bungled operation by Fliess on Eckstein. If such materials were in Freud's original draft, they might well have been censored by Fliess, who did have the opportunity to examine the manuscript. Following Schur's (1966) logic, Freud might have been trying to exculpate not merely himself for the continued miseries of Anna Hammerschlag-Lichtheim, but more significantly Fliess for his technical error and moral failures.[25] Freud thus has provided us with a rich yet frustrating treasure: we have publicly available more materials about his life and more dream materials than about any other character, and thus any serious student of his work must be attracted to speculate about the meanings of his dreams. Yet, at the same time, we lack what would be critical to the clinical interaction—namely, the responses of the dreamer to the tentative interpretations of the analyst-interpreter. So, his readers have been provided with abundant opportunity for speculation (and his opponents have a great field for personal and professional criticism).

Freud argues that each dream has a single meaning, which is the expression of a wish, and he proceeds as if discerning this wish is a relatively simple and straightforward procedure, provided the dreamer is willing to free-associate and the analyst is alert to the basic drives of the unconscious and to the mechanisms by which an organic need fuels the composition of a dream. Thus, for Freud, the perplexing question (which he addressed in Chapter 7) is not how to interpret a dream but rather the (psychic-neurological) process by which the dream is formed. Rather than being the free creation of the human spirit, the dream should be understood as the consequent of a determinate lawful—biologically anchored—process. Innately combative, Freud expends considerable effort toward rebutting arguments against his theory of the dream as a wish fulfillment. He is then in the rhetorical position of arguing that either the dream fulfills a wish or it has no meaning, from which it could follow that the subtleties of meaning, such as those we have outlined in the case of "Irma's Injection," are irrelevant. His book purports to be about the interpreting of dreams, but, given his approach to that interpretive process, Freud's true interest is in how the dream is created, not as the free expression of the human psyche but as a bioenergetic process that must be subject to scientific law.[26] So, there is a curious sense in which the book and its title are not quite harmonious. *Deutung* has to do with *meaning*, so *Die Traumdeutung* is about the meaning of dreams.[27] Freud was devising a formal process for discerning meaning, and that very formalism made it usable by him and plausible to the biomedical community, but the same formalism also foreclosed the exploration via narrative, past or potential.

As a nineteenth-century neurologist and as a physician treating "hysterics," Freud sought the meaning of a dream in relation to the present condition of the patient. In that book, and in related early essays, he did not attempt to place dreams within the context of foretelling in the style of the biblical Joseph or of many other traditional peoples. It is true that Freud did toy with the ideas of extrasensory perception in later essays (1921, posthumously published; 1922; 1925; Chapter 2 of *The New Introductory Lectures* [1933] is titled "Dreams and the Occult"), but, despite his identification with Joseph, he omitted these speculations from the earlier work. Given his intention to bring the interpreting of dreams into the biomedical and literate communities, he was surely tactful to eliminate such speculations; but, again, the decisive character of his achievement foreclosed a fruitful avenue of investigation—namely, how individuals disclose and attune themselves to each other in ways that are outside normal awareness. This would include how an individual becomes aware of the potential stories involving self and others.

Here we are not only in the realm of the shaman and the fortune-teller but into another aspect of the role of dreams (see Eisenbud's report of the telepathic *rêve à deux* of two patients in analysis [O'Flaherty 1984:75f.]).[28] So, we might ask, was the dream of "Irma's Injection" telling Freud something about Anna Hammerschlag-Lichtheim and Martha Freud, their feelings about him, and the consequences of possible conduct by him toward them, that he had not permitted himself to acknowledge and confront? And, while he contends that the Dr. M. of the dream is basically his former mentor, Josef Breuer, is there not a sense in which he is also Wilhelm Fliess, whose medical opinions—the dream informs him—should be regarded as worthless, the equivalent of "dysentery will follow, and the poison eliminated"?[29]

Some Commentary

It still strikes me as strange that the case histories I write should read like short stories and that, as one might say, they lack the serious stamp of science. . . The nature of the subject is evidently responsible for this, rather than any preference of my own. . . . The detailed presentation of psychic processes is one that we are used to from a poet. (Freud 1893: Epicrisis; GW 1:227) . . . . In my mind, I always construct novels, using my experience as a psychoanalyst; my wish is to become a novelist—but, not yet; perhaps in the later years of my life. (Freud as quoted in Stekel 1950:66)

Psychoanalysis itself revives the situation of oral narrative exchange. Freud's strictures on traditional therapies for hysteria and on traditional reports of case histories suggest his Benjaminian valorization of the situation of live interlocution in the construction of a story, its investments of desire, its effects of truth. (Brooks 1994:101)

Based on the scientific medicine of his time, Freud postulated that the purpose of the dream was to protect sleep by offering a fantasied fulfillment of the desires that arose during sleep. The thirsty sleeper is allowed to continue in sleep because the dream presents a vision of crossing the desert and reaching an oasis. Inasmuch as the ability physically to enact our desires is minimal during normal sleep, the content of our dreams is less inhibited than during waking. Freud's postulate assumes that sleep is the necessary vital function, whereas dreaming is its facilitator. Subsequent research on sleep and dreams has revealed that dreaming is vital for our psychic well-being. Because dreaming is revealed by the presence of rapid eye movements during sleep, it is experimentally possible to disrupt that activity whenever it occurs; when that is systematically performed, the individual begins to exhibit psychotic behavior (see Hunt 1989; Lavie 1996; States 1997). It would follow that, rather than the dream protecting sleep, it is sleep that facilitates the dream.

From a psychodynamic point of view, the dream integrates the emotionally dense experiences of the previous day together with vital events of the past. Desires will certainly be manifest, but it is misleading to regard these as "the meaning" of the dream. One could as well contend that dreaming is a variety of problem solving at the deepest levels of the psyche, resonating with the earliest and most profound emotional experiences from infancy onward. The attempt to resolve these emotional tangles is not always successful, but, to the extent that it is, the individual is provided with guidance.

Because dreams are akin to poetry, drama, myth, ritual, and the visual arts, any attempt to explain and reduce them, bioenergetically, is bound to fail. Nonetheless, we can detect within them the operation of processes that also occur within ritual and the arts: symbolism, condensation, displacement of accent, projection, metonymy, and so forth. On that assumption, a given dream has a range of meanings, interconnected with significant persons and crucial events in the life and living of the dreamer. (Plausibly, the *Irma* of the dream fused: Anna Hammerschlag-Lichtheim, Emma Eckstein, Martha Freud, Sigmund Freud, and Amalia Nathanson Freud, with echoes of yet others.) We are thus confronted with the question of the role of dreams—and their interpreting—within small intimate groups, such as the Huron of the seventeenth century or the contemporary Dunne-za—and within the therapeutic dyad (see Mendelsohn 1990).

Final Reflections on Freud's Dream

Die Spaltung der Persönlichkeit im Traume, welche z.B. das eigene Wissen auf zwei Personen verteilt, von denen die fremde das eigene Ich im Traume korrigiert. [In dreams the personality may be split—when, for instance, the dreamer's own knowledge is divided between two persons, and when in the dream, the extraneous ego corrects the actual one.] (Freud 1900: G.W., II/III:96; 1900:123; citing Radestock [1879])

Within the sleeping Freud is a dream theater. Although the theater is uniquely his, within its dramas Sigmund himself is but one of the actors. In earlier chapters, I proposed a conceptual distinction between the *psyche* and the *self,* deriving from the insightful arguments of Cooley, Mead, Sullivan, and others who have reflected about human nature. To mark this distinction in our illustrative discussion of "Irma's Injection," I shall speak of the dreamer as "Freud" and the actor in his dream theater as "Sigmund."

Whence the cast of characters in Freud's dream theater? In a trivial sense, these are persons well known to himself, for he has immediately identified them as such on recording the dream: Anna Hammerschlag-Lichtheim, Joseph Breuer, Oscar Rie, and so on (given pseudonyms in the published version). They are "within" Freud's psyche as dreamer, as are the characters of a novel or drama within the writer, not passively as puppets under "his" control, but as characters who assume lives of their own. The autonomy of the dream characters parallels what occurs within the creative process: in a work of aesthetic quality, the author may have begun with a scenario in mind, but the characters soon become independent. Again, this simple fact is a testimony of the *social* nature of the human psyche, and the strength and limits of the self-system.

I have contended that Freud's dream characters are complex, that each actor synthesizes or represents several actual figures who have been actors within key dramas (or narratives) of his life. Although Freud noted this possibility in other chapters of *The Interpretation of Dreams,* he did not make that analysis in his published interpretation of "Irma's Injection." However, when challenged by Karl Abraham about the apparent absence of an erotic component in the published interpretation, he then revealed that he realized that *Irma* stood not only for herself but for several other women toward whom he had feelings of desire.

Irma is the dream figure given most attention by Freud, and by subsequent commentators. Initially, Freud identified her (in effect) as his patient, Anna Hammerschlag-Lichtheim. Subsequently, Schur associated *Irma* with Emma Eckstein. Agreeing with the emphasis on *Irma,* I have added and emphasized Martha Freud, his wife pregnant with their sixth child. Erikson has further reminded us that the text also points to Freud's own identification—as a man whose symptoms seemed to him to denote heart trouble—with Irma, whose chest is being examined by the coterie of dream physicians. Further, I have suggested the identification—from early childhood—of *Irma* with pregnant women, in particular, his mother, Amalia Nathanson Freud. In total, then, the dream would suggest that Freud had a marked feminine component, one that echoed a woman suffering a variety of conditions and complaints. Finally, the dream conveys that Sigmund was impatient with this feminine component and prone to dismiss its suffering.

The dream and Freud's associations offer few clues to the possible complexities of other characters. Freud identified Dr. M. with Josef Breuer, while I (and a few others) have suggested Wilhelm Fliess, about whom Freud was coming to be ambivalent. I am inclined to suggest that this figure (who looks unprofessional and offers foolish prognoses) might historically correspond to one of the male adults in his childhood: father Jakob Freud or half-brothers, Emanuel or Philip, who were of the same age as Amalia. In any case, the dream portrait of Dr. M. highlights the scornful attitude of Freud toward Breuer, although we have fewer clues to confirm this identification.

Mead spoke of the actor "taking the role of the other"; this is surely what happens in the dream theater. One might add that these figures of the dream theater are *the (Meadian) others* who view and judgmentally assess the conduct of the actor. In the case of "Irma's Injection" their combined judgment absolves Sigmund of responsibility for the pains and distress of *Irma.* Yet this finding is paradoxical. Whereas the manifest dream absolves Sigmund by offering multiple scapegoats, the latent thoughts bear a multiple indictment: on the one hand, against Fliess for his mishandling of the case of Eckstein; on the other hand, against Freud for invasive behaviors: as clinician toward Anna, as male authority toward his own feminine aspect, and as husband toward Martha, so inducing an unwanted pregnancy.

Sullivan argued that *the self-system* was like a microscope: by focusing one's vision so closely on particular aspects of one's conduct, it thereby caused one to be inattentive to other aspects. This is patent in "Irma's Injection," in which Sigmund is so focused on who or what—other than himself—is responsible for Irma's plight that the moral issue—*what ought a responsible person do now?*—is quite neglected. A century later and with hindsight, it is easy to pose such dilemmas, but it is the dream that remains evocative.

Objects and Archetypes

Going beyond the arguments of Cooley, Mead, and Sullivan, I suggest that deriving from infancy and childhood, there becomes established within the psyche a set of archetypical figures—*others*—who become the nuclei for the subsequent emotional dramas of the actor. In the language of orthodox Freudianism, these others are designated as *objects.*[30] Freud's exemplary dream sharply distinguishes the actor Sigmund (his *self*) from the other characters who, by being present in that theater, must therefore be actively present within his psyche-and-soma).

To speak in this fashion is not intrinsically revolutionary, for psychotherapeutic discourse notes the presence in the subject of various alternative persons: mother, child, teenager, and so forth. The limitation of orthodox psychoanalysis was the insistence that the basic inner scenario had to be the oedipal configuration with parental actors (objects) and appropriately simplistic motivations. Holding before us a particular dream and dreamer (Freud), we are encouraged to consider much greater complexities.

The fact that the dreamer can so identify with *Irma* that he feels the infiltration in his own chest can be linked to the ability of a stage-actor to so attune to another as to portray him or her within a public drama or recitative. The more that the actor surrenders his (or her) self and becomes the other, the more gripping is the stage performance. While this is a trained ability for professional actors, it is implicit within dreams and is consonant with the discussions in earlier chapters of dissociation and multiplicities of personality. In principle, Freud or any other dreamer has the capacity to enact the role of a dream character. Other parallels are the psychoanalyst in the reverie state of communion with an analysand, and the shaman, who with the aid of drugs, or rhythmic singing or dancing, enters into a trance and assumes a derivative character. Whether we deal with trained specialists—actors, shamans, psychotherapists—or with ordinary mortals, the potentials are present in the form of well-organized *others* within the psyche-soma.

The discussion of "Irma's Injection" thus bears closely on the contention of the first chapter that dreaming is a psychic mechanism that enables group life. By being able to assume the roles of others, whether in dreaming or in reflective analysis, the actor is able to adjust his (or her) conduct. I am not evaluating the process positively or negatively: whether as adaptation, manipulation, or gaining insight into self or others. Within the dream of "Irma's Injection," Freud was considering and reconsidering his interactions with his intimates. The dream therefore was offering a perspective on his and their behaviors. So far as the data allow, one cannot say that, because of the dream, he came to act either better or worse. In subsequent years Freud broke with Fliess, and he transformed daughter Anna into his disciplinary alter and heir.

Potentialities and Pathologies

Bien que les sources de la créativité soient toujours mystérieuses, je centerai ma réflexion sur l'idée que le coeur de l'art *est le corps* et que le processus créatif dépend en partie de la façon dont les élans pulsionnels sont organisés dès le début de la vie psychique. Je veux parler en particuler de la bisexualité psychique, pour mieux comprendre son rôle dans l'acte créateur.[31] (McDougall as cited in Menahem 1997:93)

Between potentialities and pathologies the boundaries vary, not only among different cultures but among the occupations and statuses within a complex culture such as the United States. If it be the involuntary leap of a nonspecialist, switching from one personality to another is considered a *dissociative disorder,* especially if there is amnesia between the one state and the other. Note that it is not considered to be pathological for there to be total or partial amnesia in the parallel movement from the state of dreaming to that of awakening.[32] Nor would it be considered pathological for a person to be so engrossed in either the anticipation of a significant activity or its performance that he (or she) might later have but little recall of some ancillary activity, as in the case of a person so oriented toward the events that might occur on arrival that he (or she) cannot later recall the details of traveling to that point, which may even include as demanding a performance as driving in traffic.

What is again patent in "Irma's Injection" is the interactions and interrelationships among the dream actors. In Freud's dream, a consensus seems to emerge. In other dreams—whether of Freud or others—there is disagreement, dispute, even slayings. It is not too much of a jump to suggest that within some persons at some times, there can be an internal disagreement that paralyzes.

In her clinical work, McDougall (1995: Part II; Menahem 1997:92f.) perceived that artistic creativity depends on a balance between the gendered portions of the personality: masculine and feminine. When the balance is disturbed, the result is creative blockage:

> In whatever field, we each create with masculine as well as feminine aspects of ourselves, whichever offers us a sublimatory pathway for our impossible desire to be and to own both sexes. As I like to say: we are father and mother of our creations. (McDougall, cited in Menahem 1997:93)

McDougall's is an important observation but in the present context incomplete. Creativity depends on the capacity to mobilize as much as possible of the various others (archetypes, Kohutian self-objects) within the psyche-soma, including but not limited to gender. In Freud's case, it would follow that his great productivity was based on his having achieved an equilibrium among his internalized family of others. A number of his essays are shaped almost as dialogues.

Some of the greatest writers—Plato, Galileo, Diderot—have preferred the format of the dialogue (and obviously playwrights). A dialogue neatly captures the tensions among the internal personae, and is most engrossing when the alternates are evenly matched. Although Freud's essays do hold one's attention, the alternate—the skeptic of psychoanalytic verities— is never Sigmund's equal. As he himself recognized, his temperament was that of a crusader who thrived on combatting enemies, so that many of his writings were designed not to reflect and refine his inner tensions but to counter those who had become disaffected or apostates.

Notes

1. Born July 1923 at Melun, Seine-et-Marne, Didier Anzieu was a member of the class of 1944 at the Ecole Normale Supérieure and began analysis with Lacan in January 1949. Anzieu's teacher, Daniel Lagache, suggested the research project that eventuated in the encyclopedic volume (1975/1986). An early version (1959) was expanded by the effort of a group whose membership included several German-speaking psychoanalysts and Eva Rosenblum. Although I am critical of some aspects of the project, the book is invaluable and a fine achievement.

2. An alternative translation of this passage:

As to your mother's marriage bed—don't fear it.
Before this, in dreams too, as well as oracles,
many a man has lain with his own mother. (Sophocles, Grene, trans., 1942 in Grene and Lattimore)

3. Proceeding as a psychoanalytic clinician, Devereux (1976) then interprets the dreams presented in the Hellenic tragedies by the characters Atossa, Io, Menelaos, Klyteimestra, and others.

4. Outre les desirs que nous avons communément, qui nous sont libres, ou au moins volontaires, qui proviennent d'une connoisance precedente de quelque bonté qu'on ait conceu estre dans la chose desirée, les Hurons croyent que nos ames ont d'autres desirs, comme naturels et cachez; lesquels ils disent prouenir du fond de l'ame a de certain objets.
Or ils croyent que nostre ame donne a connoistre ces desirs naturels, par les songes, comme par sa parole, en sorte que ces desirs estant effectuez, elle est contente; mais au contraire si on ne luy accorde ce qu'elle desire, elle s'indigne, non seulement ne procurant pas a son corps le bien et le bon-heur qu'elle vouloit lue procurer, mais souvent mesme se reuoltant contre luy, luy causant diuerses maladies et la mort mesme. (Lalement 1648 in Lincoln 1935:37; Wallace cites editor Rageneau)

5. Once one accords meaning and reality to dreams (and significance to their recitation to others), the issues become epistemological rather than simply psychological (see O'Flaherty 1984 and the contributions to Wautischer 1995).

6. Critics of the authorized translations of Freud's German into English have noted that Freud consistently spoke of *die Seele,* translated by Strachey as "mind" (cf. the discussions in the volume edited by Ornston [1992], especially pp. 64–67 of the editor's rejoinder to Bettelheim). Freud was a careful writer, a master of

German prose, who seldom employed words such as *der Sinn* or *das Gemüt,* which might appropriately have been translated as "mind." *Die Seele* has a range of meanings including "soul, spirit, psyche, heart" and is indeed more appropriate to a discipline in which mind and body are integrated. I shall translate it as "psyche."

To provide some notion of the connotations of *die Seele* to Freud and the German-speaking folk of his time, consider the following excerpt from the Psalms (84:2):

Meine Seele verlanget und sehnet sich
nach dem Vorhöfen des Herrn;
mein Leib und Seele freuen sich
in dem lebendigen Gott.
[My soul longeth, yea, even fainteth
for the courts of the Lord;
my heart and my flesh crieth out
for the living God.] (King James translation)

The passage was used by Brahms in his "A German Requiem" (op. 45), and so would have been especially familiar to cultivated readers.

7. "Throughout his life, Freud tended to write about dreams (his own and others') and the associations to them in the present tense, thus scriptively (re)presenting their hallucinatory nature. . . . Unfortunately, Strachey habitually translated dreams in the past tense, thus flying in the face of Freudian dream theory" (Mahony in Ornston 1992:38). The volume edited by Ornston contains much further detail about the translations of Freud. Overall, I should say that Strachey transformed a Viennese Jew into a British gentleman.

8. In U.S. orthodox institutes, candidates for psychoanalytic training were required to purchase the complete set of the authorized translation by James Strachey of Freud's psychoanalytic writings. And in professional writing, citations were exclusively to this, rather than any other, edition.

9. One peculiar feature of the book is an element of deliberate but well concealed provocation. At that time the word *Traumdeutung* was used to designate the popular interpretation of dreams by fortune tellers. . . . To contemporary scientists the title *Traumdeutung* held something intriguing and shocking. . . . In a letter to Fliess, on February 9, 1898, [Freud] writes that he is enjoying in thought all the "headshaking" over the indiscretions and impudences' the book contains. (Ellenberger 1970:452)

10. Although this is the text of the dream as given in *The Interpretation of Dreams,* Freud indicates later in the book (1900/1965:327) that there was more:

The principal figure in the dream content was my patient Irma. She appeared with the features which were hers in real life, and, thus, in the first instance, represented herself. But the position in which I examined her by the window was derived from someone else, the lady for whom, as the dream-thoughts showed, I wanted to exchange my patient. In so far as Irma appeared to have a diptheritic membrane, which recalled my anxiety about my eldest daughter, she stood for that child and, behind her, through her possession of the same name as my daughter, was hidden the figure of my patient who succumbed to poisoning. *In the further course of the dream* [!] the figure of Irma acquired still other meanings, without any alteration occurring in the visual picture of her in the dream. She turned into one of the children whom we had examined in the neurological department of the children's hospital, where my two friends revealed their contrasting characters. The figure of my own child was evidently the stepping-stone toward this transition. The same Irma's recalcitrance over opening her mouth brought an allusion to another lady whom I had once examined and, through the same connection, to my wife. Moreover, the pathological changes which I discovered in her throat involved allusions to a whole series of other figures. (my emphasis)

11. The final sentence of Chapter 2 is given in emphatic type: "Nach vollendeter Deutungsarbeit lässt sich der Traum als eine Wunscherfüllung erkennen" (G.W. II/III:126).

12. One of the minor tragedies of the psychoanalytic community has been its willingness to accept this level of interpretation of "Irma's Injection" (e.g., Reiser 1990: Part II). We have an abundance of detailed information about Freud's life and the psychoanalytic author's recognition that "the wish fulfillment in the Irma dream appears to be superficial. . . . If Freud were only intent upon vindicating himself in the manner implied by the dream, he could probably have done just as well during the waking state" (Sloane 1979/1990:73). Nonetheless, he leaves matters at that point. "We can surmise that further analysis might . . . lead to painful misunderstandings if exposed to general view. In this connection Freud was inclined to say with Mephistopheles in Goethe's *Faust,* 'After all, the best of what you know may not be told to boys' " (Sloane 1979/1990:68). Such interpretive caution (cowardice?) betrays the profession and leaves the field to venomous critics such as Crews.

13. "Freud was wondering whether dreams were really wish fulfillments. The Irma dream confirmed that hypothesis for him. . . . The dream of 'Irma's Injection' is a programme dream for the whole series of subsequent discoveries that were to constitute psychoanalysis" (Anzieu 1975/1986:140, 155).

Given their clinical orientation, psychoanalysts have tended to minimize or overlook the great number of instances where dreams assisted scientists in creative discoveries. Van de Castle (1994) devotes a chapter to impressive examples. For example: "A Hindu goddess named Namakkal would appear to the Indian mathematician Srinivas Ramajuan in his dreams and present him mathematical formulae which he would verify after waking" (35). Ramajuan's discoveries were of the highest order of mathematical genius.

14. I want to know for what a man is preparing himself. This is what I read out of his dreams. . . . The unconscious seems to be able to examine and to draw conclusions from facts, much as the consciousness does. It can even use certain facts, and anticipate their possible results, just because we are not conscious of them. (Carl Jung, as cited in Van de Castle 1994:158, 174)

15. "I am obliged to add. . . that in scarcely any instance have I brought forward the *complete* interpretation of one of my own dreams" (1900/1965:138n).

16. My explication of the meanings of this dream is particularly indebted to

the discussions by Anzieu (1975/1986) and Erikson (1954). As noted earlier, Anzieu places the extant dreams of Freud in the context of an insightful personal and professional biography. Erikson comments revealingly on the German text of this dream, whose meanings might not always be evident to someone perusing a translation. Anzieu also provides a thorough multilingual bibliography.

17. "Martha had been expecting (or hoping) to enter menopause, even though she was only thirty-five years old. Instead, her suspected menopause turned out to be her last child, Anna" (Anzieu 1975/1986:282–3).

18. Anzieu (1975/1986:141) cites André Berge: "The wish that is fulfilled in the dream is that of (Martha's) miscarriage."

19. Fliess had elaborated a complex theory of male and female periodicities, and, given his interest in sexual physiology, it is likely that he would have speculated about what now is labeled a "safe period," when sexual intercourse is unlikely to result in conception. It would seem plausible that he and Freud would have discussed the particularities of timing in relation to the menstrual cycle. Nevertheless, the hypothesis that Freud might have following such a Fliessian theory, only to find that Martha was again pregnant, seems disconfirmed by the contents of his letter to Fliess of May 25, 1895, in which he writes, "If you really have solved the problem of conception, just make up your mind immediately which kind of marble is most likely to meet with your approval. For me [us?] you are a few months too late, but perhaps it can be used next year" (Masson 1985:129). Anna Freud was born December 3, 1895.

20. In the testimony of Eva Rosenfeld (1892–1977): "Frau Professor [Freud] 'never loved' Anna; it was 'the tragedy of Anna's life.' Her mother had not wanted her sixth child" (Roazan 1995:208). I encountered this text long after I had perceived in the dream Sigmund's ambivalence about the pregnancy. It might also be noted that Minna (Martha's sister) joined the household in 1896, when Anna was yet an infant.

21. The effect on the development of Anna Freud of this family background and of the relationship with her father is insightfully noted by Jessica Benjamin (1995: chap. 4). The analytic relationship of Sigmund and Anna evidently lasted four years (Roazan 1993:110).

22. Trimethylamin has a doubly tripartite chemical structure, $N\text{-}(CH_3)_3$, which Anzieu proposes as the basic paradigm for "Irma's Injection" (e.g., three recalcitrant patients; three fellow professionals; three pregnant women; three families in Freiberg).

23. It is intriguing that Anzieu perceives a connection between "Irma's Injection" and a childhood in which Sigmund was surrounded by reproductively active women yet does not venture a connection between the Irma of the dream and Amalia. It is tempting to speculate that the small boy located insemination in the oral cavity.

24. Freud always insisted that he was (a natural scientist), and that psychoanalysis was the same sort of science as physics and chemistry, always claiming that the interpretations he made of, for instance, dreams and symptoms were ideas already present, albeit unconsciously, in the mind. As a result he maintained that the interpretations he made after having or being told a dream were formulations in words of non-verbal unconscious ideas that had been present before the dream and had caused it. (Rycroft 1992:60–61)

25. [In his associations to the Irma dream, Freud] delineated two groups of people to whom he attached opposing sets of ideas. One group consisted of those who "didn't know"; who made silly diagnoses; who, like Otto, gave injections with dirty syringes; who gave presents of smelly liqueur; who, like M., made silly remarks while examining the patient. The second group actually consisted of just one person—the exalted figure of his friend Fliess, "whose agreement" Freud recalled "with satisfaction" whenever he "felt isolated in his opinions"; who *did* understand Freud and "played so large a part" in his life; who "had a special knowledge of the nose and its accessory cavities"; who had drawn Freud's attention "to some very remarkable connections between the turbinal bones and the female sex organs." . . . All these connections with the Emma episode indicate that the main wish behind Freud's Irma dream was not to exculpate *himself* but Fliess. It was a wish not to jeopardize his positive relationship with Fliess. (Schur 1972:87)

26. The idea that psychoanalysis is not a causal theory but a semantic one is not original . . . the majority of Freudian analysts disclaim it entirely. They thereby lay themselves open to attack from critics like Professor Eyseneck who see quite clearly that psychoanalysis cannot satisfy the canons of those sciences which are based on the experimental method but who believe that if they can demonstrate its inadequacy as a causal theory they have proved that it is nonsense. . . . The analysts are claiming that analysis is what it is not, and Eyseneck is attacking it for failing to be what it claims to be. And both parties are assuming that it is only the natural sciences which are intellectually respectable. (Rycroft 1985:44–45)

This trenchant comment would apply today vis-à-vis the criticisms of Grünbaum, Crews, and others.

27. Bettelheim (1982: chap. 9) expounds the differences between *Deutung* and "interpretation" and attributes the loss of nuance to the bias of the translator, rather than to the tensions within Freud's own reasoning. So, Bettelheim contends that "What Freud intended to indicate with the title *Die Traumdeutung* was that he would attempt to point out the many-layered nature to dreams. . . . He did not mean to promise that he would be able 'to make clear and explicit' (the OED's definition of 'interpret') the meaning of dreams, because that would be impossible." Thus, for Bettelheim, the bias in Strachey's authorized translation is motivated by the desire for respectability within the Anglophone community, rather than reflecting a tension within the master himself, who after all approved the project and authorized the translations. *"Die Psychoanalyse war vor allem eine Deutungskunst"* (Freud 1920 as cited in Brooks 1994:9).

28. The psychoanalyst, Jules Eisenbud

interpreted what he called "a telepathic *rêve à deux*" dreamt by two of his patients: The first dreamt that she was walking in a heavy downpour and took shelter at the home of her neighbor; the second dreamt, on a subsequent night, that the first patient sought refuge in her home from a heavy downpour. . . . Once we admit the possibility of telepathic activity in dreams, we are no longer at liberty to assume that a given dream is the exclusive property of the dreamer who had it. (Eisenbud as quoted in O'Flaherty 1984: 75–76)

O'Flaherty perceives the apparently separate dreams as bits of a broken message that must be fitted together, like the separate versions of a myth. This would correspond with the views expressed by Carl Jung. . . . A more dramatic illustration of intercommunication via dreams may be found in the ethnographic report of Marianne George (1995).

29. "I can only answer the question, 'What am I do to?' if I can answer the prior question, 'Of what story or stories do I find myself a part?' " (MacIntyre 1984:216).

30. The original source of the usage was *The Three Essays toward a Theory of Sexuality* (1905), in which Freud distinguished "aim" and "object" of the sexual drive. The usage became institutionalized to the point where disciple Melanie Klein could focus on the relations between the actor and others but denoted these as *object relations,* a term that then has been employed as a label for her clinical subschool. The reliance on *object* encourages an impoverished vocabulary of affect. Heinz Kohut enlarged the orthodox vision by introducing the concept of *self-object,* regarded as interactive process rather than structure. In their *The Language of Psychoanalysis,* LaPlanche and Pontalis (1973) have headings for "Object," "Object-Choice," and "Object-Relation(ship)," although none for "Other," "Self," or "Self-object."

31. Although the sources of creativity are always mysterious, I will focus my thoughts on the idea that the very core of art is the body, and that the creative process partly depends on how the impulses become organized at the very beginning of psychic life. I refer particularly to psychic bisexuality, in order to understand better its role within the creative act.

32. Thoughtful clinical research has been performed by Barrett (1996a, 1996b, 1997).

Chapter 7

Lost in a Strange City

Dora's Dreams, Freud's Fantasies

> Freud seems to authorize us to read the case as a fragment of the analysis of *his* [own] case of hysteria . . . actively involved in a powerfully ambivalent countertransference. Resisting not only his desire for Dora but also his identification with her, Freud rejects as other and aberrant the feminine side of himself. (Bernheimer 1985:17)

> Organized as it is along multiple analytic perspectives, all converging upon Dora's repressed desires, the case has a sheer brilliance which is still breathtaking. Freud pushes the protesting girl back through her inner history—of which she is largely unaware. . . . When the dazzled reader finally arrives at Frau K., he will be ready to admit that few greater pieces of detection have been written. (Rieff 1963:10-11)

The preceding chapter illustrated the possible meanings of a dream. It also showed how even a person of some psychological and clinical sophistication, as was Freud at the turn of the century, might be led toward a simplistic interpreting and how his psychoanalytic disciples allowed the most relevant meanings to be obscured, so that a century later, authors confidently identify "Irma" with only one of the salient persons in Freud's life (Anna Hammerschlag-Lichtheim, Emma Eckstein), while ignoring the most central (Amalia Nathanson Freud, Martha Freud, Sigmund Freud) and minimizing the complexities of psychic identities.[1] These failings testify to the disciplinary rigidity that led Freud and his "orthodox" analysts to situate dreaming in the same category as neurotic symptoms, rather than with drama, poetry, and dance in a societal context.

As a clinical art and a scholarly discipline, some schools of psychoanalysis have made spectacular progress in the century since that famous dream. Accompanying this has been a critical ferment about Freud's case histories, especially that of "Dora": *Fragment of an Analysis of a Case of Hysteria* (1905). Nevertheless, what is startling is that, for almost a century, there was not just a valiant defense but an enthusiastic endorsement of Freud's handling of the case, despite his blatant failure to deal with her problems and his tendentious misinterpreting of the dreams that emerged in the clinical process.

The first edition of *The Interpretation of Dreams* was oriented about Freud's own dreams, as he had recorded and worked on them during the process of his self-analysis. Later editions were to contain the dreams of others (patients, associates, disciples); but, in reporting these, Freud had to strip much of their context, lest by narrating the intimate details of the dreamer's life, he violate privacy. To demonstrate his theoretical and clinical arguments, he needed a case, such as had been presented in his contributions to *Studies in Hysteria* (1895), but a case now in which the interpretation of a patient's dreams played a salient role. It had then to be a case in which he could write frankly, while yet preserving the anonymity of the patient. Initially written just after the publication of *The Interpretation of Dreams, The Fragment of an Analysis of a Case of Hysteria* ("Dora") can be considered as its supplement or counterpart.

In chapter 5, I noted how Freud assimilated the interpreting of dreams from folk tradition into biomedicine by using a template from comparative neurology. The achievement was brilliant, but the cost was significant: into the very basis of psychoanalysis he imported a system of bioenergetics, and a belief that biochemical toxins were ultimately at the root of every psychic disorder. From his interpretation of evolutionary theory, together with his physiological bias, he regarded the individual as fundamental, while society—and social relations—were secondary (note Freud's mythological scenario in *Totem and Tabu* [1912] of the origin of civil society). Rather than looking at the clinical situation as the encounter between two persons, he defined it as akin to biomedical treatment in which the therapist became a species of psycho-surgeon (see note 4). That which interfered with the functioning of that configuration, he defined as *resistance* or *transference* (i.e., as disruptive phenomena) rather than attempts by the patient to cope with the clinical interaction. Because the therapist was modeled on the surgeon, the very phenomenon of *countertransference* was for years hardly thinkable.

Dora Regains her Voice

The potentially liberating feature of the clinical encounter was the invitation and requirement to free-associate: to speak utterly frankly and fully, expressing all portions of the psyche. One of Dora's symptoms had been *aphonia*, an inability to speak; now, in Freud's consulting chambers, she seemingly is urged to speak. Her first dream is not only an eloquent statement about the disorders of her familial situation; it is also a powerful communication about her response to Freud. When he fails to perceive that part of her communication and instead continues to impose his agenda, Dora responds by bringing a second dream, one of whose messages is that she has come to reject his misguided efforts as therapist. When he disregards that message and ruthlessly imposes his agenda, she departs, feeling again unheard, rejected, and sacrificed to someone else's interests.

As the first psychoanalyst, as a brilliant, troubled, fallible human being—preoccupied with developing a novel technique of psychotherapy and building a practice to support a family—his failure may be understood. What was tragic was that in the decades after their encounter, his version of events was not only accepted but extolled, and extolled not merely by analysts within the movement but by others also. Until recently most commentators—and even today some commentators—fail to perceive the hidden message of her first dream, and the not so hidden message of her second dream, while accepting his interpretations of their meanings as if these were not only the veridical but a radiant example of psychoanalytic understanding.

Thus, in examining the case of Dora, we will again perceive the richness of a dream, how its strands weave into an artistic filigree the pain, soreness, and perplexities of living. Negatively, we will perceive how a rush toward closure, and a failure to relate the dream to the present situation and biography, result in distortion.

Exploited Teenager, Desperate Family

In October 1900, Philipp Bauer brought to Freud's consulting room his seventeen-year-old daughter, Ida, who had recently attempted suicide. Two years before, the girl had been brought because of hysterical symptoms, including chronic cough and loss of voice. At that time, she had already undergone treatment with various doctors,[2] and she had then refused to work with Freud. Now, her father was firm, instructing Freud to bring her to reason.

Desperate, exploited, multiply betrayed, Ida did now work with Freud. Quickly, he learned the hidden life of her family: Her mother (Katharina) was preoccupied with maintaining the cleanliness of their residence. Having been venereally infected by her husband and suffering also from constipation, she traveled frequently to spas in search of relief. Philipp (who had been treated by Freud for syphilis) had acquired a mistress ("Frau K" = Peppina Zellenka), who had taken a quasi-maternal interest in Ida. Her husband ("Herr K" = Hans Zellenka) also had taken an interest in Ida, but on several occasions, initially when she was thirteen, he had made direct sexual advances, and she experienced these as traumatic. When Ida complained of his actions, the adults denied her perceptions, for to have acknowledged them would have compelled them to deal frankly with issues that all hoped to suppress. "In some sense everyone was conspiring to conceal what was going on; and in some yet further sense everyone was conspiring to deny that anything was going on at all" (Marcus 1984:45). Suffocated in this miasma of deceit, neglect, and sexual exploitation, Ida had developed hysterical symptoms and, as these failed to bring the assistance she required, had now toyed with suicide. Little wonder that Philipp Bauer had beseeched Freud for assistance: "Suchen Sie sie jetzt auf bessere Wege zu bringen" (1949: 5:184).

Facing this troubled girl is a brilliant scientist, at the peak of his creative energies, hungry for fame, and needing to build the career and the medical practice that will support his extended family.[3] Having figured the meaning of dreams and solved (so he thought) the riddle of the Sphinx, he allows himself to regard Ida Bauer as a case on which to demonstrate his mastery of psychic processes. So, he writes his bosom friend, "the case has opened smoothly to my collection of picklocks." As "Dora" and he meet together, he manifests the attitude that if only she would assume an attitude of frank self-exposure, the psychic surgery would reveal the sources of her hysterical symptoms and issue in a cure:

> It is clear from his description that Freud's original way of working and reporting was determined by his professional identity as a physiological investigator: his clinical work was conceived as an analogy to clean and exact laboratory work. . . . This was his method; but how clinically alive and concrete is his question as to what more, or what else, Dora had a right to expect of him. He could not see, Freud relates, how it could have helped if he "had acted a part . . . and shown a warm interest in her." [So,] he did perceive, then, an interpersonal distance in his method. (Erikson 1964:168)[4]

Transference and Countertransference

In dreams begin responsibilities. (Yeats 1914)

As their interaction deepens, the needful girl begins to form a strong attachment to Freud, but he cannot allow himself to recognize this. Possibly he is anxious lest the treatment entangle the two of them as his mentor, Josef Breuer, with "Anna O."[5] In any event, Freud deals ruthlessly with that transference, defining it as simply sexual: she wanted a kiss from him (1905/1963:92). Of his own intense countertransference, he is unaware.[6]

After the lies disseminated by the enmeshed families—Dora's and the K's—Freud's consulting room offered truth (or a sort of truth), and this was surely a benefit to the teenage girl. But the proffered truth was framed in a format so individualistically focused and so physiologically sexual that it neglected the relational entanglements and her emotional desperation.[7] As Freud remarked defensively of his clinical procedure (and in French!), "J'appelle un chat un chat" ["I call a cat a cat" = "I call a spade a spade"][8] and "pour faire une omelette il faut casser des oeufs" ["to make an omelette, one must crack eggs"] (1905/1963:65–66). But, Dora's psyche already bore evidence of cracking, and a sexual kitten she could not be. Little wonder that Dora abandoned treatment after only a few months, leaving a therapist frustrated—and unaware of how his own needs (emotional and career oriented) had sabotaged their interchange. Gifted at detecting the ulterior interests of those claiming to be proffering assistance, Dora might well have realized that, at one level, Freud's interest was in scientific exploration rather than her personal benefit (Buckley 1989:1396).

For those willing to listen, her "Second Dream" offers remarkable evidence of this therapeutic misalliance, and so it is noteworthy that the analytic literature contains virtually no discussion of its meanings.[9] Her "First Dream" has been often reviewed, but, in following Freud's lead with its exclusively erotic emphases, much significance has been neglected.

Before proceeding further, I should note an artifact that has tended to promote confusion. Not only does Freud address his patient as if she had the social maturity of a woman ten years or more senior, but he misrepresents her age. Ida Bauer was born November 1, 1882. In 1898, at the age of fifteen, she had first been brought to Freud's office by her father but had refused treatment; Freud dates this visit as being when she was sixteen (1905/1963:37). Then, early in October 1900, she had been brought again, "in spite of her reluctance" (Decker 1991:4). Following local Viennese (but not Anglo-American) usage, Freud writes as if Dora were fully eighteen (33), when in fact she began treatment some weeks shy of that birthdate. Later in his narrative she becomes "this hysterical girl of nineteen" (68).[10] This misdating—the "aging" of Dora—is accentuated by nuances of Strachey's English translation (although any translator would likely translate *Mädchen* as "girl").

Generally, Freud wrote a German richer yet more tentative than Strachey's English. Mahony characterizes Freud's language as "processive and tentative" (in Ornston 1992:31), and Ornston notes, "The problem is that Strachey's stone-cold syntheses sometimes make Freud neat and abstract in just those contexts where his writing ambiguously approximates our real problems and is therefore clinically useful" (1992:4). I offer my own modifications of the standard translations of her dreams.[11] Among the various differences from Strachey is that of tense:

> Throughout his life, Freud tended to write about dreams (his own and others') and the associations to them in the present tense, thus scriptively (re)presenting their hallucinatory nature. According to Freud's oneiric grammar, the optative mode of the latent dream was changed into the indicative present tense, characterizing the hallucinatory nature of the dream dreamt. . . . Unfortunately, Strachey habitually translated dreams in the past tense, thus flying in the face of Freudian dream theory. (Mahony in Ornston 1992:38)

I offer the foregoing as caution to those whose only reading of the text is the standard edition.

To understand the meanings of Dora's dreams, we should have to embed our interpretations within the narrative of her life, her family, her developmental problems, and her clinical treatment by Freud. In this effort, we are severely limited, as we have only Freud's account, together with a few other materials (e.g., Decker 1991; Mahony 1996). What we do have, however, is more than enough for a critical response to the traditional and conventional psychoanalytic literature, long dominated by a worshipful attitude toward Freud's handling of the case.[12]

The First Dream

> A house is on fire. Father [*der Vater*] stands beside my bed and wakes me. I dress quickly. Mama [*die Mama*] still wants to rescue her jewelry-case, but Papa [*der Papa*] says, "I refuse to allow myself and my two children to be burnt for the sake of your jewelry-case." We hasten downstairs, and, when I am outside, I awake. (my translation)

Freud concentrates on the erotic symbolisms of this dream. The symbolisms are indeed present, and given the erotic activities of the troubled household, that interpretation has much justification. Additionally, in response to Freud's questions, Dora provided specific associations to an occasion when she awoke from an afternoon nap on her couch to find her erotic pursuer, Herr K, inside her bedchamber. All this has been discussed so thoroughly within the literature (e.g., the "jewelry-case" as symbolizing the female genitalia) that I hesitate to recapitulate but, instead, will simply agree that these meanings are indeed present.

In noting that set of erotic meanings, we should be careful to bear in mind Dora's status as someone whose emotional life has been crippled. She is the product of a rigid mother, currently preoccupied with her health and with the cleanliness of her body and her household, and of a father who is willing to sacrifice her well-being—and virginity—for his own pleasures. When he was desperately ill, Dora had devoted herself to nursing this father, yet at this critical juncture in her maturation, he finds her fidelity to be inconvenient and expendable.

What has not been discussed in the literature is the dream's reference to the analytic situation itself. "A house is on fire" is linked by Freud with such matters as bed-wetting and masturbation, but it far more drastically refers to the terrible dangers to her own and her family's integrity. Yes, the fire could well symbolize sexuality, as well as disaster, and, yes, Dora is indeed conflicted about her own sexuality, but the real danger to the house is the emotional irresponsibility and the sexual escapades of the adults.

"Father stands beside my bed and wakes me." This objectified *Vater* stands in contrast to the *Papa* of the later narrative. Yes, that figure could refer to the seductive and intrusive Herr K; but, as someone awakening her and rousing her to danger, it is also and even more likely to be the figure of Freud, who is smoking cigars and sitting (or standing) beside the Dora on the couch. "Mama wishes, yet, to rescue her jewelry-case." Especially in the context of her associations to the gifts of her father (and Herr K), "jewelry-case" could surely refer to her mother's identity as female and to Philipp's deprecatory view of this as vanity; derivatively, there could be a reference to Herr K's attempted penetration of Dora's genitals. But what conspicuously is lacking in the scenario of familial and personal danger is any vision of Katharina in a maternal, or protective, or mentoring role. Nor is Frau K visible as a guardian.

"But, Papa says, I refuse to allow myself and my two children to be burnt for the sake of your jewelry-case." This statement brings both good and tragic news. Papa is concerned about the well-being of the children, but they become exclusively *his,* and not his and Katharina's, while expressing his judgment that Katharina is failing to concern herself with the hazardous situation of their children. In saying that the children are "his," is Papa also expressing the attitude that has allowed him to barter Dora to Herr K in order that he enjoy the relationship with Frau K? Would not the normal expression be *"the* children," so that "my two children" is a denial of their autonomy? Is this Papa, in turn, expressing no concern about the welfare of his wife, as foolishly as she may be acting? Is there also a suggestion here that Dora hopes that Freud will regard her as "his child"?

"We hasten downstairs, and, when I am outside, I awake." Again, positive and negative: the family (with Dora) can escape—even though its house is burning—but it may well be that being "outside" (leaving that burning house) is so frightening that the dream cannot be allowed to continue. One set of meanings then might be that Freud is wakening her to a danger, which she has preferred to disregard, and is offering succor, but haste is essential, not only to her but to him (for Philipp expects a speedy "cure"). But a crucial problem is revealed in the image of the jewelry case. If her mother has no maternal role, so that her jewelry case is merely vanity and therefore expendable, where does that leave Dora's own sexuality and identity as woman? If, moreover, the Freud by the couch is assimilated to the dangerous Herr K and the unreliable father, then how can Dora trust him?

The Second Dream

I, being poor, have only my dreams;
I have spread my dreams under your feet;
Tread softly because you tread on my dreams.
            (Yeats 1899/1989:73)

As Dora discusses this dream with Freud, she adds additional fragments, indicated by the parenthetical numbers and appended below the primary dream text.[13]

I am walking in a city I do not know, seeing streets and squares foreign to me.(1) I come then to a house where I am living, go to my room, and find lying there a letter from Mama. She writes: "Because I have left home without the knowledge of my parents, she had not wanted to write that Papa was ill. Now he has died, and if you want to (2), you can come." Then I go to the (railroad) station [*Bahnhof*] and ask, perhaps a hundred times: "Where is the station?" The response is always, "Five minutes." Then I see a dense wood before me, into which I enter, and there I ask a man whom I meet. He says, "After two and a half hours."(3) He offers to escort me. I decline and go alone. I see the station before me but am unable to attain it. With this I have the usual feeling of anxiety that one has in dreams when one cannot move onward. Then, I am at home, so I must have travelled, but of that I know nothing. I step into the porter's lodge and ask about our apartment. The servant girl [*Dienstmädchen*] opens for me and responds: "Mama and the others are already at the cemetery [*Friedhof*]."(4)

   1. Here, the significant addition: At one of the squares I see a monument.
   2. To this the addition: By this word there is a question mark, "want?"
   3. On repeating, she said: "Two hours."

4. During the next hour, she added: "I saw myself particularly distinctly going up the stairs." And, "After her answer, I went to my room, but without any sadness, and read from a large book that lay upon my desk."[14]

Without a description of the affect accompanying the dream's recital, any attempt at uncovering its meanings must be risky. Nevertheless, its manifest content is one of loss and *being lost*. Dora is in a foreign environment.[15] She knows that she must make a journey, but she is unable to take the decisive steps that would initiate it. At one point she cannot find the railroad station; at another, she finds it but cannot attain it; and at still another, she is present at the station but cannot allow herself to act appropriately—by implication, this would mean to locate and board the right train. It is as if the therapeutic interaction has encouraged Dora to perceive that she must independently undertake the journey of personal (emotional and psychosexual) maturation, but the dream indicates that psychically she is *lost* and incapable of movement.

For Dora to find herself and thereby be capable of movement and growth, she would require inner resources. But the dream twice states that her father is dead. The man to whom she was so devoted, and whom she nursed through severe disability, has abandoned and betrayed her (as he has her mother), and now in the dream she perceives him as being interred, while she exhibits neither grief nor desire to join the funeral cortege. (One wonders whether "the monument" memorializes this loss.) The mother, of whom elsewhere she speaks with open contempt (35), is here present only as the writer of an ambiguously worded letter that in Dora's associations evokes the invitation of Frau K to the resort where occurred the fateful and seductive lakeside stroll when Herr K propositioned her (118). Thus, Mama's invitations are questionable and lead to dangerous encounters. So, Dora lacks the internalized parental objects who might sustain her on her journey, and instead, she retires to her room and a large book. (In response to a direct query from Freud (1949:263) she responds that, yes, the book was in encyclopedia [*Lexikon*] format, and he takes this as further evidence of her quest for sexual information and the sexual significance of the dream.)

Ideally, the therapeutic sessions with Freud would supply the emotional support that would allow Dora to undertake her journey. In the dream, a masculine figure does offer to escort her through the dense wood (and possibly toward the station). One may guess that this figure is a compound of Freud, Herr K, and the remnants of the once beloved father; but in any case, Dora rejects the offer, without indicating a rationale. Lacking the escort, she finds herself in the familiar dream anxiety of seeing her goal and wishing to move but being glued to the spot.

Within the dream, distance is perceived temporally, a transformation that is intelligible on several levels: in terms of personal maturation and in terms of the therapeutic sessions with Freud. Inwardly, she had given him fourteen days' notice (as one does a servant, Freud comments); so the "two and a half hours" or "two hours" could refer to the therapeutic space that she was willing to endure, beyond which she would not wait to be healed.

Freud interpreted the dream as a parable of defloration, in which various key words have actual or symbolic meanings in relation to the female genitalia: He thinks of her references to *Bahnhof* (= railroad station = railway court) and to *Friedhof* (= cemetery = peace court) as associative paths to *Vorhof* (= vestibulum = fore court) and that that interpretive judgment is confirmed by her associative reference to *Nymphae* (nymphs and wood within a picture she had viewed on the day before; labia minora).[16] He refers also to the argot obtained from technical medical books, rather than personal experience and folk discourse (119f.). In one sense, he is surely right. The life course of a teenage Viennese girl of the Jewish upper bourgeois would normally lead toward heterosexual experience, marriage, and defloration (in some sequence). Yet, in Dora's case, this journey was fraught with deep anxiety. Her father suffered from syphilis; her mother from the vaginal discharge (or "catarrh") presumably due to his venereal infection.[17] From Dora's wording, Freud judged that she suspected her father of total or partial impotence (64).[18] Nevertheless, her father's erotic infatuation with Frau K had not only divided his family but resulted in Dora's person being offered as a bribe to the restless and sexually deprived cuckold. Herr K had seemed to offer the support of a loving and concerned foster father, but to Dora's horror this had been corrupted by sexual advances in which, at the lakeside, he had employed the same self-exculpatory phrasing toward her as he had when seducing the governess of his children (127). Were she to yield to his plea, would she, too, be discarded as was the governess, rejected with contempt? Having herself been deprived of nurturance and protection as a child, how could she possibly respond to Herr K's request for emotional succor, except with repulsion? Little wonder that in Dora's associations to her second dream, she should recall how she had sat for several hours totally absorbed in contemplation of the Sistine Madonna, a figure who personifies maternal nurturance and childbirth without coitus. (The Virgin Mary was a Jewish maiden.) Possibly also of significance, even for the Jewish Ida Bauer, is the date of this dream—namely, the Christmas season (Lewin 1974), the final session, which was the third devoted to this dream, being on December 31.

The magnitude of Freud's bias becomes explicit in the footnote (126; 1949, V: 267) where he discerns great significance in what he perceives as an absence in the dream. Had the dream been properly sequential,

Freud states, then, when the dreamer comes to the porter's lodge, she should have inquired, "Does Herr ____[Bauer] live here?" or "Where does Herr ___ [Bauer] live?" The reason behind that omission, he contends, is a vulgar pun on the family name, which naturally he cannot disclose: *kalte Bauer*, which literally means "cold peasant," is a euphemism for seminal emission, as from a wet dream (Decker 1991:116). Freud's contention would only make sense if the dreamer pictured herself as a total stranger coming to the family residence. However, in the dream narrative, Dora speaks of asking at the porter's lodge about *unsere Wohnung* (= "our dwelling" or, as here appropriate, "our apartment") and not about a foreign residence. Indeed, assuming a reasonable logic to the dream, the maid servant on duty at the porter's lodge would unquestioningly have admitted the family daughter, but surely not an inquiring teenage stranger, to an apartment whose adult occupants were elsewhere. And, finally, in the "fourth addition" to the manifest dream, Dora speaks of going to *her* room, which again signifies a familial residence. Moreover, we know that in 1900 the Bauer family had an apartment on the Liechtensteinstrasse in Vienna (Decker 1991:4), so that the action in the manifest dream is consistent, and there would have been no reason for the dreaming Dora to inquire of the porter whether this was the residence of Herr Bauer.[19] In short, given the manifest dream as reported, there is not the absence judged as significant by Freud, and the dreaming Dora was not altering her journey so as to avoid the vulgar pun on her family name. The footnote by Freud thus reveals another facet of his countertransference.

However, what is noteworthy about this final episode in the dream is Dora's movement. In real life she had been displaying symptoms of lameness ("foot-dragging") so that climbing stairs had become a burden (122f.), and in the earlier dream episode she had been unable to find her way or even finally to move; but, now, in the final dream episode, without evident difficulty or comment, Dora makes her way up the stairs, into the family residence, and into her room. She cannot initiate the journey of maturation, but, with the symbolic death of her father and the absence of her mother, her only pathway is to instruct herself from books in the privacy of her own room. Some feminist commentators think of Dora as retiring to the privacy of her own room to masturbate; here they follow Freud's emphasis on overt sexual practices, while ignoring the quandary of this abused, psychically beleaguered teenager. One could also speculate that the work with Freud has relieved the psychosomatic symptom expressed in lameness.

Among Dora's associations to this dream is a reference to a young engineer who seemed interested in courting Dora. Three years later (December 6, 1903), she did marry Ernst Adler, "an unsuccessful engineer and composer" (Decker 1991:151; see Mahony 1996:14). In hindsight, she may have been developing the strategy that saw marriage as a way of detaching herself from the difficult situation with her parents and the K family, even though she was emotionally and psychosexually quite unprepared for an intimate relationship. With its imagery of being unable to move, despite her desire and need to do so, the dream may have forecast her use of that strategy and its unhappy consequence (Deutsch 1957).

More on Freud's Countertransference

Several commentators (notably Anzieu 1975/1986:531f.) have argued that Freud's dream of "*table d'hôte*" has specific reference to the case of Dora. That dream was published in the small *Über den Traum* (= *On the Dream*) published originally in 1901:

> A gathering at dinner-table or "table d'hôte." . . . Spinach was being eaten. . . . Frau E. L. sits near me, turns entirely toward me, and tenderly lays her hand upon my knee. Defensively, I remove the hand. She then says: You have always had such beautiful eyes. . . . Indistinctly, I then see a diagram of two eyes or the contours of a pair of eyeglasses. (1949, V:649; my retranslation)

The dream may reasonably be dated as having occurred in October 1900, when Freud had begun to treat Dora and also work on this small book about dreams. Freud's associations point to a connection between "Frau E.L." and his wife, Martha, but it is not unreasonable to hazard that "Frau E.L." also "represents Dora with the erotic transference with which she appeals to Freud" (Anzieu 1975/1986:543). Given that Freud's associations center about the costliness of ordering *table d'hôte* (versus *plat du jour*), Anzieu concludes that the central idea of this dream is that love—including countertransference affection—is a costly business. Possibly, there is a reference to the troubles provoked by the erotic attachment of Anna O. to Josef Breuer, including the phantom of a phantom pregnancy (see note 5, referenced earlier), and were that the case, then to give Freud his due, it is noteworthy that Dora's attack of appendicitis occurred nine months after Herr K had propositioned her at the lake (121–3).[20]

Prior Discussions of Dora

Freud was able to turn a clinical failure into a literary success. (Spence 1986:4)

In the half century following its publication, the case of Dora seems not to have been evaluated critically within the psychoanalytic literature. Discussion centered positively on the theoretical relevance of the clinical treatment of Dora. "The description of Freud's fragmentary work with Dora [had] become the classical analysis of the structure and genesis of a hysteria" (Erikson 1964:168). The major body of work consisted of appreciations of what was being discovered by Freud in those early solitary years of clinical effort and of how the case of Dora exhibited his increasing skill in interpreting dreams and symptomatic acts. Likewise, the case was valued for demonstrating his increasing recognition of clinical transference and bisexuality. Homosexuality, masturbation, repression, reaction formation (disgust toward sexual encounters) and the female version of the Oedipal complex were the topics dominating the literature.

One may guess that when the case was reviewed within the training sessions of analytic institutes, it was as exemplary, rather than critically. (Fenichel's magisterial text [1945] contains but two minor substantive references to the case.) Meanwhile, a distinguished literary critic could characterize Freud as "the Great Detective [i.e., Sherlock Holmes] in all his glory in the Dora case" (Hyman 1962:343; sadly, too, Brooks 1993:234–4).

The critical silence was breached in 1962 by Erikson, who referred to the emergence in adolescence of distinctive virtues:

> There are, of course, many ways in which a young person may express a sudden preoccupation with truth—at first perverse and obsessive, changeable and pretentious, and altogether defensive in Freud's sense, but gradually taking hold of relevant issues and productive commitments. He may come to have a personal stake in the accuracy, veracity, and authenticity, in the fairness, genuineness, and reliability of persons, of methods, and of ideas. . . . Patients such as Dora, therefore, may insist that the genetic meaning of their sickness find recognition within an assessment of the historical truth. (1961/1985:5051)

Erikson did not bluntly state that Freud had failed to deal properly with the adolescent Dora,[21] but, by directing attention to the distinctive psychic qualities of the adolescent, a direct examination and challenge became easier.

With the passage of time, as the clinical case became the focus, much attention was devoted to Freud's countertransference and to its roots in his personal history and patriarchal (and "phallocentric") culture of Viennese society. Dora herself remained a symbol, and attention continued to be directed, almost exclusively, to her first dream. The case thus became valued not just for its theoretical advances but because the psychoanalytic forefather had frankly presented what now was recognized as having been a clinical failure, rather than his version as its having been ended from the sheer spite of a neurotic teenager unable to accept the only treatment that might have benefited her. It was being recognized that, under the screen of his theories of sexuality, Freud had allowed his countertransference to distort his perceptions and thereby had misinterpreted her communications and failed her. Having failed her, he then wrote the case narrative as if she had failed him.

As feminists began to affect psychoanalysis, they used the case of Dora as a negative exemplar. They think of Dora's case as mishandled, but mishandled because of Freud's implicit heterosexual focus (and the sexual conflicts that underlay his countertransference). It would be nice to say that the feminist critics remedy his bias. Several write with grace, wit, and elegance. Yet, read carefully, they also fail to perceive Dora. Their agenda is to attack the patriarchal system of bourgeois Vienna, and Freud is their proximate target.[22] That he would speak of the importunate Herr K as "prepossessing" and suitable as a marriage partner for Dora as a resolution of her difficulties they find outrageous.[23]

Of these writers, only a few clearly perceive Dora herself: outstandingly, Mahony and the historian Hannah S. Decker. The latter traces as much of her biography as today can be discovered and revealed. I should also note the literary analysis of Steven Marcus, who does not focus on Dora but elegantly deals with the narrative, noting both its intricacies and its symptomatic revelations of its author. An even more detailed literary (and clinical) analysis was performed by McCaffrey, who reaches the conclusion:

> It is these betrayals, and Dora's reactions to them, that are the subject of her second dream. Her reaction is to dissociate herself from those [her father, Herr K, Frau K] who have betrayed her and to return to her own privacy and her solitary quest for knowledge. She practices this dissociation most thoroughly upon her father by imagining herself living independently in a strange town, by imagining him dead, and by refusing even to attend his funeral. (1984:81)

Vicissitudes of Freud's Manuscript

Vienna, January 25, 1901
Dear Wilhelm,
. . . I finished "Dreams and Hysteria" yesterday, and today I already miss a narcotic. It is a fragment of an analysis of a case of hysteria in which the explanations are grouped around two dreams, so it is really a continuation of the dream book. In addition it contains resolutions of hysterical symptoms and glimpses of the sexual-organic foundation of the whole. It is the subtlest thing I have written so far and will put people off even more than usual. Still, one does one's duty and does not write for the day alone. It has already been accepted by Ziehen. (Masson 1985:433)

What induced Freud to write the case of Dora? Having written it within the space of a month, and having had it quickly accepted by a journal for publication, what moved him to withdraw it and leave it among his files? Five years later, what caused him to exhume it, rewrite its preface (and possibly more [Marcus 1985:63–64]), and now allow its publication? We can only speculate.[24]

As a way of announcing his novel capabilities to the medical public, Freud would have wished to record a case that was clinically successful. Ideally, he would have wished for a case in which the therapy was as rapid and decisive as that of Katherina, described in *Studies in Hysteria:* An eighteen-year-old resident of the Alps, she was suffering from hysterical symptoms. Identifying the hiker as a physician, she initiated conversation, and in response to Freud's shrewd questioning, she disburdened herself of a history of sexual assaults by her father. After the prudery of bourgeois Vienna, Freud found her candid responses to be refreshing, enabling a rapid therapeutic outcome (Mahony 1989: chap. 2).

On the theoretical level, Freud would have wished to publish a text that confirmed the argument of *The Interpretation of Dreams* (1900), utilizing the dreams of a person other than himself.[25] Then, after the publication of *Psychopathology of Everyday Life* (1901) and *Three Essays on a Theory of Sexuality* (1905), he would have again been pleased to offer confirmation of their theses by a clinical case. Certainly, the *Fragment of the Analysis of a Case of Hysteria* does afford such weight to Freud's theories, but it surely could not have been presented as a clinical success.

So, early in his clinical career, Freud would have been ambivalent about adding the Dora of December 1900 to the cast memorialized in *Studies in Hysteria.* Yet, although the case had then been awkwardly terminated, by 1903 he could have appended an apparently more satisfactory terminus or a conclusion more satisfying to the bourgeoisie from among whom he drew most of his patients. For in December 1903, Ida Bauer did marry and Freud "optimistically judged it a healthy step . . . although her parents had serious misgivings about the bridegroom" (Decker 1991:151–2). Perhaps the fact that the wedding was held in Vienna's fashionable Reform Jewish temple militated against his referring to its occurrence in a case appendix. For one of the problems of presenting frank case histories is that readers may utilize them as *romans à clef* and seek to recognize the actors. Because of chronic illnesses, the families of Philipp Bauer and Hans Zellenka (= "the K's") had spent much of their time in Meran (and at various spas), so that they would not have been identifiable to the Viennese reading public.

Of course, one may guess at alternative explanations for Freud's handling of his manuscript. The intimate friendship between Freud and Wilhelm Fliess was coming to the end, possibly forecast in the dream of

"Irma's Injection" with its reference to the bungled operation on Emma Eckstein. In addition, the two men, who had shared ideas so freely, now began to quarrel bitterly about research priorities. They had jointly been theorizing about the bisexuality of the human actor, although it was the 1903 publication by Weininger, *Geschlecht und Charakter* (*Sex and Character*) that was the angry climax for Fliess, who felt that Freud had betrayed his creative innovations to another Viennese. Swales (1982) has argued that it was the dispute with Fliess that led Freud to table his case history: "I withdrew my last work from the printer because shortly before I had lost my last audience in you" (letter of March 11, 1902); so it was not until a significant passage of time that Freud felt moved to release this pertinent manuscript. However, Gay (1988:246) notes that Freud was evidently disheartened by the critical reception of the manuscript by Oscar Rie, friend, medical colleague, family physician. Also plausible is the argument that Freud needed that interval of time to assimilate the experience of (counter-)transference within the clinical situation (Ellman 1991: Part I).

Whatever its history, the final manuscript of the "Fragment" exhibits the familiar cast of Freud's inner personae: the psychotherapist, hypersensitive to words, dreams, and mechanical actions, and leaping from dazzling intuition to bewildering misinterpretation. The ironic humanist who dignifies what once was considered the humble labor with the hysterically disturbed by counterpointing with the great classics of German, Latin, and Greek literatures. The man who could refer to dreams as psychoses yet introduce his magisterial work on their meaning with a quotation from Virgil, "Flectere si nequeo superos, Acheronta movebo." There is the case narrator whose writing "has a sheer brilliance which is still breath-taking" (Rieff 1963:9). And, of equal stature, there is the physiological investigator, trained in the finest biological laboratories of his century, who believes that he must demonstrate an interconnection between the processes of the psyche and those of the bloodstream and nervous system. The prose consequence is sometimes harmonious and sometimes bizarre, as when he appends to the fantastic narrative of the "Fragment" an "Epilogue" where, after acknowledging his verbal therapy of psychoneurotic patients, he hypothesizes that the root cause of their problems is a chemical toxin, likely of sexual origin (135; 1949:276-7).[26]

The end product of these multiple personae is a complexity of discourse akin to Shakespeare. Also Shakespearian is the impact on language. Nonce words have become embedded not just in the language of psychodynamics but even in common speech (Ornston 1992:12). For Breuer and Freud of 1895, *übertragen* as an adjective could mean "figurative" (Mahony 1992:26), but now in the "Fragment" the word *Übertragung* (1949:279f.) is making its appearance as "transference" (137f.).[27]

Freud's struggle to integrate these different inner voices culminates in a remarkable text. His "creative honesty was such that it compelled him to write the case of Dora as he did. . . . his case histories are a new form of literature; they are creative narratives that include their own analysis and interpretation" (Marcus 1985:90). If the abused Dora was not properly treated by the first psychoanalyst, the evidence is in a case narrative that reveals almost as much about its author as it does of its subject.

Mahony's Critique

A supervising and training psychoanalyst and professor emeritus of English, University of Montreal, Patrick J. Mahony has been devoting himself to a reconsideration in clinical and historical depth of each of Freud's case studies. He has gained access to Freud's process notes and other clinical records and has visited crucial sites. His review of the Dora case is deeply critical of Freud's handling:

> Over the hours of their meeting, Freud conducted himself in an adversarial manner that sometimes approached the brutal. If anything, his grilling increased her resistances. Freud even proposed that yielding to Hans would have been the best solution "for all parties concerned" (108). His solution, in other words, was that she submit to a male-empowering ménage à quatre and accept herself as a female object, fashioned to male devices. (Mahony 1996:14)

Mahony is also perceptive in exposing the misstatements and distortions in Freud's texts. His concluding judgment is devastating:

> The case of Dora has an array of negative distinctions. It is one of the great psychotherapeutic disasters; one of the most remarkable exhibitions of a clinician's published rejection of his patient; spectacular, though tragic, evidence of sexual abuse of a young girl, and her own analyst's published exoneration of that abuse; an eminent case of forced associations, forced remembering, and perhaps several forced dreams (64) . . . And for roughly half a century the psychoanalytic community remained collusively blind about that abuse or, because of blind adoration, simply ignorant of it. (Mahony 1996:148–9)

I only regret that Mahony chose not to be more specific in the critique of the psychoanalytic community. He has clearly heard and read those words. Best of all, Mahony does remind us of a temptation and a responsibility: "Either within or outside analysis, courage is a rare attainment. Cowardice is easily rationalized as prudence. . . . Freud does not need idealizing protection: he is great enough to stand on his own."

Concluding Remarks

With his background in comparative neurology and his intensive training in biomedicine, Freud brought to his clinical practice a model that
was doubly reductionist: the individual was emphasized at the expense of
social relationships; the physiology of the individual was emphasized at
the expense of the psyche. So he could write that the ultimate cause of a
psychic disturbance was a biochemical toxin (likely of sexual origin) that
affected the neurological functioning of the patient:

> [N]euroses have an organic basis. . . . It is the sexual function that I look
> upon as the foundation of hysteria and of the psychoneuroses in general.
> . . . Of all the clinical pictures which we meet with in clinical medicine, it is
> the phenomenon of intoxication and abstinence in connection with the use
> of certain chronic poisons that most closely resembles the genuine psy-
> choneuroses. (135)

In the absence of a technique for directly addressing that somatic imbalance, Freud thought he could achieve a cure by inducing psychic
catharsis. In this scenario, the dream has but the meaning of a hidden
wish. By bringing to the patient her hidden (sexual) wishes, by making her
aware that the roots of her symptoms lay in the repressed status of these
wishes, a cure could be accomplished. As therapist, his role was detached,
as objectified as the physician who lances a boil, sterilizes the wound, and
awaits the somatic healing. It is this metaphorical imagery that provides
the basis for the recent devastating attacks on Freud and psychoanalytic
therapy. If "hysteria" or a neurosis are merely the equivalent of a chronic
infection or somatic imbalance, then why waste all that time and energy
on prolonged conversation within the psychoanalytic consulting room? If
the problem is taken to be the overt symptom (Dora's aphonia, tussis ner-
vosa, or threats of suicide), then psychoactive drugs are quicker and
cheaper, and more conducive to direct empirical testings.

If, instead, we perceive the ailing person as an organism within a social
environment, a being whose psychic growth has been so injured that it is
overwhelmed with pain, strangled with defensive formations, and unable
to heal itself, then we surrender the image of psychic cure on the model
of a surgical operation (or psychopharmacology). The dream becomes
an incredibly rich resource, conveying the emotional difficulties of the
patient in addressing her daily problems and touching on a broad range
of trauma and pain. Thus, a dream does not have a simple single interpretation but instead has a variety of meanings and significances. Likewise, her symptoms should be perceived as inadequate and immature ex-
pedients, rather than entities that need to be eliminated.

By imposing his agenda on Dora, Freud may have provided some partial assistance, but in a fashion that was authoritarian, phallocentric, destructive. That we can perceive this is a tribute to his efforts. To fail to act on that perception is to betray that which was positive and beneficial in his efforts.

Notes

1. An egregious example is Hopkins's chapter in Neu (1991).
2. "[T]he various methods of treatment which are usual, including hydrotherapy and the local application of electricity, had produced no result . . . [so] the child had developed into a mature young woman of very independent judgment, who had grown accustomed to laugh at the efforts of doctors" (1905/1963:37). These medical efforts, which seem barbaric and punitive, are described in Decker (1991: chap 1).
3. Freud "brooded about his income. His letters to Fliess chronicle anxiously the startings and stopping of patients' treatments. At times he was down to three or four sessions a day. The departure of any patient was a financial blow, since many relatives depended upon his earnings" (Decker 1991:92).
4. "I cannot advise my colleagues too urgently to mold themselves during psycho-analytic treatment on the surgeon, who puts aside all his feelings, even his human sympathy, and concentrates his mental forces upon the single aim of performing the operation as skillfully as possible" (Freud 1912).
5. Josef Breuer, Freud's mentor and sponsor, had treated Bertha Pappenheim, a patient who was to go into history under the pseudonym of "Anna O." An intense relationship had developed between physician and patient, which may finally have discomfited Breuer. Anzieu comments (1975/1986:543): "to defend himself against [Dora's] transference, Freud remembers, so as not to fall into the same trap, Breuer's conscious blindness and unconscious connivance when faced with Anna O's erotic transference."
Whether Anna O. actually produced a phantom pregnancy, as was later claimed by Freud, is not evident from the extant records concerning Breuer, but surely there was an intimate relation:

> What really happened with Breuer's patient I was able to guess later on, long after the break in our relations, when I suddenly remembered something Breuer had once told me in another context before we had begun to collaborate and which he never repeated. On the evening of the day when all her symptoms had been disposed of, he was summoned to the patient again, found her confused and writhing in abdominal cramps. Asked what was wrong with her, she replied, "Now Dr. B's child is coming!"
> At this moment he held in his hand the key that would have opened the "doors to the Mothers" [Goethe, *Faust*, II], but he let it drop. With all his great intellectual gifts, there was nothing Faustian in his nature. Seized by conventional horror he took flight and abandoned the patient to a col-

league. For months afterwards she struggled to regain her health in a sanitarium. (Freud, letter to Stefan Zweig, June 2, 1932)

I find more precise and more insightful the reconstruction of these events in Appignanesi and Forrester 1992:80f.), but we have to recognize what Freud thought and feared as he dealt with Dora. It is also noteworthy that, after leaving the sanitaria, Pappenheim became a leading figure in social welfare activities within Germany, and her character and contributions were recognized by persons such as Martin Buber. She died during the Nazi regime (Rosenbaum 1984).

6. Feminist critics (e.g., Moi, Ramas, Sprengnether) have been especially acute in dissecting Freud's countertransference. Scharfman (1980) has noted the sexual imagery of the "picklock" metaphor in the letter to Fliess; had it appeared in Dora's associations, he would unhesitatingly have remarked on the phallic symbolism of placing a key in a lock. Anzieu (1975/1986:531f.) approaches the issue analytically by interpreting the character of Frau E. L. in Freud's "Table d'hote" dream (*Über den Traum:* chap. 1) as representing the erotic Dora.

7. We may need to be reminded that at this stage of his thinking, Freud was convinced that "neuroses have an organic basis" in which "definite sexual substances" have an "excitant action." "It is the phenomenon of intoxication and abstinence in connection with the use of certain chronic poisons that most closely resembles the genuine psychoneuroses" (1905/1963: 135; 1949, V: 276–7). Swales (1983) argues that experiences with cocaine provided Freud with the model for this reasoning.

8. Yet this French phrase was hardly "direct." At the very least, Freud was opting for a roundabout way to make his point as well as choosing substitute, seemingly innocuous nouns as replacements for the "technical names" he said he had used. But perhaps even more was involved. *Chat* or *chatte* is also vulgar slang for female genitalia. Freud had taken "a French detour and call(ed) a pussy a pussy." This interpretation holds up well in German. (Decker 1991:119, referencing Gallop's witty dissection [1985:209] of Freud's prose)

9. More precisely, it is the literature in the English language that contains little discussion of the second dream. Lacan and his disciples do interpret that dream but from within their own distinctive theoretical framework, focused on the body and on the orientation toward the father: "For Dora to be able to acquire knowledge about sex, or to accede to sex inasmuch as it has to do with knowledge, her father must be dead. . . . Her father is no longer the homosexual accomplice of her games; he is dead. Thus she can usurp his place, not so as to continue to masturbate but so as to explore the sexual order" (David-Ménard 1983/1989:124–5). Her second dream will be printed and discussed later in this chapter.

10. One suspects that Freud's consistent reference to Dora as a year older than she really was lay in his identification with Mr.K. and unconsciously buttressed his suggestion that Dora marry K. It is not only that Freud referred to Dora as being nineteen, although she was not even eighteen when she began the treatment and quit the therapy less than two months after her eigh-

teenth birthday. Freud also wrote that she was fourteen when K. kissed her in his office, although she was still thirteen. He said she was sixteen when the scene by the lake occurred, but she was only fifteen. (Decker 1991:118)

11. Here, as elsewhere, I consulted about issues in translating Freud's German with Elizabeth Welt Trahan and Erika Bourguignon, both native Viennese.

12. "The Dora case is also noteworthy because it contains a masterful demonstration of clinical dream interpretation" (Jennings 1986:607–8).

13. I go walking in a city that I do not know, and I see streets and squares that are strange to me. Then I come into a house where I live, go to my room, and find Mama's letter lying there. She writes: Since I [Dora] am away from home without my parents' knowledge, she didn't wish to write me that Papa took ill. Now he has died, and if you [Dora] want, you can come. So I go to the station and ask perhaps 100 times: Where is the station? I always receive the answer: Five minutes. Then I see a thick wood in front of me and I go into it and ask a man whom I meet there. He says to me 2½ hours more. He offers to accompany me. I refuse and go alone. I see the station in front of me and cannot reach it. At the same time I have the usual feeling of anxiety when one cannot go farther in a dream. Then I am home; in the meantime I must have traveled but I know nothing about that.—I step into the porter's lodge and ask him about our apartment. The maidservant opens for me and replies: Your mom and the others are already at the cemetery. (translation by Mahony 1996: 87)

14. Translation by Elizabeth Welt Trahan and Murray Wax.

15. "My analysis of the second dream is somewhat different from Freud's. To begin with, Dora, following her self-exile from her family at the end of the first dream, is now completely alienated from them. At the outset of the second dream, she is literally a stranger in a strange land" (Lewin 1974:526). Lewin is the only author who perceived this fundamental theme.

16. Citing such materials as the 1899 essay on "Screen Memories" and the earlier correspondence with his fiancee, Swales (1983:9) comments on "the persistent nature of Freud's defloration fantasies." So, too, Appignanesi and Forrester (1992:25): "It is not going too far to say that the defloration fantasy is the crux, the authentically Freudian sexual fantasy."

Vorhof is not in the manifest dream, nor is *verkehr* (119). These are Freud's associations.

17. In Decker's (1991:52) judgment, Katherina Bauer had been infected with gonorrhea by Philipp.

18. Freud was not able to trace the source of this judgment by Dora, but it could only have been her mother or Frau K, and the latter is far more likely.

19. A minor questionable item in Freud's text and Strachey's translation concerns the "large book," from which Dora reads in the fourth addendum to her second dream. In a subsequent footnote (1949, V:267), Freud refers to Dora's consulting a *Wörterbuch* (= dictionary, but translated by Strachey as "encyclopedia"), and in a still later footnote, he refers to her reading a *Lexikon* (also translated as "encyclopedia") in quest of sexual information. In one version of the manifest

dream, she speaks of going *ruhig* (= quietly, tranquilly; Strachey translates as "calmly") to her room; in the other version she speaks of going *gar nicht traurig* (= "without the least sadness," which would be significant in view of the death and burial of her father) and there reading the large book on her desk. Most commentators have assumed with Freud that, in her final dream image of consulting a large book, Dora was referring to her bookish quest for sexual knowledge. Certainly, this is plausible, but it may be an oversimplification of Dora's interests, neurotic or otherwise. She herself indicated consulting such a work to learn about appendicitis, which was subsequently to appear among "her hysterical productions" (121). As an intelligent young woman, frustrated in her desires for education, she would in dream space have been seeking information about her situation and her miseries, sexual and otherwise. What is notable in the manifest dream is that although she cannot attain the (railroad) station, she does manage to return to a deserted family residence and to solitary and tranquil preoccupation with a book.

Freud thinks she is consulting the encyclopedia to learn sexual secrets. He may be projecting, for his interest seems to be her sexual secrets.

McCaffrey offers the intriguing suggestion that "The book has to do with the betrayals [of Dora who must now] move backwards, in the sense that she must study the past, not only to understand the trauma and its aftermath but in order to investigate and perhaps begin to repair the psychical foundations that were undermined by the betrayals" (1984:85–86).

Additionally, we may need to bear in mind Dora's intelligence, curiosity, and desire for mastery. Having somehow passed through adolescence—with considerable trauma and with help and misdirection from her work with Freud—this woman reappears in Viennese society in her middle age, as a master of contract bridge, who gave lessons to middle-class women (Decker 1991:175).

20. Appignanesi and Forrester (1992:143f.) perceive a different referent for Frau E.L. Given the limited associations presented by Freud, it is difficult to present any interpretation with assurance, except that the eyeglasses could connote that the interactions—his with another woman—were being observed.

21. Even Erikson can only permit himself the mild, "But I wonder how many of us can follow without protest Freud's assertion that a healthy young girl would, under such circumstances, have considered Mr. K's advances 'neither tactless nor offensive'" (1964:169). A few pages later, Erikson does permit himself to advocate a different posture for a contemporary therapist, while remaining cautious in his references to Freud:

> Young patients in particular appoint and invest the therapist with the role of mentor, although he may strenuously resist expressing clinically what he lives and stands for. His patient's demands do not obligate him, of course to "play a part," as Freud so firmly refused to do. True mentorship, far from being a showy form of conventional sympathy, is always part of a discipline of outlook and method. (173–4)

22. [F]or Hélène Cixous, the French theorist, Dora's case history has become an "urtext in the history of woman." She has become the symbol of that character-type of the nineteenth century, the hysterical woman, symbol of the "silent revolt against male power over women's bodies and women's

language." . . . "To that must be added that in Dora there is a very beautiful feminine homosexuality, a love for women that is astounding." (Appignanesi and Forrester 1992:146)

The obvious caveat is that Dora was not only abused, exploited, and betrayed by her father and Herr K but had been gravely neglected by her mother and betrayed by Frau K. So, once again, the real Dora is lost, as now she becomes a feminist icon.
   23. Freud: "Ich kenne zufällig Herrn K.; er ist dieselbe Person, die den Vater der Patientin zu mir begleitet hat, ein noch jugendlicher Mann von einnehmendem Äussern" (1949, 5:187, n.2). "I happen to know Herr K.; a still youthful man of engaging presence, he is the same person who accompanied Dora's father to me" (Philipp Bauer had previously come to Freud to be treated for syphilis). *Einnehmend* means captivating, charming, engaging; Strachey translates it as "prepossessing" (44).
   Dora: "[The governess of the K's children] told me that Herr K had made advances to her at a time when his wife was away for several weeks; he had made violent love to her and implored her to yield to his entreaties, saying that he got nothing from his wife ["er habe nichts von seiner Frau" (1949:268)]. . . . She had given way to him, but after a little while he had ceased to care for her, and since then she hated him" (127). Freud's paraphrase of Dora's statement of Herr K's words is "Ich habe nichts an meiner Frau" (1949:269). Either formulation is a declaration that he receives no sex from his spouse and so is free (or entitled) to solicit sexual intimacies elsewhere.
   Lacan's mistranslation (1951/1985:101) of Herr K's words leads to a sequence of dubious interpretations:

> [W]e need only stick to the text to understand it. Herr K. could get in only a few words, decisive though they were: "My wife is nothing to me." The reward for his effort was instantaneous: a hard slap (whose burning aftereffects Dora felt long after the treatment in the form of a transitory neuralgia) gave back to the blunderer: "If she is nothing to you, then what are you to me?"

   24. The following items are relevant but do not unravel the entirety of the enigma: Letter to Fliess, March 13, 1901 (Masson 1985:438): "At his request I let Oscar [Rie] read 'Dreams and Hysteria,' but I derived little joy from it" (seemingly because Rie did not endorse the treatment and its narrative). Letter to Fliess, March 11, 1902 (Masson 1985:456): "I withdrew my last work from publication because just a little earlier I had lost my last audience in you." While the editor of the letters takes Freud's text at face value (an unusual stance for Masson), one might also note that Freud had just achieved his great professional desire, the award of a professorship at the University of Vienna, and so he no longer required the published case to bulwark his theory, for as he continues in this penultimate letter to Fliess: "Congratulations and flowers are already pouring in, as though the role of sexuality has suddenly been officially recognized by His Majesty, the significance of the dream certified by the Council of Ministers, and the necessity of a psychoanalytic therapy of hysteria carried by a two-thirds majority in Parliament" (457).
   25. Bernheimer (1985:17) notes that in his correspondence with Fliess, Freud

explicitly called the case history of Dora "a continuation of the dream book." He then goes on to suggest that "Freud seems to authorize us to read the case as a symptomatic continuation of his ongoing self-analysis, as a fragment of the analysis of *his* case of hysteria. To view the text in this way is to see Freud as actively involved in a powerfully ambivalent countertransference."

26. "It is well known that gastric pains occur especially often in those who masturbate. According to a personal communication made to me by W. Fliess, it is precisely gastralgias of this sort which can be interpreted by an application of cocaine to the 'gastric spot' discovered by him in the nose, and which can be cured by cauterization of the same spot" (1905/1963:97).

27. [Freud] considered the language of [psychoanalytic] theory figurative, not literal. Only by means of such distorting figurative language could he be aware of unconscious processes, which was further complicated by the fact that the distorting nature of the language itself can never be fully known. . . . [T]he central determinant of the patient's associations is transference, whose verbalization is by its very nature figurative. The earlier Freud used to spell this out, calling transference "a false connection"—*eine falsche verknüpfung*—hence a kind of relation definable by the past participle of a German word now used for the English word transference—*Übertragung*. Used as an adjective, *übertragen* may also mean figurative. (Mahony 1992:25–26)

Note then Freud's comment "In dem zweiten Traume Doras is die Übertragung durch mehrere deutliche Anspielungen vertreten" (1949:283).

PART THREE

CONCLUSIONS

Chapter 8

Dreams within Human Group Life

Western Rationality and the Angel of Dreams

Anthropologists Victor and Edith Turner and their children lived among the Ndembu of southern Africa during the 1950s. Describing how his vision became enlarged, Victor wrote:

> In the field [among the Ndembu], I was at a loss how to proceed further. . . . [Then] I rediscovered (after about twenty years' latency period) Freud's *Interpretation of Dreams*. This great paradigmatic work is concerned with dream symbols and their interpretation. I was also concerned with symbols, but with cultural symbols. . . . These sociocultural symbols had at least one important property in common with dream symbols as Freud conceptualized these. They were "multivocal," susceptible of many meanings . . . multireferentiality was a central characteristic of certain kinds of symbols. (Turner 1978/1992:18–19)

Multivocality—multireferentiality—is indeed characteristic of the symbols of dreams, the actions and matériel of rituals, as well as of objects viewed aesthetically. Victor Turner's explication of the range of meanings of Ndembu symbols is convincing and dramatic because he situated the symbols within the lives and specific concerns of a people he and his family knew, loved, and appreciated. As but one example of this symbolism, *blood* signifies that which is shed by the hunter at the kill and by the menstruating woman (1967:41f.). For, in the latter case, the blood also symbolizes a death, since among the highest values of the Ndembu is that a woman should become the mother of numerous and lively children. A second example comes from a healing ritual (observed later by Edith Turner) in which the shaman extracted from an ailing person an *ihamba*, the equivalent of a poisonous tooth (E. Turner 1992). The *ihamba* incarnated the grudge of another person.

123

Both instances noted by the Turners are evocative, amplifying the reports of ethnographers about other peoples. What is notable is that the symbolisms and rituals communicate instantly across the cultural and linguistic barriers, even though they are anchored in the practices of a people otherwise so different.

Multireferentiality may be taken as thematic within this book. Western epistemology has been anchored in the Aristotelean axiom of binary opposition: either the proposition *p* is true or *p* is false—for example, either "All A is B" ("All men are mortal") or "Some A is not B" ("Not all men are mortal"). As applied to conventional logic and science, the axiom has been invaluable, even when the phenomena of nature are as elusive as those of quantum mechanics (or the paradox of light as wave or corpuscle). (In the face of quantum theory, Einstein could bolster his confidence by declaring that God does not play dice with the universe.)

However, as applied to the character of *Irma* or to the *dominant* symbols of Ndembu ritual, the Aristotelean axiom becomes not so much meaningless as irrelevant. Within the symbolic systems of dreams, rituals, magical practices, and art, binary contrasts exist but these are not the binary oppositions of Aristotle. The figure of *Irma* is compound, being condensed from a variety of persons, including the dreamer Freud, yet Sigmund is the contrastive person who invades her body. In Pawnee mythology, the protagonist, Without-wings, engages in magical combat with the chief of the bison herd, and they each assume a multiplicity of animal forms (Wax 1962). Accordingly, the inherent significations can only be approached hermeneutically. Claude Lévi-Strauss, exponent of structural analysis of myth, hoped to avoid the hermeneutic resolution by the appeal to the methods of structural linguistic analysis—as he interpreted them. However, binary *contrasts* should not be seen as binary *oppositions* in the linguistic sense, for binary oppositions are fundamental to the intelligibility of a spoken language.

The study of dreams and dreaming challenges the epistemology and rationalistic vision of Western civilization, in which the natural sciences are the apex of knowledge. The differences in discourse and in reasoning between this high tradition and that of alien and exotic peoples (such as the Ndembu) has long been noted by observers (travelers, explorers, missionaries) and in the twentieth century by cultural anthropologists. The anthropological discussion has become particularly heated and politicized, because the key assumption was implicit, namely that only the Western high tradition was valid, and therefore to note any such differences in the operations of the psyche and the modality of reasoning was to declare that non-Western peoples were irrational and inferior.

A brilliant philosopher, Lucien Lévy-Bruhl (1857–1939), analyzed the ethnographic data then available upon alien peoples and published a series of essays on "primitive mentality" (notably, *Les Fonctions mentales dans les sociétés inférieures* [1910]; *La Mentalité primitive* [1922/1923]). Referring to the beliefs such as a human being related to an animal, or even assuming its form and becoming the animal, or dreams constituting messages from other beings (1922/1923: chap. 3), he employed the analytic framework of neo-Kantian epistemics and thereby concluded that the *collective representations* of "primitive" peoples were prelogical and mystical.

Lévy-Bruhl's essays provoked a storm of protest among the American anthropologists associated with Franz Boas. For these scholars, Lévy-Bruhl's categorizations were invidious. Although unfamiliar with neo-Kantian categorizations, these anthropologists did not challenge their universal applicability. What they presumed was that if the reasoning of these other peoples could be classified as "mystical" and "prelogical"—even heuristically—then these peoples were indeed "primitive" and "inferior." Accordingly, the American anthropologists assembled quantities of ethnographic data demonstrating that the peoples in question (no longer labeled as "primitive") could be as sensible in their reasoning and behavior as their Western counterparts (which, incidentally, Lévy-Bruhl had never denied). Note the very title of Paul Radin's *Primitive Man as Philosopher* (1927).

In the same period, the Polish-born anthropologist Bronislaw Malinowski published "Magic, Science and Religion" (1925/1955), which contended that the native peoples of the Trobriand Islands practiced "science." The Trobriand Islanders were indeed sensible and practical folk, capable of remarkable feats such as navigating via canoes from one Pacific island to another. But they were not "scientists," nor did they reason according to the canons and presuppositions of the natural sciences. In these polemical responses to Lévy-Bruhl, basic terms such as *magic, science, logic,* and *philosophy* were twisted, and data were tendentiously misunderstood and misinterpreted. (Also, disregarded in the fracas was American anthropologists' unfamiliarity with the neo-Kantian concept of "collective representations.")

A generation later, the British anthropologist E. E. Evans-Pritchard described the Zande system of reasoning about causation (*Witchcraft, Oracles and Magic among the Azande* [1937/1976]). In the climate of opinion set by the foregoing debate, he appended a lengthy interpretation of "why Azande do not perceive the futility of their magic." That he should have felt it necessary to provide a response of twenty-two reasons is testimonial to the response he was encountering from critics. His field data would have confirmed the analysis of Lévy-Bruhl (whose work he saluted).

Among the Azande, Evans-Pritchard lived according to their logic and precepts, finding them quite workable:

I always kept a supply of [oracular] poison for the use of my household and neighbours and we regulated our affairs in accordance with the oracles' decisions. I may remark that I found this as satisfactory a way of running my home and affairs as any other I know of. (1937/1976:126)[1]

The *Rationality* of Western Civilization

Rycroft sees Freudian psychoanalysis as contaminated by "the pathology of the Western intellectual tradition," even when it is attempting to account for those aspects and attributes of mind which are most at odds with that pathology. (Fuller 1985:23)

Parallel to social anthropology, in the field of comparative sociology, the great German sociologist Max Weber (1864–1920) had concluded that, in comparison with other civilized societies, Western civilization was uniquely *rational.* Weber was led to this judgment after prodigious comparative investigations that included traditional India and China, ancient Israel, and the Roman empire. Two examples employed by Weber are worthy of mention. All civilized societies had produced aesthetic compositions in the plastic arts, but only in the West had there been a prolonged effort to *rationalize* painting by subjecting its depictions to the *laws of perspective* (in mathematics the field of projective geometry). Throughout the Renaissance and thereafter, painters had prided themselves on their ability to transfer onto canvas the ocular *perspective* that today we would associate with the basic mechanisms of lens and screen (as in a camera obscura or a modern camera with long depth of focus). Likewise, only in the West had there been a prolonged effort to *rationalize* music in a fashion leading to the tempered (diatonic) scale, the related system of printed notation, the organization of a symphony orchestra, and the composition of scores to determine performance. These key examples help us to understand the specific nature of Western *rationality:* magnificent painting may be done regardless of conventionalized perspective; superb music may be performed even though not in the tempered scale nor representable in a conventional musical score.

Allusion and Clarity in Discourse

From Descartes and Locke to the present day, the predominant goal of many philosophers has been to clarify discourse, to reduce knowledge to a basis in "clear and distinct ideas" (Levine 1985). These scholars hoped thereby to eliminate classical paradoxes and dilemmas by demonstrating that via strict analysis these would prove to be meaningless. A primary target was the theological system of the Roman Catholic Church. As contrasted to many other systems of ritual and worship, the Church had evolved an ortho*doxy* (i.e., a creedal system to be *believed*) rather than an ortho*praxis*. Among most peoples of the world, even those participating in "world religions," the emphasis has been on proper ritual practice rather than creedal assent. (Even Orthodox Judaism, which has a great body of sacred literature, focuses on the use of the literature to determine praxis.) However, the Catholic Church emphasized adherence to a statement of *belief*, and this orthodoxy had been defended and explicated by a distinguished body of theology and philosophy. By establishing a *univocal* discourse (McKeon 1952), the critical philosophers hoped not only to undermine the theology but to arrive at certainty and truth, comparable to the achievements of mathematics and the natural sciences.

In the present century, this philosophical endeavor was epitomized by the school denominated as analytic philosophy. Its partisans have ranged over all discourse but have been especially preoccupied with two tasks: eliminating propositions (particularly those of "metaphysics") by demonstrating that they are either "meaningless" or have a limited range of meaning; and elucidating the meaning of moral expressions, such as "X is good" or kindred expressions within esthetics.[2] This program is wholly within the rationalistic spirit that Weber perceived as characterizing Western civilization. Although the analytic school originated earlier in this century, its efforts would be consonant with the contemporary interest in artificial intelligence and machine translation of natural languages. Humanly speaking, the analytic program has been not only sterile but misdirective and misleading (MacIntyre 1966, 1984) and rather like programming a computer to write poetry.

Viewed historically and cross-culturally, the philosophical program is peculiar. In most societies a premium has been placed on a subtlety of discourse employing allusions to some body of symbols, images, and metaphors. Within the great civilizations of India, China, Japan, and classical Greece, there has been a common core of valued texts, cherished by the literati and employed for discreet and nuanced conversation. Auditors unfamiliar with the texts would hear only a superficial message. Of course, such vocal indirection would be especially useful within an authoritarian institution, but it would be a mistake to restrict its practice to such limited realms. A kindred discretion has also characterized the discourse within arcane disciplines, where the knowledge of adepts was not suitable to be apprehended by commoners. Literati and adepts would find the program of analytic philosophy bizarre.

As reported by anthropologists, many folk peoples value an allusiveness of discourse:

Amhara culture presents a case where the love of ambiguity appears particularly pronounced. This is so much the case that one is considered a master
of spoken Amharic only when one's speech is leavened with ambiguous nuances as a matter of course. . . . The basic manner of communicating is indirect, often secretive. . . . The written literature is suffused with parable and
protracted symbolism. (Levine 1985:25)

It is not my goal to value one style of discourse over the other: simple
declarative clarity versus complex allusiveness. Rather, I mention this an-
tinomy to note (1) the language of dreams is much closer to this complex
allusiveness, and (2) the rationalistic spirit of Western civilization is an-
tipathetic to such language. In short, the difficulties in discussing dreams
and dreaming stem from the *presumed* canons of scientific discourse,
rather than from the oddities of a phenomenon present throughout human history.

Critical Voices

During recent decades, a profusion of books and essays have focused critically on Freud. Whereas earlier critiques had been mounted by authors ignorant of his work, this present generation was learned—indeed, more
learned than the typical American psychoanalyst. I note only a few: Adolf
Grünbaum was an eminent philosopher who heretofore had specialized in
the natural sciences; now, as compared with the frivolous judgments on
psychoanalysis of fellow-philosopher Karl Popper, he had truly engaged
the Freudian texts. Jeffry Masson had earned the doctorate in a scholarly
field, been trained as an analyst at a recognized institute, and had labored
in the Freudian archives. Peter Swales, Frank Sulloway, Henri Ellenberger,
and Paul Roazan had conducted historical researches in depth. Frederick
Crews was a literary critic of some distinction, gifted with a rapier-like pen.

In retrospect, this joint volume of critique could have had the most
salutary effect on psychoanalysis: liberating it from its rigid orthodoxies
and cultish subservience to the figure of Sigmund Freud. The latter could
have been elevated to the position of a Charles Darwin or Isaac Newton,
a historical star of the first magnitude, but not a figure whom one would
cite to support a contemporary argument. No serious critic of evolution
hopes to controvert it by attacking the work of Darwin; no serious re-
searcher in biology hopes to defend his investigations by citing a relevant
passage from Darwin.

What was amazing about these critiques and their counterdefenses was
that the figures of Freud and his patients, and even Josef Breuer and
"Anna O." remained crucial, despite the passage of a century and despite

the profound changes in psychoanalytic theories and practices. In his "Clark University Lectures" (1909) and elsewhere, Freud had recognized Breuer's work with Anna O. as the inspiration for his development of psychoanalysis. The case does remain a fascinating historical adventure, especially since the youthful "Anna O." surfaced as the mature Bertha Pappenheim, who created a remarkable and innovative career in social welfare, until her death during the Nazi regime. But, since her (Bertha's) treatment by and work with Breuer in the 1890s, there had been thousands (likely tens of thousands) of kindred patients treated by hundreds of therapists, practicing a psychodynamic art that could be linked to her case only genealogically. Purely psychoanalytic cases—(supposedly) nondirective therapeutic encounters, four to five times per week—must number in the thousands. Moreover, during the twentieth century, there had been profound modifications in clinical practice and the gradual emergence of different subschools of psychoanalysis. Hence, for Grünbaum (or other critics) to make the case of Anna O. fundamental for the validity of contemporary psychoanalysis is bizarre. For any psychoanalyst to accept this as a reasonable basis of debate was a mark of cultic insanity.

A generation ago, dealing with a similar but less learned critique by Hans Eysenck, Rycroft stated that "analysts are claiming that analysis is what it is not, and Eysenck is attacking it for failing to be what it has no need to claim to be" (1966/1985:45). Rycroft found that he could not alter institutionalized psychoanalysis in Great Britain. (One is not surprised to learn that subsequently he dissociated himself from its activities.)

Institutionalized psychoanalysis is vulnerable to critics such as Grünbaum only because it has insisted on defending what cannot be defended and should not be defended.

Rationalizing the Study of Dreams

Unmentioned by Weber but culturally similar was the attempt to rationalize the understanding of dreams. Over the millennia, this attempt has taken several forms. The most basic was the production of manuals of dream interpretation, as exemplified in the classical Mediterranean by Artemidorus, where a given event within a dream had a specific and particular interpretation. In this sustained rationalistic effort, Freud represented a cultural climax, because he managed persuasively to situate the human psyche within biomedicine and to explain dreams as an activity of a creature viewed in post-Darwinian terms. Freud oscillated between the interpretive approach of universalistic symbols and an hermeneutic in which the associations of the dreamer revealed significances. One of his greatest achievements was to perceive that the psychic processes visible in dreams were akin to those of psychoneurotic symptoms and to the mechanisms visible in works of art. He also perceived that these in turn were akin to the strange phenomena then being reported of non-Western peoples (and which had become the data for the philosophical analyses of Lévy-Bruhl). As indicated earlier, these achievements were limited by Freud's physiological predilections and individualistic orientations.

In the sections that follow, I will sharpen the differences in orientations toward dreaming among various cultural groups. For, although dreams are universal among human beings, cultures vary widely in judging their significance. Overall, one can distinguish three major orientations, which I will term (1) communal attunement: dream sharing (and vision seeking); (2) individual guidance: the dream as personal message; (3) the dream as mental noise (electrical static) to be disregarded or misinterpreted: alienation of the dreaming self (or what Weber called "the disenchantment of the world").

Dream Sharing (and Vision Seeking)

There is something to be learned about dreams from cultures that take dreams seriously. People in such cultures have spent their lives giving considerable attention to dreams, and the theories they have developed about them often contain some of the fruits of their lifetimes of observations. (Kracke 1991:203)

Dreams, like myths, in Kagwahiv culture, are to be told. Waking at daybreak, or in the middle of the night at 2 or 3 A.M., one may then hear someone narrating a dream to a few others as they warm themselves by the fire. . . . Dreams are not only told on a regular basis . . . but are earnestly discussed to ascertain what they 'mean'; what event or development they augur, or what state of the spiritual surround they reflect. (Kracke 1987:32–33)

There have been many societies in which people regularly recite their dreams to each other. Typically, these were or are small communities of close kin, sustained by hunting-and-gathering or nomadic (transhumant) pasturage, where men work together under conditions of hardship and danger and women depend crucially on each other. The emotional nexus of the community is children, not just their nurturance and care but as sources of enjoyment and pleasure (Briggs 1970). Oriented about children and living intimately and interdependently, group members are already emotionally attuned, and dream narration intensifies and facilitates that attunement. Because the group shares so much in the way of symbols, language, and culture—not as ethnological abstractions but as concrete realities—its members are able to "read" the significance of a dream without specialist assistance.

Socially and emotionally, these small communities integrate themselves with rites and ceremonies, myth and dance. Although people plan, prepare, and discuss these events, they do not seek for their "meaning" in the demythologizing or deconstructive stance of modern interpretive schema. Their ritual specialists (e.g., "Muchona the Hornet" [Turner 1959]) are aware of the multivocality of communal symbols, but their interpretive discourse is not to disenchant but rather to accentuate, illuminate, and elaborate by poetic resonance: emotional sensibilities dulled in urban industrial life are here exercised. From a psychoanalytic perspective, the exegetical process is the more effective because significant meanings are implicit. Within this emotional milieu, a narrated dream will have an effect like a rite or communal dance: more influential when apprehended unconsciously.

Within the family of the biblical Jacob, no dream specialists were needed to read the meaning of Joseph's dreams (chap. 4). Indeed, so universal is the symbolism of those dreams—the sun, moon, and planets bowing to the star of Joseph—that the interpreting by his kin seems a commonplace. Once Joseph's recitation of the dreams confirmed his brothers in their assessment of familial dynamics, they took steps to curb or destroy this threat to their status and welfare. The biblical tale is at an extreme, but it reminds us that small intimate groups harbor powerful passions: rivalry and hatred as well as love and tender concern. In similar fashion, the traditional Iroquois (Seneca or Huron [Lalemont 1648 in Wallace 1958]) regarded dreams as manifesting desires that demanded fulfillment, and members went to great lengths to ensure that this occurred, whether in actuality or in symbolic form. The Iroquois might thus have found an alternate route for defusing the tensions aroused by the dreams of a Joseph.

Phrased more abstractly, dream interchange facilitates the adjustment of group members to each other and so can be especially beneficial in those areas where cooperation and interdependence must proceed easily, unreflectively, harmoniously, as among the small band who collectively confront a harsh world and must live, hunt, and, on occasion, fight as a unit, entrusting their lives to each other.

As becomes manifest in a dream, human beings are able to read each other's emotional predispositions, unconsciously. The consequence is that dreams become instruments of divination, clairvoyance and precognition, prophetically revealing the events which are about to happen:

> Whatever the dream may be it appears patent to Tangu that a man cannot lie down and dream whatever he might like to dream; and that when he does dream it is up to him to take notice. He must act on the dream. For a dream carries an imperative, is never experienced for nothing, and tends to realize the future. (Burridge 1965:242)

The guidance of dreams or dreamlike states is therefore sought, and members of the group will deliberately engage in rituals likely to elicit visions. Thus, the traditional Plains Indians encouraged their young men to embark on an isolated four-day fast, in which the novice prayed to the deities for guidance: the resulting vision provided guidance for the kind of life and *virtues* (potencies) he then would have, as well as the kinds of ritual trainings and precautions that he would have to undergo. Other Plains rituals, like the Sun Dance, used fasting, fatigue and pain to induce visions.

The Personal Message—Classical, Jewish, and Islamic

A dream uninterpreted is like a letter unopened (R. Hisda). Whoever goes seven days without a dream is called evil (R. Zera). Once I dreamt a dream and I went round to [the twenty-four interpreters of dreams in Jerusalem], and they each gave different interpretations, and all were fulfilled (R. Bana'ah). (Berakot, chap. 9, modified from Harris 1994: chap. 1)

Within the urbanized world of the classical Mediterranean, dreams became items for individual attention rather than group concern. No longer a rite of communion and attunement among intimates, they were regarded as messages to individual dreamers.[3] The function and symbolism of the dream thus became problematic. Previously influential or transparent within the shared living of the group, the language of the dream now became obscure: the dream bore a significant message; but, if that message were to be understood, an *interpretation* was needed. So emerged dream specialists among the retinue of monarchs, as the biblical Pharaoh or Nebuchadnezzar; the specialist's knowledge of the monarch, his public and personal lives, gave background for understanding the significances of his dreams.

Whether monarch or layperson, the dreamer's use of the language and culture of the time is always basic, especially the rituals and metaphors, the riddles and jokes, the personal crises and rites of passage (note the initial epigraph from Turner's work among the Ndembu). For the rabbinical exegetes of the Talmudic era, the symbolisms and associations of Holy Scripture provided the key to interpretation: "An ass means salvation on the basis of Zechariah 9:9"; wheat means peace on the basis of Psalm 147:14; barley means that one's sins will depart (Isaiah 6:7); a goose signifies wisdom because "Wisdom crieth aloud in the streets" (Proverbs 1:20). So, like the multiple rabbinical interpretations of scriptural text, there could be twenty-four interpretations of a dream, and each be correct (foregoing based on Harris 1994: chap. 1).

Thus, within an urbanized community of common language, ritual, and symbolism, the systems of interpretation could become codified and public. In the world of the classical Mediterranean, this is exemplified in the magisterial exposition of Artemidorus of Daldia, living in the second century B.C.

> Both Artemidorus and Freud assume what moderns call the cleavage of the subject (conscious/unconscious), with the unconscious (psyche) either talking to the dreamer, as in Artemidorus, or waiting to be discovered down the "royal road" of dreams, as in Freud. Both interpreters agree with Aristotle that dreams are not heaven-sent. Both privilege allegorical dreams that require decoding—dreams that use condensation and displacement to veil significant events—over direct dreams. And both recognize the notion of the "day's residues," already a topos in Epicurean literature. As Artemidorus puts it: "A man will not dream about things to which he has never given a thought." (Wilson 1993:60)

In a world influenced by Freud's theories, especially fascinating is that for Artemidorus (as for the Kagwahiv [Kracke]), dreams with an overt sexual content are usually interpreted to have a nonerotic significance: for a male Kagwahiv, sexual dreams presage the nature of the day's hunting (what kind and variety of animal, if any); for Artemidorus, the nature of success or failure in one's occupation: because the penis alternately expands and contracts, it may correspond to "wealth and possessions" or to "poverty, servitude, and bonds" (Krauss trans. I, 45). Or, as an alternate example, should a childless woman dream that her breasts fall off, this signifies financial embarrassment (I, 41).

What makes a dream book like that of Artemidorus possible is a commonality of symbolism, ritual, and language (in this case, the *koine* Greek of the Hellenistic world). Basically treated as prophetic, dreams thus can be "interpreted" by an outsider—or even by consulting a manual. But, as contrasted with the dream interchange of the small intimate group, the avenue of influence and understanding has been sharply restricted. Dreams are no longer a vehicle of unconscious attunement within the group, possibly requiring collective response, but rather they reveal the fate of the individuated dreamer. And, of course, once the dream manual is translated for use within a different society with different cultural symbols, its grammar of interpretation becomes particularly obscure.

Another compiler of an encyclopedic guide to dream interpretation was 'Abdalghani an-Nabulusi (1614–1731):

> Man sees dreams with the spirit and understands them with the intelligence. . . . When a man sleeps, his spirit spreads like the light of a lamp or the sun. By this light and the brightness of God he sees that which the angel of dreams shows him. . . . When the senses are reawakened to their activities, the spirit is reminded of what the angel of dreams has shown and suggested to it. (Nabulusi as cited by von Grunebaum 1966:9)

Like Artemidorus, Nabulusi links the dream elements and "objective" reality associatively. The preferable links are to passages from the Koran but may also be found in current sayings and current expression.

Alienation from the Dreaming Self

A dream is a psychosis with all the absurdities, delusions and illusions of a psychosis. (Freud 1940/1969:29)

Alexithymia (from Greek *a:* "without," *lexis:* "word," *thumos:* "heart" or affectivity") means . . . having no words for emotions. . . . It includes not only the difficulties that [these analysands] have in attempting to describe their affective states but also the incapacity to distinguish one affect from another. It should be noted that the apparent disavowal of affectivity is not limited to painful affects. In these afflicted people, there is an equally profound inability to experience satisfaction or pleasure. (McDougall 1982/1991:159–60)

If one now focuses on modern urbanized life, the functioning and telling of dreams again becomes altered. With the diminution of common rites and symbols, the detachment of children from the sphere of communal social life, the multiplication of secondary contacts, and the ever sterner insistence on dispassionate, rationalized, relationships at work and play, individuals become alienated from their emotions and bodies. The emotional density of the intimate group is confined to limited arenas, such as sexuality, suitably privatized. Or, alternatively, emotional life may be expressed in violence or addictive behaviors.

This section might have been titled "A *Mental* Process of Questionable Value," because the resonances of "mental" convey the disregard of dreaming. In the modern world, "mental" betokens the computer screen displaying the operations of the "black box" that is "the mind," whereas dreams are experiences of an emotional human animal who interacts with like animals. So alienated from their bodily selves and emotional lives do people become, that it becomes plausible to entertain the notion that dreams are meaningless. Disregarding popular belief from many cultures and throughout history, scientists can solemnly declare that dreams are erratic excitation of the nervous system, and have no significance.

Living within an isolated intimate group (such as the traditional Inuit or Seneca or the family of the biblical Jacob) is far from being an emotional utopia, and the detachment of urbanized life can seem preferable. The former, however, does have an emotional density that seems more compatible with the potential of the human spirit. For in the contemporary milieu, dreams now become so privatized as to be imparted only within the therapeutic dyad and then unilaterally: from analysand to analyst. The analyst's professional responsibility is to become attuned to the analysand. (The analysand does attune to the analyst, but it is the distortions of that attempt—the transference—that become a central focus of the analysis.) The dream may then be produced in relationship to the analytic encounter, but it would be simplistic to regard it exclusively in that vein.

Within the sleeping person, the dream is an event, an experience, sometimes attended by powerful affects, occasionally visible by muttering and bodily movement. The dream may be recalled or translated into words, and then narrated, with an interpretation sought. Dreams reflect powerful emotional needs, problems, desires, deeply rooted in the body, as well as the psyche.

> *Die Traumdeutung* [*The Interpretation of Dreams*] (1900): the title itself already links, indeed irrevocably unites, the dream and its interpretation. Freud, at the same time as he totally revises it, places himself in the tradition of the various seers, secular and religious, where the dream is consecrated to its meaning, thus to some extent neglecting the dream as *experience:* the subjective experience of the dreamer dreaming and the intersubjective experience in therapy, when the dream is brought to the analyst, both offered yet withheld, speaking yet silent. Perhaps when with Freud the dream travels to a definitive status through interpretation, and the dream *dreamt in images* is converted into the dream *put into words,* something is lost: every victory is paid for by exile and possession by loss. (Pontalis 1974/1993:108)

In a radical effort to combat cultural insistence on alexithymia, Fromm (1951) wrote of dreams as "a forgotten language." The metaphor of "language" is evocative and provocative but, like the title and contents of Freud's opus (*Die Traumdeutung*), it too biases toward the rational and objective. Were the dream to be a communication within a language, then we are at the level of Artemidorus, seeking for a key to translation (i.e., interpretation), and we have done justice to the dream neither as affect-ridden event nor as a vehicle of interpsychic attunement.[5]

The Misinterpretation of Dreams

> Working with dreams is not only an enlightening experience for the patient, but it may also be a source of new clinical and theoretical insights for the analyst, if he has an open mind. Furthermore, there are some analysts who have no ear or eye for dreams, like people who find it hard to hear and visualize the beauty of poetry, or like the tone-deaf who cannot appreciate the special imagery and language of music, or those who have no facility for wit and humor. (Greenson 1970/1993:75)

Bitter, angry polemicists though they may be, critics of psychoanalysis such as Karl Popper and Frederick Crews might reasonably have focused on the analytic interpreting of dreams. I will reframe their contentions, using the case materials of chapters 6 and 7. What are we to make of the fact that a particular dream of a particular individual (e.g., "Irma's Injection" of Freud, or the second dream, "Lost in a Strange City," of Dora) might have several different meanings and that a reasonable case could be advanced for each such meaning? Worse yet, what are we to make of Freud's cavalier dismissal of Dora's negative to his proffered interpretations?

> My expectations were by no means disappointed when this explanation of mine was met by Dora with a most emphatic negative. The "No" uttered by a patient after a repressed thought has been presented to his conscious perception for the first time does no more than register the existence of a repression and its severity . . . If this "No," instead of being regarded as the expression of an impartial judgment (of which indeed the patient is incapable) is ignored, and the work continued, the first evidence soon begins to appear that in such a case "No" signifies the desired "Yes." (Freud 1905/1963: 76)

For an analyst so to deal with an analysand is spectacularly destructive. To believe that a dream has a single definite meaning, which can be explicated according to a psychoanalytic grammar, is misleading and often in error. Most analysts no longer accept this formulation (Rycroft 1979/1996; Mendelsohn 1990), but insofar as it had been maintained within the psychoanalytic community, it was theoretically and clinically limiting.

Like a poem, a dance, a piece of music, or a ritual performance, a dream has significances and meanings; but, neither poem, dance, music, ritual, nor dream can be considered equivalent to its verbal "interpretation." Were we to regard Dora's second dream, "Lost in a Strange City," as a poem, musical composition, or dance she performed in Freud's consulting room, we would not presume that it would lead to a unique "interpretation." Instead, we would attempt to identify the emotions and images aroused within us as viewers, as we related the elements of the performance to cultural symbols, on the one hand (e.g., the Sistine Madonna and the Virgin Mary; the railroad station), and, on the other hand, to the private symbols emerging from her free associations and depiction of familial life (e.g., ailing Father). These would lead us to ask, How then is she commenting on the dyadic relationship, and where is she trying to move it and herself? Via the dream, Dora declares that she cannot accept Freud's assistance in the form offered, yet by presenting the dream, she has provided a final opportunity for him to attune to her psyche and its needs, while she forecasts her inability to do other than retreat to the privacy of herself.

While I have rejected the notion that dreams are to be regarded as a language, and I have alluded to the fact that dreaming is an aspect of our mammalian heritage, I must qualify by noting that dreaming is an occurrence before an audience. On the one hand, dreams are performed on an inner stage before an inner audience; on the other hand, dreams may be shaped by the anticipation of an exterior audience, particularly within the therapeutic situation. So, analysts have noted that dreams become a way by which analysands bring unconscious materials—affects, anxieties, desires, traumatic memories—to the attention of the analytic dyad. I have referred to the attunement that takes place via the recitation of dreams, but I have not emphasized that dreams may be oriented, and in a sense directed. I do not mean that dreaming is a deliberated action but rather am referring to the fact that when or as the dreamer anticipates an external audience, then the dream seems somehow shaped to reach that audience (Blechner 1995).

When Freud spoke of the interpretation of dreams as the royal road to knowledge of the unconscious activities of the psyche, he was conjuring up a vision of the investigative journey by the analyst, rather than a conjoint enterprise of the therapeutic dyad.

Le Rêve à Deux within the Laboratory

Insofar as dreams have to do with the emotional attunement of intimates, the project reported by Krippner (1991) is worthy of review. Analysands of two of his psychoanalytic colleagues had had dreams that revealed "anomalous" knowledge of their analysts (Ehrenwald 1954; Eisenbud 1946). These experiences led Ullman to organize a dream laboratory and to enlist Honorton and Krippner as colleagues in a series of investigations. In the basic design there was an agent and a subject who was to sleep in the laboratory. Early in the night the agent—suitably isolated from the subject—was presented with a randomized stimulus, and the question was whether what the subject then dreamed indicated a transferring of thought.

In terms of my argument in this book, the research procedure is remarkably misdirected. What I have emphasized is the unconscious attuning of persons to each other; the attuning is not between strangers but among intimates, exemplified by either the members of a small residential community, such as a hunting-and-gathering group, or the psychotherapeutic dyad. The process of attuning is facilitated by the reciting of dreams, with the consequence that the several parties come to develop insight about each others and to "know" materials that have not been brought into conscious communication. Thus, it would not be surprising were both analyst and analysand to possess "latent knowledge" of the other and that this might then be manifested in dreams.[6]

Dreams as Art

So-called absolute music can be regarded as both a form of expressive behavior and also as a kind of communication:

> Of course, the composer does hope for listeners and may therefore work hard at making his expressive behavior perfect, using the most recondite devices of harmony, counterpoint, musical architecture, and instrumentation. . . . [Nevertheless], he does not seek to teach the listener counterpoint, nor even in an alleged piece of program music like Debussy's *La Mer*, does he seek to initiate the listener into the mysteries of oceanography. (Devereux 1965/1980:112)

Dealing with a work of art, an interpretive critic can perform a thematic analysis, and this may become a technique for ensuring that the various elements each receive appropriate recognition. Thematic analysis can be revealing; it can also be misleading. Reiser (1990: chap.3) performs a careful thematic analysis of Freud's "Dream of the Botanical Monograph." The attempt at precision is marred by clinging to the text of the Anglicized standard edition to which Reiser refers when he invites his readers to "consult the original text"! But, disregarding that common failing of the Anglophone, we can observe that Reiser's efforts reveal the inherent limitations of this sort of analysis. From his outlines and diagrams, we learn no more than what Freud had already made clear in his text; and what Freud could or would relate was such (as remarked by Sloane), that Freud would not have needed to dream to arrive at this (self-) portrait. Throughout *Die Traumdeutung* Freud acknowledged that he was withholding materials from his readers (and he challenged readers critical of this suppression to be more frank in print about their own intimate lives). That reticence does not fault Freud but does fault Reiser insofar as he presents the thematic analysis of this dream as if it were exemplary for clinical work, as held to the standards of biomedicine. Since I have already demonstrated a different order of interpretive process with a dream of Freud's (as well as of Dora's), it would be unnecessary here to perform a parallel interpretation of "The Botanical Monograph," but I do feel it essential to note the limitations of Reiser's technique, and so I will refer to Anzieu's critical exposition of various interpretations of this dream (by Fromm, Roazan, et al.), each of which he eliminates, thus leading him to conclude (1975/1986: 293f.) with Eva Rosenblum:

[I]t is a dream of wonderment—the wonderment of a child at the colour illustrations of a traveller's tale, the wonderment of a boy at the body of his young mother, who is as attractive as a multi-coloured picture-book, the wonderment of the male at the mystery of femaleness, and the wonderment of the connoisseur at the weaver's masterpiece. . . . But at the same time, to possess is to deflower, to read is to tear up, and to create is to destroy. A certain wish to destroy is also part of the passions that cause suffering.[7]

I would only add that these creative and destructive impulses characterize *Die Traumdeutung*, as well as Freud's case of Dora, and that only by recognizing and appreciating them can psychoanalysis recognize its art and find its soul. "Freud's flight to sanity could be something we psychoanalysts are trying to recover from" (Winnicott 1964/1989:483).

Concluding Remarks

I began this work as an attempt to clarify and reconstruct the understanding of dreams, to replace Freud's biomedical paradigm with one that was not only social and cultural, but liberated from the authoritarianism, biases, and rigidities that constricted psychoanalysis as it institutionalized. Although I had begun with a focus on dreams and dreaming, I soon found that I had to deal with issues of the self and the psyche, and thereby I had recourse to the American Pragmatist tradition of social psychology and to cross-cultural comparisons, insofar as data were available. In the research process I found that I was confronting the rationalistic tradition of Western intellectual life. In opposition I was creating—or endeavoring to create—a cultural psychology different from any I had encountered.

The universality of dreaming, and the high regard that most peoples have had for dreams, sustained my intuition that dreaming is essential, not just for the well-functioning of the individual dreamer but as a stabilizing element of group life. Humanity has lived and evolved within small intimate groups. The stability and endurance of a small group, its capacity for intricate cooperative activities, including the bearing and rearing of children, is founded on the dreaming of its members, together with kindred activities: collective dancing, singing, drumming; the reciting of dreams to intimates; the seeking of visions and trance states; the narrating and enacting of myth. For these small human groups, the differentiation between mundane existence and revelations of dreams is the inverse of the Western intellectual tradition: these groups seek dreams and visions, and they value their messages more than they do the knowledge obtained through pseudo-objective scientism.

In modern urbanized society, the actor gains freedom, but at the cost of losing contact with body and emotions. The achievements of modern natural science have been remarkable, but the results are potential for both human growth and destructiveness. While human destructiveness is scarcely novel, the conditions of urban civilization not only provide the armamentarium but facilitate malevolent psychic organization. Various countercultural movements have been attempts at reversing this course.

As formulated by Sigmund Freud, psychoanalysis fitted dreams (and related activities) onto a biomedical template and so made their investigation respectable, but at the cost of severe distortion. Worse yet, the cultic orthodoxy of the Freudian movement foreclosed the possibility of moving beyond naive scientism, while the biomedical identification confirmed the authoritarianism within and without the consulting chamber. Dreams were assimilated to neurotic symptoms, and valuable human potentialities were labeled as "psychopathologies." The current depreciation of psychoanalysis is not the result of the venomous critiques of Frederick Crews or Jeffry Masson but the outcome of the therapeutic limitations and theoretical misdirection.

In Freud's evocative metaphor, dreams were a royal road to understanding the workings of the unconscious of the individualized dreamer. That metaphor guides us in the wrong direction. I have argued that dreams should be viewed as aesthetic productions akin to poetry, dance, and even possession-trance. Grounded in myth, the great tragedies of classical Greece were ritual performances. Recognizing their transformative power, Aristotle spoke of them as inducing a catharsis of pity and fear. We can follow his lead, while altering his vocabulary. Like the great tragedies, dreams offer a potential for self-understanding and growth. For, in Yeats's words, "in dreams begin responsibilities."

Notes

1. I learnt from African 'primitives' much more than they learnt from me, much that I was never taught at school, something more of courage, endurance, patience, resignation, and forbearance that I had no great understanding of before. . . . I learnt more about the nature of God and our human predicament from the Nuer than I ever learnt at home. (Evans Pritchard 1937/1976:244–5)

2. The reductio ad absurdum of this quest was G. E. Moore's celebrated analysis that *good* is the name of "a simple unanalyzable [and "nonnatural"] property" (Moore 1903). Note MacIntyre 1966: chap. 18.

3. From Mesopotamia in the fourth century B.C.E. come the cycle of stories about the deity, Dumuzi. Within a dream, he foresees disaster, so that on awak-

ening he takes precautions, but these prove counterproductive because of betrayal by a comrade, and the destruction symbolically represented in that dream comes to pass (Jacobsen 1976:48f.).

4. Further discussion of the Islamic tradition of dream interpreting may be found in the contributions by Fahd, Lecerf, Corbin, Rahman, Meier, and von Grunebaum in the volume edited by the latter and Caillois (1966). These do not modify the basic argument of this chapter.

5. What has been overlooked by psychoanalytic commentators is a particular verbal technique used by Freud when dealing with the obsessional ideation inherent in compulsive acts. Not only did he interpret the general meaning at various strata underlying these acts, but he also strove to coin orally marked, aphoristic formulae of which these acts were the *immediate* translation. At one point in the Rat Man case, for example, Freud suggests: "Our present patient's obsessive fear, therefore, when restored to its original meaning, would run as follows: 'If I have this wish to see a woman naked, my father will be bound to die.' " (1909, p. 63) Part of the contemporary unawareness of Freud's technique is reflected in Strachey's English rendering of one of the subheadings in the Rat Man case: "Some obsessional Ideas and Their Explanation" (p. 186). In truth, "explanation" should be "translation, the English meaning of the German." (Mahony 1986: 205–6)

6. An appropriate illustration together with an insightful discussion of the *Rêve à Deux* with special reference to Hindu culture may be found in O'Flaherty (1984:75–80); even more dramatic is the experience from anthropological fieldwork, described by George (1995). An experimental but nonlaboratory project of dream intercommunication is described in Mogollón and Shor (1990).

7. The "Botanical Monograph" text has been so worked over that expectations of novel motive formulations are perhaps unrealistic, but SSLS does highlight a rare, and therefore, interesting feature of the motive-packed free-association chain F, in which Freud himself found "the ultimate meaning of the dream" (1900, p. 191). This feature is the perceived interconnectedness of several modes of relationship such that, for instance, involvement and creation are equated with destruction. (Foulkes 1978:296)

Appendix
The Magic of Learning and Teaching

[I]nformants tend to stress the harmonious, cohesive aspects of the milk tree symbolism. They also stress the aspect of dependence. The child depends on its mother for nutriment; similarly, say the Ndembu, the tribesman drinks from the breasts of tribal custom. Thus nourishment and learning are equated in the meaning context of the milk tree. I have often heard the milk tree compared to "going to school"; the child is said to swallow instruction as the baby swallows milk . . . Do we not ourselves speak of "a thirst for knowledge"? (Turner 1967:22)

With its course numbering systems and "credit hours," and its textbooks of predigested scholarship, undergraduate education has departed from the Ndembu intimacy. Its rationalized and bureaucratized ideal would be interchangeable instructors offering the identical subject matter in identically denominated courses at institutions differing only in name. Teaching and learning bear a magical potential, but this rationalization is a "disenchantment of the world," in the phrase of Max Weber.

Faced with the bureaucratic pressure, instructors must find a path to teach what they know and love. As a student, I had the wondrous experience of exploring original texts. As an instructor, I tried to provide my students with the same opportunities. Encountering the originals, students perceive science and scholarship as a critical but disciplined discourse, a conversation conducted across the millennia and the generations, and among radically distinct ethnicities and nationalities, whose ideal is to solicit and appreciate distinctive contributions.

The present book emerged from my experiences in introducing cross-cultural materials on childhood, family, and adolescence to bright and skeptical undergraduates. This appendix is a memoir of that experience, presented as a guide to those who might use this book as a centerpiece in a similar course. In the design of such a course, practicalities are important, notably the availability of texts at modest prices, and I have indicated my decisions.

Family and Childhood

"Yes, truly remarkable, how one must rejoice in this sad sight," remarked Freuchen's Eskimo mother-in-law. The children were happily sliding down Greenland's rocks, a sport whose side effect was wear and tear of their trousers, sewn from the furs laboriously processed by womenfolk from the animals secured by menfolk running trap lines in the arctic winter:

> Children ruin things without giving it a thought; they have no cares. But every day of their lives they become wiser and wiser. Soon the time will come when they never will do that sort of thing. They will remember their unnecessary wear on their pants and regret it. Everyone must rejoice by recalling that we start out as thoughtless children, but with every day the good sense increases in us. Just imagine if it were the other way round. (Freuchen 1961:118)

The family life of the traditional Inuit (circa 1850–1950) has been well documented. The accounts of adventurers (e.g., Peter Freuchen) who married Eskimo women have been augmented by the ethnographic detail of fieldworkers, notably Jean Briggs but including numerous others. These are complemented by the vivid films of the annual cycle of the traditional Netsilik, as recorded with their cooperation, under the direction of Asen Balicki. For ethnohistorians there are the volumes of the Fifth Thule Expedition (Rasmussen 1929) and the account of the youthful Boas (1901–1907). Briggs's narrative account is exceptionally frank, wondrously detailed; it has a powerful appeal to students and is available in paperback.

Not merely do students encounter the familial life of "another culture"; they also find themselves challenged by the Inuit child training: at once loving and "permissive" yet stern and harsh to a level that seems sadistic. On the one hand, the children are accorded the freedom not only to damage valuable garments but even to risk their lives in dangerous games; on the other hand, their Inuit elders engage in a process that we would denominate as *teasing*, whose effects would seem traumatic. Briggs's account is vivid:

> Adult, to a girl who has just acquired a baby brother: "Have you seen your baby brother?"
> Child, smiling happily: "Yes."
> Adult: "Do you love him?"
> Child, smiling, as before: "Yes."
> Adult: "You *do*? Ugh, *I* don't. *I* think he's disgusting. You *love* him?"
> Child looks blank and says nothing.
> Adult: "Did you carry your brother in your parka?"
> Child, smiling proudly: "Yes."

Adult, in a persuasive voice: "Why don't you tip him out and kill him? Like this"—and she demonstrates the technique by jerking her head and shoulders forward.

Child looks blank and says nothing. (Briggs 1990:35)

Dreams, Rites, Symbols: Some Concepts

To deal with the issues raised by both Briggs's descriptions and the forthcoming accounts of puberty rites and adolescent development, the students need concepts, not as "God's truth" but as ways of grasping phenomena so they can reason, evaluate, debate. The works of Freud offer case materials from Austria-Hungary a century ago, together with a corresponding set of concepts and theories. Again, the availability of inexpensive paperback editions of his works is a potent factor.

From *The Interpretation of Dreams* (1900), I choose chapter 2, Freud's recital of his dream of "Irma's Injection" together with his "interpretation." Many of the students have had some exposure to Freudian theory and to the voices of the critics, and so they follow the assignment passively. At that juncture, I begin to supply the information contained in the chapters in this volume: about Vienna, its Jewish community, Freud's family and career, and his problems as an ambitious physician, so transforming the reading from an authoritative theory to a rich and problematic text. I urge the students to liberate their intuition on the meanings of this dream, and in so doing some experience an epiphany.

Simultaneously with my course, many of the students were enrolled in courses in the Department of Psychology, where they were exposed to laboratory experiments, neurobiology, and injunctions to be faithful to objectivity and the scientific method. Now, suddenly, they share a profound understanding that seems indubitably valid, yet beyond these behavioristic exhortations. The transformation is completed when they decide themselves to monitor their own dreams.

The ethnographic materials enable students to perceive the emotional demands of group living, the complexities of affect, and the culturally specific nature of the labels that Euro-Americans apply to affect. *Never in Anger* contains a glossary of traditional Inuit terms for emotion; what is particularly valuable is not only the imparting of cultural relativity but the implicit Inuit emphasis on emotions as qualities of relating, rather than as states of an detached and individuated body. The foregoing example from Briggs foregrounds both. Love may be accompanied by jealousy, hate, or antagonism: within the child who is encountering a younger sibling, and within the person who is "teasing" her. Briggs hypothesizes that the teasing makes the child aware of its ambivalences. The teasing also has other potent effects.

These portraits do not recount Inuit dreams. Briggs does inform us of the nightmares suffered by some of the children; we do not learn their content but only that the children cannot be aroused from these experiences.

Puberty: Interpretations and Misinterpretations

Freud writes, "A gynaecologist, after all, under the same conditions, does not hesitate to make them submit to uncovering every possible part of their body. The best way of speaking about such things *is to be dry and direct"* (my italics). Freud concludes his argument thus: "I call bodily organs and processes by their technical names, and I tell these to the patient if they—the names, I mean—happen to be unknown to her.

"*J'appelle un chat un chat.*"[1] . . . At the very moment [Freud] defines nonprurient language as direct and noneuphemistic, he takes a French detour into a figurative expression. By his terms, the French sentence would seem to be titillating, coy, flirtatious. And to make matters more juicy (less "dry"), *chat* or *chatte* can be used as a vulgar (vulvar) slang for the female genitalia. So in this gynaecological context, where he founds his innocence upon the direct use of technical terms, he takes a French detour and calls a pussy a pussy. (Gallop, "Keys to Dora," in Bernheimer & Kahane 1985:209)

To enlarge this exercise in social and intellectual history, I assign the case of "Dora" (*Fragment of the Analysis of a Case of Hysteria,* 1905). Freud's narrative introduces us into the problems of adolescent girls of that ethnicity (orthodox Jewish) and place (fin-de-siècle Vienna), as viewed by a man who judged himself emancipated. In that context we gain a deepened understanding of puberty as a gendered transition. As evident from the chapter in this volume, Freud's narrative centers on two dreams, which the girl brings to their sessions and which he misinterprets. So sexualized are his interpretations, and so dominating his clinical posture, that the case becomes a wonderful text to stimulate discussions of gender and authority and of the hazards of ignoring the voice of the dreamer (analysand). So, incidentally, the clinical encounter provides an understanding of *transference* and *countertransference.*[2]

Puberty Rites

Victor and Edith Turner lived and worked among the Ndembu of southern Africa during the 1950s, and their accounts supplement each other. Particularly illuminating is Victor's insight that a symbol encompasses a range of meanings from the physiological to the ideological, so that *mudyi* (the milk tree) encompasses breast and breast milk, matrilyny, learning, and the unity and persistence of Ndembu society (1967: chap. 1). Edith's description (1987) of the field experience makes a wonderful complement. The Turners' exposition of Ndembu ritual and symbolism is particularly instructive.

To the extent that time allows (and that the students have the inclination to read), I counterpose her and his descriptions of the puberty rituals: the girl's (*Nkang'a*) and the boy's (*Mukanda*). Her *The Spirit and the Drum* (1987) describes both. His *The Forest of Symbols* (1967) describes the male ritual, but for Nkang'a one would have to go to *The Drums of Affliction* (unfortunately not currently available in paperback).

Victor's descriptions of each ritual are ethnographically detailed, occupying over sixty dense pages. So, I usually deal only with one of these rituals, and even so do not propose that students master the ethnographic and linguistic details. Nevertheless, I remind them that while ritual detail is significant, one must not expect a meaningful ceremonial to have the dramatic impact of a theatrical performance. (An anthropological wit remarked that an observer may be assured that the ritual is authentic if it is boring.) Nevertheless, the rituals help us to comprehend Ndembu symbolism, whereas ritual and symbolism reveal the tensions in their lives, including the particular tensions surrounding the developmental process. (V. Turner also emphasizes the tension between matrilineal descent and virilocal marriage and the rituals that address this.)

Both puberty rituals serve to detach the initiates from their natal families, to reposition them as reproductively adult, and to establish stronger linkage with their genders. In N'Kang'a the pubescent girl lies motionless beneath the mudyi tree while the women of the community (initially not including her mother) dance about her. In Mukanda a cohort of boys jointly undergoes circumcision. Traditionally, the girl's ritual climaxed in her marriage, whereas the boys' ritual established their maturity as sexual beings. In interpreting the symbolism, one could focus on the matrilineal, maternal, and nurturant symbolisms for the girl. One could also focus on the various possible meanings of circumcision, including the implicit rivalry between the generations (and possibly the waning potencies of the older generation), and the wound they inflict upon the younger. One might also note how the series of rituals enforces solidarity (*communitas* is the term used by V. Turner) among the cohort of initiates.

Peer Societies

From the *communitas* of the boys undergoing circumcision, it is but a small step to the peer societies of teenagers, and a particularly dramatic account is *Formal Education in an American Indian Community: Peer Society and the Failure of Minority Education* (Wax et al. 1989). Again, our students are dealing with another culture, that of twentieth-century Plains Indians. Nevertheless, the students recognize the dynamic process: including teasing and threats, on the one hand, and peer emulation, on the other hand. The Sioux children were organizing themselves into a solidary peer society, one of whose achievements was countering—even sabotaging—the authority of the school, its educators, and the ontology implicit in its lessons.

Traditionally, Plains Indians not only have valued dreams and visions but have perceived the nature of time and *the self* quite differently than Euro-America:

> Historic events happen once and are gone forever. Mythic events return like the swans each Spring. . . . Mythic events are true in a way that is essential and eternal. In mythic time a person can be a frog or a fox and still be a person. In mythic time a person can follow a trail of song to another county. In mythic time a child can be led toward the place where knowledge and power will come naturally. (Ridington 1988:72)

Puberty, Adult Hostility, Homosexuality

What next becomes extremely effective with students are readings on the tribal peoples in highland Papua–New Guinea. Available and vivid are the works of Gilbert Herdt, especially *The Sambia* (1987). The status of the warrior male and the demand for unity among warriors, the homosexual practices enforced on adolescents, the suspicion between the genders, the ritualized nose bleedings, the mythical power of semen, the difference between male and female maturing—all these provoke student thought and discussion. (There is a weird resonance between the Sambian eroticization of the nose—including nose bleedings—and the bizarre theories of Wilhelm Fliess about the relationship between the nose and the genitals, and this point is echoed in "Irma's Injection.")

The violent rituals inflicted by Sambian men on their offspring may be counterposed to the Greek myth of Oedipus (and the Sophoclean tragedy), which were initiated by the deadly actions of Laius toward his son. Freud's exposition of the Oedipus complex concentrated on the inverse: the antagonism of Oedipus toward Laius, but that distorts the patent content of the Greek narrative. A parallel, although limited, antagonism is Ndembu *mukanda,* the circumcision inflicted by Ndembu fathers on their male offspring.

In addition to Herdt's essays there are the observations of this same people by Lidz and Lidz (1989) and by Herdt and Stoller (1990). There are also studies of peoples with similar customs (e.g., Read 1965, 1986; Herdt 1982; etc.).

With the materials on these rituals, symbolisms, and familial tensions, the course dramatically coheres, as the semester's readings integrate powerfully while resonating with the student's personal experience.

What then must be faced is the weakness of our knowledge of the Sambia (and adjacent peoples), as the various readings so emphasize the male gender, and we are given so little about what it means to be a Sambian woman. How does she cope with a husband whose adolescence has been sexually focused on homosexual fellatio? How much does she know about the male rituals? Where does she gain emotional balance and security? What rituals do these women practice—with menstruation, sexuality, fertility and infertility, pregnancy and childbirth, suckling and nurturing? And, finally, how does a woman cope with having to lose her juvenile male offspring to the men's lodge (forbidden to her) and her nubile female offspring to virilocal marriage (into a hamlet with which that of her husband has a relationship of suspicion or even overt hostility)? For such information, we need women ethnographers (note Gillison 1993 and Meigs 1988). Herdt and others have brought fascinating materials about ritual and symbol, but unfortunately, dream materials are lacking.

Feminist Critiques

The essays by Karen Horney (1967) make a convenient packet along with those by Nancy Chodorow (1989). Together, they offer psychodynamic interpretations of gendered anxieties and rituals: whether of the Sambian males, or of males generally, including Euro-American; and the corresponding problems of women. Most students, and especially, the women, appreciate these essays. An occasional student may judge Horney's essays to be dated, for the earliest were drafted in the 1920s. However, the course is designed to use historical as well as ethnographic materials, and indeed much of the latter have become historical.

Self, Psyche, Interpersonal Concepts and Theory

The foregoing outlines what the students and I might accomplish in a conventional college semester. In a year-long course, I am next able to initiate discussions of the social psychological tradition of Cooley, Dewey, Mead, James, and Sullivan, as presented in the chapters on the self. I am also able to bring a variety of other relevant readings. It would be especially relevant to deal with issues of *possession* and *possession-trance*, as, for example, manifested in vodou (whether in the Caribbean or New York City). Likewise, the comparative literatures on dreams, dream interpreting, and symbolisms could be instructive.

Pedagogics

Dividing the class into two, I assign biweekly short essays. I also announce that on the due date, each student may then be called on to speak about the classwork. A person who has drafted a thoughtful essay will then be eager to respond orally.

This regular assignment has several consequences. It prepares students for discussing materials, rather than passively attending lectures. It encourages the quiet ones to participate in the discussion and the students to listen to each other. Since students are more concerned about their appearances and performance before each other, they prepare more carefully and, after a brief experience, begin to outline more lively presentations. Finally, the announcement of these assignments discourages the free-loading idlers, who seek a course in which all they have to do is cram the night before the final exam.

Of course, the instructor has to read and respond to the papers, which is valuable in providing information about the students' intellectual and emotional status and where they are misunderstanding the class materials. For the instructor, this reading and responding is an investment of energy, but the rewards can be great. Students acknowledge one's dedication, appreciate the course, and look back on it as an experience that has helped them to grow. The growth was also mine, and this book is the visible product.

Notes

1. A direct translation of the French is "I call a cat a cat," which is equivalent to the Anglo-Saxon "I call a spade a spade," but in the context of Freud's case study, the connotations become particularly significant.

2. The literature on "Dora" is vast, and the appraisals of Freud's treatment have gone from veneration by his early disciples to intense criticism, notably and wittily by French feminists (see the essays by Jane Gallop, Maria Ramas, Toril Moi, and Madelon Sprengnether in Bernheimer and Kahane 1985). Note especially Mahony (1996) and Decker (1991).

Bibliography

Aboulafia, Mitchell. *The Mediating Self: Mead, Sartre, and Self-determination.* New Haven, Conn.: Yale University Press, 1986.

Abraham, Hilda C., and Ernst L. Freud, eds. *A Psycho-Analytic Dialogue: The Letters of Sigmund Freud and Karl Abraham, 1907–1926.* London: Hogarth, 1965.

Adams, Abigail E. "Dyke to Dyke: Ritual Reproduction in a U.S. Men's Military College." *Anthropology Today* 9, no. 5 (October 1993):3–6.

Anzieu, Didier. *L'Auto analyse de Freud et la découverte de la psychanalyse.* 2 vols. Paris: Presses Universitaires de France, 1975. Trans. Peter Graham as *Freud's Self-Analysis.* London: Hogarth, 1986.

———. *Une Peau pour les pensées.* Paris: Gallimard, 1986. Trans. Daphne Nash Briggs as *A Skin for Thought.* London: Karnac, 1990.

Appignanesi, Lisa, and John Forrester. "Dora: An Exemplary Failure." Pages 146–57 in *Freud's Women.* New York: Basic Books, 1992.

———. *Freud's Women: Family, Patients, Followers.* New York: Basic Books, 1992.

Armstrong, Judith. "Reflections on Multiple Personality Disorder as a Developmentally Complex Adaptation." Pages 349–64 in *The Psychoanalytic Study of the Child,* vol. 49, ed. Alber J. Solnit et al. New Haven, Conn.: Yale University Press, 1994.

Artemidor von Daldisca. *100 BCE Traumbuch,* übertragung von F. S. Krauss. Basel: Schwabe, 1965.

Baldwin, James Mark. *Mental Development in the Child and the Race, Methods and Process.* New York: Macmillan, 1893.

Balicki, Asen. *The Netsilik Eskimo.* New York: Natural History Press, 1970.

Barrett, Deidre. "Dreams in Multiple Personality Disorder." Pages 68–81 in *Trauma and Dreams,* ed. Deidre Barrett. Cambridge, Mass.: Harvard University Press, 1996.

———, ed. "The Relationship of Dissociative Disorders to Sleep and Dreaming." Pages 216–229 in *Broken Images, Broken Selves: Dissociative Narratives in Clinical Practice,* ed. Stanley Kripppner and Susan Marie Powers. New York: Brunner/Mazel, 1997.

———, ed. *Trauma and Dreams.* Cambridge, Mass.: Harvard University Press, 1996.

Benjamin, Jessica. *The Bonds of Love: Psychoanalysis, Feminism, and the Problem of Domination.* New York: Pantheon, 1988.

Bernheimer, Charles, and Claire Kahane, eds. *In Dora's Case: Freud—Hysteria—Feminism.* New York: Columbia University Press, 1985.

Bernheimer, Charles. Introduction: Part One. Pages 1–18 in *In Dora's Case,* ed.

Charles Bernheimer and Claire Kahane. New York: Columbia University Press, 1985.

Bernstein, Isidor. "Integrative Summary: On the Re-viewings of the Dora Case." Pages 83–91 in *Freud and His Patients,* ed. Mark Kanzer and Jules Glenn. Northvale, N.J.: Aronson, 1993. (Originally published 1980)

Bettelheim, Bruno. *Freud and Man's Soul.* New York: Vintage, Random House, 1982.

Bharati, Swami Agehanada. *The Ochre Robe.* London: Allen & Unwin, 1961.

———. *The Tantric Tradition.* London: Rider, 1965.

Blechner, Mark J. "The Patient's Dream and the Countertransference." *Psychoanalytic Dialogues* 5, no. 1 (1995):1–25.

Bloomfield, Leonard. *Language.* New York: Holt, 1993.

Blumer, Herbert. *Symbolic Interactionism.* Upper Saddle River, N.J.: Prentice Hall, 1969.

Bourguignon, Erika. "Multiple Personality, Possession Trance, and the Psychic Unity of Mankind." *Ethos* 17, no. 3 (1989):371–84.

———. *Psychological Anthropology.* New York: Holt, Rinehart & Winston, 1979.

———, ed. *Religion, Altered States of Consciousness, and Social Change.* Columbus: Ohio State University Press, 1973.

Brame, Gloria G., William D. Brame, and Jon Jacobs. *Different Loving: The World of Sexual Dominance & Submission.* New York: Villard, 1996.

Braude, Stephen E. "Multiple Personality and Moral Responsibility." *Philosophy, Psychiatry and Psychology* 3, no. 1 (March 1996):37–54.

Brenner, Ira. "Trauma, Perversion, and 'Multiple Personality.'" *Journal of the American Psychoanalytic Association* 44, no. 3 (1996):785–814.

Bremner, J. Douglas, and Charles R. Marmer, eds. *Trauma, Memory, and Dissociation.* Washington, D.C.: American Psychiatric Press, 1998.

Breuer, Josef, and Sigmund Freud. *Studien über Hysterie.* Reprinted in Sigmund Freud, *Gesammelte Werke,* vol. 1. London: Imago, 1895.

Briggs, Jean L. *Never in Anger: Portrait of an Eskimo Family.* Cambridge, Mass.: Harvard University Press, 1970.

———. "Playwork as a Tool in the Socialization of an Inuit Child." *Arctic Medical Research* 49 (1990):34–38.

Brooks, Peter. *Body Work: Objects of Desire in Modern Narrative.* Cambridge, Mass.: Harvard University Press, 1993.

———. *Psychoanalysis and Storytelling.* Oxford: Blackwell, 1994.

Brown, Karen McCarthy. *Mama Lola: A Vodou Priestess in Brooklyn.* Berkeley: University of California Press, 1991.

Buckley, Peter. "Fifty Years after Freud: Dora, the Rat Man, and the Wolf Man." *American Journal of Psychiatry* 146, no. 11 (November 1989):1394–1403.

Burridge, Kenelm. "Tangu, Northern Madang District." Pages 224–49 in *Gods, Ghosts and Men in Melanesia,* ed. P. Lawrence and M. J. Meggitt. Melbourne: Oxford University Press, 1965.

Byck, Robert, ed. *Cocaine Papers: Sigmund Freud.* New York: New American Library, 1975.

Chapman, A. H. *Harry Stack Sullivan: The Man and His Work.* New York: Putnam's, 1976.

Chase, Trudi. *When Rabbit Howls.* New York: Jove, 1987.

Chodorow, Nancy J. *Feminism and Psychoanalytic Theory.* New Haven, Conn.: Yale University Press, 1989.

Cohen, David. *Alter Egos: Multiple Personalities.* London: Constable, 1996.

Cohen, Jonathan A. "The Moral Landscape of Psychoanalysis." *Journal of the American Academy of Psychoanalysis* 22, no. 4 (1994):699–725.

———. *Freud's Subversion of Meaning.* Unpublished manuscript, 1998.

Cohen, Lewis, Joan Berzoff, and Mark Elin, eds. *Dissociative Identity Disorder.* Northvale, N.J.: Aronson, 1995.

Condon, Richard G. *Inuit Youth: Growth and Change in the Candian Arctic.* New Brunswick, N.J.: Rutgers University Press, 1987.

Cook, Gary A. *George Herbert Mead: The Making of a Social Pragmatist.* Urbana: University of Illinois Press, 1993.

Cooley, Charles Horton. *Social Organization: A Study of the Larger Mind.* New York: Schocken, 1962. (Originally published 1909)

———. *Human Nature and the Social Order.* Rev. ed. New York: Schocken, 1964. (Originally published 1922)

Cortina, Mauricio, and Michael Maccoby, eds. *A Prophetic Analyst: Erich Fromm's Contribution.* Northvale, N.J.: Aronson, 1996.

Crabtree, Adam. *From Mesmer to Freud: Magnetic Sleep and the Roots of Psychological Healing.* New Haven, Conn.: Yale University Press, 1993.

Cuddihy, John Murray. *The Ordeal of Civility: Freud, Marx, Levi-Strauss, and the Jewish Struggle with Modernity.* Boston: Beacon, 1974.

David-Ménard, Monique. *L'Hystérique entre Freud et Lacan: Corps et langage en psychanalyse,* trans. Catherine Porter as *Hysteria from Freud to Lacan: Body and Language in Psychoanalysis.* Ithaca, N.Y.: Cornell University Press, 1989. (Originally published 1983)

Davies, Jody Messler. "Dissociation, Repression, and Reality Testing in the Counter-transference." Pages 45–75 in *Memories of Sexual Betrayal: Truth, Fantasy, Repression, and Dissociation,* ed. Richard Gartner. Northvale, N.J.: Jason Aronson, 1997.

Davis, Madeleine, and David Wallbridge. *Boundary and Space: An Introduction to the Work of D. W. Winnicott.* New York: Brunner/Mazel, 1981.

Davy, Georges. *Emile Durkheim: Choix de textes avec étude du système sociologique.* Paris: Alcan, 1927.

Decker, Hannah S. *Freud, Dora, and Vienna 1900.* New York: Free Press, 1991.

Deren, Maya, ed. *Divine Horsemen: The Voodoo Gods of Haiti.* New York: Chelsea House, 1970. (Originally published 1951)

Deutsch, Felix. "A Footnote to Freud's 'Fragment of an Analysis of a Case of Hysteria.'" *Psychoanalytic Quarterly* 26 (1957):159–67. Reprinted (pp. 35–43) in *In Dora's Case,* ed. Charles Bernheimer and Claire Kahane. New York: Columbia University Press, 1985.

Devereux, George, ed. *Basic Problems of Ethnopsychiatry.* Trans. Basia Miller Gulati and George Devereux. Chicago: University of Chicago Press, 1980.

———. *Dreams in Greek Tragedy: An Ethno-Psycho-Analytical Study.* Berkeley: University of California Press, 1976.

———. "Pathogenic Dreams in Non-Western Societies." Pages 274–88 in *Basic Problems of Ethnopsychiatry,* ed. George Devereux, trans. Basia Miller Gulati and

George Devereux. Chicago: University of Chicago Press, 1980. (Originally published 1966)

———. "Psychoanalysis as Anthropological Fieldwork: Data and Implications." Pages 305–20 in *Basic Problems of Ethnopsychiatry*, ed. George Devereux, trans. Basia Miller Gulati and George Devereux. Chicago: University of Chicago Press, 1980. (Originally published 1957)

———. *Psychoanalysis and the Occult.* New York: International Universities Press, 1970.

———. "The Voices of Children: Psychocultural Obstacles to Therapeutic Communication." Pages 105–21 in *Basic Problems of Ethnopsychiatry*, ed. George Devereux, trans. Basia Miller Gulati and George Devereux. Chicago: University of Chicago Press, 1980. (Originally published 1965)

Durkheim, Emile. *Les Règles de la méthode sociologique.* Paris: Alcan. Trans. W. D. Halls as *The Rules of the Sociological Method.* New York: Free Press, 1982. (Originally published 1901)

Edgerton, Robert N. *Sick Societies: Challenging the Myth of Primitive Harmony.* New York: Free Press, 1992.

Ehrenwald, J. *New Dimensions of Deep Analysis.* New York: Grune & Stratton, 1954.

Eisenbud, Jule. "The Dreams of Two Patients in Analysis as a Telepathic *Rêve à Deux.*" Pages 262–76 in *Basic Problems of Ethnopsychiatry*, ed. George Devereux, trans. Basia Miller Gulati and George Devereux. Chicago: University of Chicago Press, 1980. (Originally published 1970)

———. "Telepathy and the Problems of Psychoanalysis." *Psychoanalytic Quarterly* 15 (1946):32–37.

Ellenberger, Henri. *The Discovery of the Unconscious: The History and Evolution of Dynamic Psychology.* New York: Basic Books, 1970.

Ellman, Steven J. *Freud's Technique Papers: A Contemporary Perspective.* Northvale, N.J.: Aronson, 1991.

Erikson, Erik H. *Childhood and Society.* 2d ed. New York: Norton, 1965.

———. "The Dream Specimen of Psychoanalysis." *Journal of the American Psychoanalytic Association* 2 (1954):5–56. Reprinted in *A Way of Looking at Things: Selected Papers,* ed. Stephen Schlein. New York: Norton, 1987.

———. "Psychological Reality and Historical Actuality." Chap. 5 in *Insight and Responsibility.* New York: Norton, 1964.

Evans-Pritchard, E. E. *Witchcraft, Oracles and Magic among the Azande.* Abridged by Eva Gillies. Oxford: Clarendon, 1976. (Originally published 1937)

Fenichel, Otto. *The Psychoanalytic Theory of Neurosis.* New York: Norton, 1945.

Flanders, Sara, ed. *Dream Discourse Today.* New Library of Psychoanalysis. London: Routledge, 1993.

Foulkes, David. *Dreaming: A Cognitive Psychological Analysis.* Hillsdale, N.J.: Erlbaum, 1985.

———. *A Grammar of Dreams.* New York: Basic Books, 1978.

Freuchen, Peter. *Book of the Eskimos.* Cleveland: World, 1961.

Freud, Sigmund. *Briefe 1873–1939.* Ausgewählt und herausgegeben von Ernst L. Freud. Frankfurt am Main: Fischer, 1960.

———. "Bruchstück einer Hysterie-Analyse." Pages 161–286 in *Gesammelte Werke (Chronologisch Geordnet), Fünfter Band, Werke aus den Jahren 1904–1905.* London:

Imago, 1948. Trans. James Strachey, ed. Philip Rieff, and published as *Dora: An Analysis of a Case of Hysteria*. New York: Collier, Macmillan, 1963. (Originally published 1905)

———. 1887–1904. *The Complete Letters of Sigmund Freud to Wilhelm Fliess*. Trans. and ed. Jeffrey M. Masson. Cambridge, Mass.: Belknap, Harvard, 1985.

———. "Dreams and Telepathy." Pages 196–220 in S.E.18. (Originally published 1922)

———. *Five Lectures on Psychoanalysis*. Trans. James Strachey. New York: Norton, 1989. (Originally published 1910)

———. *Gesammelte Werke: Chronologisch Geordnet*. London: Imago, 1949. (Herein abbrveiated as G.W.)

———. *Letters of Sigmund Freud*. Ed. Ernst L. Freud. New York: Dover, 1992.

———. "New Introductory Lectures on Psycho-Analysis." In S.E. 22. (Originally published 1933)

———. *An Outline of Psychoanalysis*. New York: Norton, 1940.

———. "Psycho-analysis and Telepathy." Pages 175–195 in S.E. 18. (Originally published 1921)

———. "Recommendations to Physicians Practicing Psycho-analysis." In S.E. 12:111–20. (Originally published 1912)

———. "Some Additional Notes on Dream-Interpretation as a Whole: The Occult Significance of Dreams." Pages 135–140 in S.E. 19.

———. *Standard Edition of the Complete Psychological Works of Sigmund Freud*. London: Hogarth, 1953. (Customarily designated as S.E.)

———. *Die Traumdeutung*. Vienna: Deuticke, 1900. Reprinted as *Gesammelte Werke II/III*. London: Imago, 1948. Trans. (from 8th ed.) by James Strachey as *The Interpretation of Dreams*. New York: Avon, 1965.

———. "Über Coca." Pages 47–74 in *Cocaine Papers: Sigmund Freud*, ed. Robert Byck. New York: New American Library, 1975. (Originally published 1884)

———. "Über den Traum." Pages 643–703 in *Gesammelte Werke II/III, Werke aus den Jahren 1900–1901*, trans. James Strachey as "On Dreams." New York: Norton, 1952. (Originally published 1901)

———. *Das Unbehagen in der Kultur*. Trans. James Strachey as *Civilization and Its Discontents*. London: Imago, 1948. (Originally published 1930)

Freyd, Jennifer. *Betrayal Trauma: The Logic of Forgetting Childhood Abuse*. Cambridge, Mass.: Harvard University Press, 1996.

Fromm, Erich. *Escape from Freedom*. New York: Farrar & Rinehart, 1941.

———. *The Forgotten Language: An Introduction to the Understanding of Dreams, Fairy Tales, and Myths*. New York: Grove, 1951.

———. *Man for Himself*. New York: Rinehart, 1947.

Fuller, Peter. "Introduction." Pages 1–38 in Charles Rycroft, *Psychoanalysis and Beyond*, ed. Peter Fuller. Chicago: University of Chicago Press, 1986.

Gackenbach, Jayne, and Anees A. Sheikh, eds. *Dream Images: A Call to Mental Arms*. Amityville, N.Y.: Baywood, 1991.

Galatzer-Levy, Robert M., and Bertram J. Cohler. *The Essential Other: A Developmental Psychology of the Self*. New York: Basic Books, 1993.

Gallop, June. "Keys to Dora." Pages 200–20 in *In Dora's Case*, ed. Charles Bernheimer and Claire Kahane. New York: Columbia University Press, 1985.

Gartner, Richard B., ed. *Memories of Sexual Betrayal: Truth, Fantasy, Repression, and Dissociation.* Northvale, N.J.: Aronson, 1997.

Gay, Peter. *Freud: A Life for Our Time.* New York: Norton, 1988.

George, Marianne. "Dreams, Reality, and the Desire and Intent of Dreamers as Experienced by a Fieldworker." *Anthropology of Consciousness* 6, no. 3 (September 1995):17–33.

Gillison, Gillian. *Between Culture and Fantasy: A New Guinea Highlands Mythology.* Chicago: University of Chicago Press, 1993.

Gilman, Sander L. *The Case of Sigmund Freud.* Baltimore: Johns Hopkins University Press, 1993.

Glenn, Jules. "Freud's Adolescent Patients: Katharina, Dora and the 'Homosexual Woman.'" Pages 23–47 in *Freud and His Patients,* ed. Mark Kanzer and Jules Glenn. Northvale, N.J.: Aronson, 1993. (Originally published 1980)

———. "Freud, Dora, and the Maid: A Study of Counter-transference." *Journal of the American Psychoanalytic Association* 34, no. 3 (1986):591–606.

Goldberg, Arnold, ed. *The Future of Psychoanalysis.* New York: International Universities Press, 1983.

Gori, R. "Le Rêve n'existe pas." Pages 139–55 in *Le Bloc-Notes de la psychanalyse,* no. 15, "Freud, Le Rêve et son Interprétation." Geneva: Georg, 1998.

Graham, Laura. *Performing Dreams: Discourses of Immortality among the Xavante of Central Brazil.* Austin: University of Texas Press, 1995.

Greenson, Ralph R. "The Exceptional Position of the Dream in Psychoanalytic Practice." Pages 64–88 in *The Dream Discourse Today,* ed. Sara Flanders. London: Routledge, 1993. (Originally published 1970)

Grinstein, Alexander. *On Freud's Dreams.* Detroit: Wayne State University Press, 1968.

Grolnick, Simon. "The Relationship of Winnicott's Developmental Concept of the Transitional Object to Self and Object Constancy." Pages 107–134 in *Self and Object Constancy: Clinical and Theoretical Perspectives,* ed. Ruth F. Lax, Sheldon Bach, and Alexis Burland. New York: Guilford, 1986.

Grosso, Michael. "Inspiration, Mediumship, Surrealism: The Concept of Creative Dissociation." Pages 181–98 in *Broken Images, Broken Selves: Dissociative Narratives in Clinical Practice,* ed. Stanley Kripppner and Susan Marie Powers. New York: Brunner/Mazel.

Grünbaum, Adolf. *The Foundations of Psychoanalysis.* Berkeley: University of California Press, 1984.

Guntrip, Harry J. S. *Psychoanalytic Theory, Therapy, and the Self.* New York: Basic Books, 1971.

Hacking, Ian. *Rewriting the Soul: Multiple Personality and the Sciences of Memory.* Princeton, N.J.: Princeton University Press, 1995.

Hallowell, A. Irving. *Contributions to Anthropology: Selected Papers.* Chicago: University of Chicago Press, 1976.

———. "The Role of Dreams in Ojibwa Culture." Pages 449–74 in *Contributions to Anthropology: Selected Papers,* ed. A. Irving Hallowell. Chicago: University of Chicago Press, 1976. (Originally published 1966)

Harrelson, Walter. *Interpreting the Old Testament.* New York: Holt, Rinehart, & Winston, 1964.

Harris, Monford. *Studies in Jewish Dream Interpretation.* Northvale, N.J.: Aronson, 1994.

Hegeman, Elizabeth. "Reconstruction and the Psychoanalytic Tradition." Pages 149–77 in *Memories of Sexual Betrayal: Truth, Fantasy, Repression, and Dissociation,* ed. Richard B. Gartner. Northvale, N.J.: Aronson, 1997.

Herdt, Gilbert, ed. *Rituals of Manhood: Male Initiation in Papua New Guinea.* Berkeley: University of California Press, 1982.

———. *The Sambia: Ritual and Gender in New Guinea.* New York: Harcourt Brace Jovanovich, 1987.

Herdt, Gilbert, and Robert J. Stoller. *Intimate Communications: Erotics and the Study of Culture.* New York: Columbia University Press, 1990.

Hirsch, Samson Raphael. *Der Pentateuch übersezt und erlautert,* trans. Isaac Levy, 2d rev. ed. New York: Judaica Press, 1971. (Originally published 1867–1868)

Hirschmüller, Albrecht. *The Life and Work of Josef Breuer.* New York: New York University Press, 1978.

Hook, Sidney, ed. *Psychoanalysis, Scientific Method and Philosophy.* New York: New York University Press, 1959.

Hoopes, James. *Consciousness in New England: From Puritanism and Ideas to Psychoanalysis and Semiotic.* Baltimore: Johns Hopkins University Press, 1989.

Hopkins, James. "The Interpretation of Dreams." Pages 86–135 in *The Cambridge Companion to Freud,* ed. Jerome Neu. New York: Cambridge University Press, 1991.

Horney, Karen. *Feminine Psychology.* Ed. Harold Helman. New York: Norton, 1967.

Hughes, Charles. *Eskimo Boyhood: An Autobiography in Psychosocial Perspective.* Lexington: University of Kentucky Press, 1974.

Hughes, Judith M. *From Freud's Consulting Room.* Cambridge, Mass.: Harvard University Press, 1994.

Hume, David. *A Treatise of Human Nature.* New York: Dutton, 1939. (Originally published 1738)

Hunt, Harry T. *The Multiplicty of Dreams: Memory, Imagination, and Consciousness.* New Haven, Conn.: Yale University Press.

Hunter, Mic. *The Sexually Abused Male,* Vol. 2. Lexington, Mass.: Lexington, 1990.

Hyman, Stanley Edgar. *The Tangled Bank: Darwin, Marx, Frazer and Freud as Imaginative Writers.* New York: Atheneum, 1962.

Irwin, Lee. *The Dream Seekers: Native American Visionary Traditions of the Great Plains.* Norman: University of Oklahoma Press, 1994.

Jacobsen, Thorkild. *The Treasures of Darkness: A History of Mesopotamian Religion.* New Haven, Conn.: Yale University Press, 1976.

Jennings, Jerry L. "The Revival of Dora: Advances in Psychoanalytic Theory and Technique." *Journal of the American Psychoanalytic Association* 34, no. 3 (1986): 607–35.

Joas, Hans. *G. H. Mead: A Contemporary Re-examination of His Thought,* trans. Raymond Meyer. Cambridge: MIT Press, 1985. (Originally published 1980)

———. *Praktische Intersubjektivät: Die Entwicklung des Werkes von George Herbert Mead.* Frankfurt: Suhrkamp, 1980. Trans. Raymond Meyer as *G. H. Mead: A Contemporary Re-examination of His Thought.* Cambridge, Mass.: MIT Press, 1985.

Junod, Henri A. *The Life of a South African Tribe. Vol. 2: Mental Life.* New Hyde Park, N.Y.: University Press, 1962. (Originally published 1927)

Kafka, Helene. "Incest Survival, Memory Disruption, and Authenticity of the Self." Pages 113–27 in *Memories of Sexual Betrayal: Truth, Fantasy, Repression, and Dissociation,* ed. Richard B. Gartner. Northvale, N.J.: Aronson, 1997.

Kanzer, Mark. "Dora's Imagery: The Flight from the Burning House." Pages 72–82 in *Freud and His Patients*, ed. Mark Kanzer and Jules Glenn. Northvale, N.J.: Aronson, 1993. (Originally published 1980)

———. "Freud's 'Specimen Dream' in a Widening Context." Pages 241–54 in *The Future of Psychoanalysis*, ed. Arnold Goldberg. New York: International Universities Press, 1983.

Kanzer, Mark, and Jules Glenn, eds. *Freud and His Patients*. Northvale, N.J.: Aronson, 1993.

———. *Freud and His Self-Analysis*. Northvale, N.J.: Aronson, 1979.

Kaplan, Bert, ed. *Studying Personality Cross-Culturally*. Evanston, Ill.: Row, Peterson, 1961.

Katz, Joseph. "The Joseph Dreams Anew." *Psychoanalytic Review* 50, no. 2 (1963): 92–118.

Kelman, Harvey. "The Day Precipitate of Pharaoh's Dreams." *Psychoanalytic Quarterly* 55, no. 2 (1986):306–9.

Kenny, M. G. "Multiple Personality and Spirit Possession." *Psychiatry* 44 (1981): 337–58.

———. *The Passion of Ansel Bourne: Multiple Personality in American Culture*. Washington, D.C.: Smithsonian Institution Press, 1986.

Keyes, Daniel. *The Minds of Billy Milligan*. New York: Random House, 1981.

Kiell, Norman. *Freud without Hindsight: Reviews of His Work: 1893–1939*. Madison, Conn.: International Universities Press, 1988.

Klein, Dennis B. *Jewish Origins of the Psychoanalytic Movement*. Chicago: University of Chicago Press, 1981.

Kleinman, Arthur. "Culture and Clinical Reality: Commentary on Culture-bound Syndromes and International Disease Classification." *Culture, Medicine, and Psychiatry* 11 (1987):49–52.

———. *Writing at the Margin: Discourse between Anthropology and Medicine*. Berkeley: University of California Press, 1995.

Kohut, Heinz. *Self Psychology and the Humanities: Reflections on a New Psychoanalytic Approach*. Ed. Charles Strozier. New York: Norton, 1985.

Kracke, Waud. "Dreaming in Kagwahiv: Dream Beliefs and Their Psychic Uses in an Amazonian Indian Culture." Pages 119–71 in *Psychoanalytic Study of Society*, Vol. 8, ed. Werner Munsterberger, Aaron Esman, and L. Bryce Boyer. New Haven, Conn.: Yale University Press, 1979.

———. "Myths in Dreams, Thought in Images." Pages 31–54 in *Dreaming: Anthropological and Psychological Interpretations*, ed. Barbara Tedlock. New York: Cambridge University Press, 1987.

Krippner, Stanley. "Dissociation in Many Times and Places." Pages 3–40 in *Broken Images, Broken Selves: Dissociative Narratives in Clinical Practice*, ed. Stanley Krippner and Susan Marie Powers. New York: Brunner/Mazel, 1997.

———, ed. *Dreamtime and Dreamwork: Decoding the Language of the Night*. Los Angeles: Tarcher, 1990.

Krippner, Stanley, and Susan Marie Powers, eds. *Broken Images, Broken Selves: Dissociative Narratives in Clinical Practice*. New York: Brunner/Mazel, 1997.

Kris, Anton O. *Free Association: Method and Process*. New Haven, Conn.: Yale University Press, 1982.

LaBarre, Weston. *Muelos: A Stone Age Superstition about Sexuality.* New York: Columbia University Press, 1985.

Lacan, Jacques. *Ecrits: A Selection.* Trans. Alan Sheridan. New York: Norton, 1977.

———. "Intervention on Transference." Trans. Jacqueline Rose, pages 92–104 in *In Dora's Case,* ed. Charles Bernheimer and Claire Kahane. New York: Columbia University Press, 1985. (Originally published 1951)

———. "The Mirror Stage as Formative of the Function of the I as Revealed in Psychoanalytic Experience." Pages 1–7 in *Ecrits: A Selection,* trans. Alan Sheridan. New York: Norton, 1977.

Lalemant, Père, S.J. *Relations du Jésuites dans la Nouvelle France.* Quebec: [n.p.] 1858. (Originally published 1648)

Langs, Robert J. "The Misalliance Dimension in the Case of Dora." Pages 58–71 in *Freud and His Patients,* ed. Mark Kanzer and Jules Glenn. Northvale, N.J.: Aronson, 1993. (Originally published 1980)

Lantis, Margaret. *Eskimo Childhood and Interpersonal Relationships.* Seattle: University of Washington Press, 1960.

LaPlanche, J., and J. B. Pontalis. *Vocabulaire de la Psychanalyse.* Paris: Presses Universitaires de France, 1967. Trans. Donald Nicholson-Smith as *The Language of Psychoanalysis.* New York: Norton, 1973.

Lasky, Richard. "The Psychoanalytic Treatment of a Case of Multiple Personality." *Psychoanalytic Review* 65 (1978):355–80.

Lavie, Peretz. *The Enchanted World of Sleep.* New Haven, Conn.: Yale University Press, 1996.

Lax, Ruth F., Sheldon Bach, and J. Alexis Burland, eds. *Self and Object Constancy.* New York: Guilford, 1986.

Lerman, Hannah. *A Mote in Freud's Eye: From Psychoanalysis to the Psychology of Women.* New York: Springer, 1986.

Levin, Jerome D. *Theories of the Self.* Washington, D.C.: Hemisphere, 1992.

Levine, Donald N. *The Flight from Ambiguity.* Chicago: University of Chicago Press, 1985.

Lévy-Bruhl, Lucien. *Les Fonctions mentales dans les sociétés inférieures.* Paris: Alcan, 1910. Trans. Lilian A. Clare as *How Natives Think.* New York: Washington Square Press, 1966. (Originally published 1910)

———. *La Mentalité primitive.* Paris: Alcan, 1922. Trans. Lilian A. Clare as *Primitive Mentality.* Boston: Beacon, 1923.

Lewin, Karl Kay. "Dora Revisited." *Psychoanalytic Review* 60, no. 4 (Winter 1973–1974):519–32.

Lidz, Theodore, and Ruth Wilmanns Lidz. *Oedipus in the Stone Age.* Madison, Conn.: International Universities Press, 1989.

Lincoln, Jackson Stewart. *The Dream in Primitive Cultures.* New York: Johnson Reprint, 1970. (Originally published 1935)

Lippmann, Paul. "The Greatness and Limitations of Fromm's Thought: On Dreams." Pages 133–50 in *A Prophetic Analyst: Erich Fromm's Contribution,* ed. Mauricio Cortina and Michael Maccoby. Northvale, N.J.: Aronson, 1996.

Littlewood, Roland. *Reason and Necessity in the Specification of the Multiple Self.* Occasional paper #43. London: Royal Anthropological Institute of Great Britain and Ireland, 1996.

Ludwig, A. M., et al. "The Objective Study of a Multiple Personality, or Are Four Heads Better Than One?" *Archive of General Psychiatry* 26 (1972):298–310.

MacIntyre, Alasdair. *After Virtue*. 2d ed. Notre Dame, Ind.: University of Notre Dame Press, 1984.

———. *A Short History of Ethics*. New York: MacMillan, 1966.

Magid, Barry, ed. *Freud's Case Studies: Self-Psychological Perspectives*. Hillsdale, N.J.: Analytic Press, 1993.

Mahony, Patrick J. *Freud as a Writer*. New York: International Universities Press, 1982.

———. *Freud's Dora: A Psychoanalytic, Historical, and Textual Study*. New Haven, Conn.: Yale University Press, 1996.

———. *On Defining Freud's Discourse*. New Haven: Yale University Press, 1989.

———. "The Oral Tradition, Freud, and Psychoanalytic Writing." Pages 199–214 in *Freud: Appraisals and Reappraisals. Contributions to Freud Studies, Vol. 1*, ed. Paul Stepansky. Hillsdale, N.J.: Analytic Press, 1986.

———. "A Psychoanalytic Translation of Freud." Pages 24–47 in *Translating Freud*, ed. Darius Gray Ornston, Jr. New Haven, Conn.: Yale University Press, 1992.

Malinowski, Bronislaw. "Magic, Science, and Religion." Reprinted in *Magic, Science and Religion and Other Essays*, ed. Robert Redfield. New York: Doubleday Anchor, 1955. (Originally published 1925)

Marcus, Steven. "Freud and Dora: Story, History, Case History." Pages 56–91 in *In Dora's Case*, ed. Charles Bernheimer and Claire Kahane. New York: Columbia University Press, 1985.

Marcus, Paul, and Alan Rosenberg, eds. *Psychoanalytic Versions of the Human Condition and Clinical Practice*. New York: New York University Press, 1997.

Masson, Jeffrey Moussaieff, trans. and ed. *The Complete Letters of Sigmund Freud to Wilhelm Fliess, 1887–1904*. Cambridge, Mass.: Belknap, 1985.

Matthis, Iréne, and Imre Szecsödy, eds. *On Freud's Couch: Seven New Interpretations of Freud's Case Histories*. Northvale, N.J.: Aronson, 1998.

McCaffrey, Phillip. *Freud and Dora: The Artful Dream*. New Brunswick, N.J.: Rutgers University Press, 1984.

McDougall, Joyce. *The Many Faces of Eros*. New York: Norton, 1995.

———. *Théâtre du Je*. Paris: Gallimard, 1982. Translated as *Theaters of the Mind*. New York: Brunner/Mazel, 1991.

McGrath, William J. *Freud's Discovery of Psychoanalysis: The Politics of Hysteria*. Ithaca, N.Y.: Cornell University Press, 1986.

McKeon, Richard. *Freedom and History*. New York: Noonday, 1952.

Mead, George Herbert. "The Definition of the Psychical." *Decennial Publications of the University of Chicago*, 1st series, 3 (1903):77–112. Reprinted (pp. 25–59) in *Selected Writings of George Herbert Mead*, ed. Andrew J. Reck. Indianapolis: Bobbs-Merrill, 1964.

"The Mechanism of Social Consciousness." *Journal of Philosophy* 9 (1912):401–6. Reprinted (pp. 134–41) in *Selected Writings of George Herbert Mead*, ed. Andrew J. Reck. Indianapolis: Bobbs-Merrill, 1964.

———. *Mind, Self and Society*. Ed. Charles W. Morris. Chicago: University of Chicago Press, 1934.

———. "The Social Self." *Journal of Philosophy* 10 (1913):374–80. Reprinted (pp.

142–59) in *Selected Writings of George Herbert Mead,* ed. Andrew J. Reck. Indianapolis: Bobbs-Merrill, 1964.

Meigs, Anna. *Food, Sex, and Pollution: A New Guinea Religion.* New Brunswick, N.J.: Rutgers University Press, 1988.

Menahem, Ruth. *Joyce McDougall.* Paris: Presses Universitaires de France, 1997.

Mendelsohn, Roy M. *How Can Talking Help?* Northvale, N.J.: Aronson, 1992.

———. *The Manifest Dream and Its Use in Therapy.* Northvale, N.J.: Aronson, 1990.

Merkur, Dan. *Gnosis: An Esoteric Tradition of Mystical Visions and Unicorns.* Albany: State University of New York Press, 1993.

Métraux, Alfred. *Le Vaudou haïtien.* Paris: Gallimard, 1958. Translated as *Voodoo in Haiti.* New York: Schocken, 1972.

Miller, David L. *George Herbert Mead: Self, Language, and the World.* Austin: University of Texas Press, 1973.

Miller, David L., ed. *The Individual and the Social Self: Unpublished Work of George Herbert Mead.* Chicago: University of Chicago Press, 1982.

Mogollón, Linda Lane, and Barbara Shor. "Shared Dreaming: Joining Together in Dreamtime." Pages 252–60 in *Dreamtime and Dreamwork: Decoding the Language of the Night,* ed. Stanley Krippner. Los Angeles: Tarcher, 1990.

Moore, George Edward. *Principia Ethica.* Cambridge: Cambridge University Press, 1903.

Moore, Marianne. *Collected Poems.* New York: Macmillan, 1952.

Moser, Brian, and Donald Tayler. *The Cocaine Eaters.* New York: Taplinger, 1967.

Mullahy, Patrick. *The Beginnings of Modern American Psychiatry: The Ideas of Harry Stack Sullivan.* Boston: Houghton Mifflin, 1973. (Originally published 1970)

Munsterberger, Werner, Aaron Esman, and L. Bryce Boyer, eds. *Psychoanalytic Study of Society, Volume 8.* New Haven, Conn.: Yale University Press, 1979.

Murray, Stephen O. *American Gay.* Chicago: University of Chicago Press, 1996.

Muslin, Hyman, and Merton Gill. "Transference in the Dora Case." *Journal of the American Psychoanalytic Association* 26 (1978):311–28.

Nelson, Benjamin, ed. *Freud and the Twentieth Century.* New York: Meridian, 1957.

Neu, Jerome, ed. *The Cambridge Companion to Freud.* Cambridge University Press, 1991.

O'Flaherty, Wendy Doniger. *Dreams, Illusion and Other Realities.* Chicago: University of Chicago Press, 1984.

Oliner, Marion Michel. *Cultivating Freud's Garden in France.* Northvale, N.J.: Aronson, 1988.

Olson, David R. "Review of 'The Ethnography of Reading, edited by Jonathan Boyarin (University of California Press, 1993).'" *Contemporary Sociology* 23 (July 4, 1994):609–10.

Oppenheim, A. Leo. *The Interpretation of Dreams in the Ancient Near East.* Philadelphia: American Philosophical Society, 1956.

Oring, Elliot. "Victor Turner, Sigmund Freud, and the Return of the Repressed." *Ethos* 21, no. 3 (September 1993):273–94.

Ornstein, Paul H. "Did Freud Understand Dora?" Pages 31–86 in *Freud's Case Studies: Self-Psychological Perspectives,* ed. Barry Magid. Hillsdale, N.J.: Analytic Press, 1993.

Ornston, Darius Gray, Jr. "Improving Strachey's Freud." Pages 1–23 in *Translating*

Freud, ed. Darius Gray Ornston, Jr. New Haven, Conn.: Yale University Press, 1992a.

———. "Obstacles to Improving Strachey's Freud." Pages 191–222 in *Translating Freud*, ed. Darius Gray Ornston, Jr. New Haven, Conn.: Yale University Press, 1992b.

Ornston, Darius Gray, Jr., ed. *Translating Freud*. New Haven, Conn.: Yale University Press, 1992c.

Ostow, Mortimer, ed. *Judaism and Psychoanalysis*. New York: Ktav, 1982.

Parker, Sue Taylor, Robert W. Mitchell, and Maria L. Bocca, eds. *Self-Awareness in Animals and Humans: Developmental Perspectives*. New York: Cambridge University Press, 1994.

Pendergrast, Mark. *Victims of Memory: Incest Accusations and Shattered Lives*. Hinesburg, Vt.: Upper Access, 1995.

Polanyi, Michael. *Science, Faith and Society*. Chicago: University of Chicago Press, 1964.

Pontalis, J.-B. "Dream as an Object." Reprinted (pp. 108–21) in *The Dream Discourse Today*, ed. Sara Flanders. London: Routledge, 1993. (Originally published 1974)

———. *Entre le rêve et la doleur*. Paris: Gallimard, 1977. Trans. Catherine Cullen and Philip Cullen as *Beyond the Dream and Psychic Pain*. London: Hogarth, 1981.

Prince, Morton. *The Dissociation of a Personality*. New York: Longmans, 1908.

Radestock, P. *Schlaf und Traum*. Leipzig: (n.p.), 1878.

Radin, Paul. *Primitive Man as Philosopher*. New York: Dover, 1957. (Originally published 1927)

Ramas, Maria. "Freud's Dora; Dora's Hysteria." Pages 149–80 in *In Dora's Case*, ed. Charles Bernheimer and Claire Kahane. New York: Columbia University Press, 1985.

Rappoport, Angelo S. *Myth and Legend of Ancient Israel*. New York: Ktav, 1966. (Originally published 1928)

Rasmussen, Knud. *Report of the Fifth Thule Expedition, 1921–24*. Vol. 7, no. 1, *Intellectual Culture of the Iglulik Eskimos*. Copenhagen: Glydendalske Boghandel, Nordisk Forlag, 1929.

Rayner, Eric. *The Independent Mind in British Psychoanalysis*. Northvale, N.J.: Aronson, 1991.

Read, Kenneth E. *The High Valley*. New York: Scribner's, 1965.

———. *Return to the High Valley*. Berkeley: University of California Press, 1986.

Reck, Andrew J., ed. *Selected Writings of George Herbert Mead*. Indianapolis: Bobbs-Merrill, 1964.

Reiser, Morton F. *Memory in Mind and Brain: What Dream Imagery Reveals*. New York: Basic Books, 1990.

Ridington, Robin. *Trail to Heaven: Knowledge and Narrative in a Northern Native Community*. Iowa City: University of Iowa Press, 1988.

Rieff, Philip. *Freud: The Mind of the Moralist*. 3d ed. Chicago: University of Chicago Press, 1979. (Originally published 1959)

———. "Introduction." Pages 7–20 in *Dora: An Analysis of a Case of Hysteria*. New York: Collier Books, Macmillan, 1963.

Riesman, David. *The Lonely Crowd*. New Haven, Conn.: Yale University Press, 1950.

Rigaud, Odette Mennesson. "Appendix A: Notes on Two Marriages with Voudoun Loa." Pages 263–70 in *Divine Horsemen: The Voodoo Gods of Haiti*, ed. Maya Deren. New York: Chelsea House, 1970.

Roazan, Paul. *Freud and His Followers*. New York: Knopf, 1971.

———. *How Freud Worked: First-Hand Accounts of His Patients*. Northvale, N.J.: Aronson, 1995.

———. *Meeting Freud's Family*. Amherst: University of Massachusetts Press, 1993.

Rosenbaum, Max. "Anna O. (Bertha Pappenheim): Her History." Pages 1–25 in *Anna O: Fourteen Contemporary Reinterpretations*, ed. Max Rosenbaum and Melvin Mueoff. New York: Free Press, 1984.

Rosenbaum, Max, and Melvin Muroff, eds. *Anna O: Fourteen Contemporary Reinterpretations*. New York: Free Press, 1984.

Rosenzweig, Saul. *Freud, Jung and Hall the King-Maker: The Expedition to America (1909)*. St. Louis: Rana House Press, 1992.

Roth, Paul. "Self-Deception, Danger Situations, and the Clinical Role of Narratives in Roy Schafer's Psychoanalytic Theory." In *Psychoanalytic Versions of the Human Condition and Clinical Practice*, ed. Paul Marcus and Alan Rosenberg. New York: New York University Press, 1997.

Rycroft, Charles. *The Innocence of Dreams*. New York: Pantheon, 1979.

———. *Psychoanalysis and Beyond*. Ed. Peter Fuller. Chicago: University of Chicago Press, 1986.

———. "Why Freud and Jung Could Never Agree." Pages 59–61 in *Rycroft on Analysis and Creativity*. New York: New York University Press, 1992.

Sarna, Nahum N. *Understanding Genesis: The Heritage of Biblical Israel*. New York: Schocken, 1966.

Sayers, Janet. *The Mothers of Psychoanalysis: Helen Deutsch, Karen Horney, Anna Freud, Melanie Klein*. New York: Norton, 1991.

Scharff, Judith Savege, ed. *The Autonomous Self: The Work of John D. Sutherland*. Northvale, N.J.: Aronson, 1994.

Scharfman, Melvin A. "Further Reflections on Dora." Pages 48–57 in *Freud and His Patients*, ed. Mark Kanzer and Jules Glenn. Northvale, N.J.: Aronson, 1993. (Originally published 1980)

Schoenewolf, Gerald. *Jennifer and Her Selves*. New York: Fine, 1991.

Schreiber, Flora Rhea. *Sybil*. New York: Warner, 1973.

Schur, Max. *Freud: Living and Dying*. New York: International Universities Press, 1972.

———. "Some Additional 'Day Residues' of 'The Specimen Dream of Psychoanalysis.'" Pages 45–85 in *Psychoanalysis: A General Psychology: Essays in Honor of Heinz Hartmann*, ed. R. M. Loewenstein et al. New York: International Universities Press, 1966.

Singer, Milton B. "A Survey of Culture and Personality Theory and Research." Pages 9–92 in *Studying Personality Cross-Culturally*, ed. Bert Kaplan. Evanston, Ill.: Row, Peterson, 1961.

Sloane, Paul. *Psychoanalytic Understanding of the Dream*. Northvale, N.J.: Aronson, 1990.

Smith, David M. "An Athapaskan Way of Knowing: Chipewaya Ontology." *American Ethnologist* 25, no. 3 (1998):412–32.

Smith, Joseph H., and William Kerrigan, eds. *Pragmatism's Freud: The Moral Disposition of Psychoanalysis*. Baltimore: Johns Hopkins University Press, 1986.

Sophocles. *Oedipus the King*. (1) Trans. Peter D. Arnott. Arlington Heights, Ill.: Crofts Classics, 1960. (2) Trans. David Grene, in *The Complete Greek Tragedies: Vol. 3*, ed. David Grene and Richmond Lattimore. New York: Modern Library.

Spain, David H., ed. *Psychoanalytic Anthropology after Freud*. New York: Psyche, 1992.

Spence, Donald P. "When Interpretation Masquerades as Explanation." *Journal of the American Psychoanalytic Association* 34, no. 1 (1986):3–22.

Spiro, Melford E. *Oedipus in the Trobriands*. Chicago: University of Chicago Press, 1982.

Sprengnether, Madelon. "Enforcing Oedipus: Freud and Dora." Pages 254–76 in *In Dora's Case*, ed. Charles Bernheimer and Claire Kahane. New York: Columbia University Press, 1985.

Stanner, W. E. H. *The Dreaming*. Reprint series 1–214. Indianapolis: Bobbs-Merrill. (Originally published 1956)

States, Bert O. *Seeing in the Dark: Reflections on Dreams and Dreaming*. New Haven, Conn.: Yale University Press, 1997.

Stepansky, Paul E., ed. *Freud: Appraisals and Reappraisals*. Contributions to Freud Studies, vol. 1. Hillsdale, N.J.: Analytic Press, 1986.

Stern, Daniel N. *The Interpersonal World of the Infant: A View from Psychoanalysis and Developmental Psychology*. New York: Basic Books, 1985.

Sternberg, Meir. *The Poetics of Biblical Narrative*. Bloomington: Indiana University Press, 1987.

Sullivan, Harry Stack. *Clinical Studies in Psychiatry*. Ed. Helen Swick Perry et al. New York: Norton, 1956.

———. *Conceptions of Modern Psychiatry*. Washington: D.C.: William Alanson White Psychiatric Foundation, 1987.

Sulloway, Frank J. *Freud: Biologist of the Mind; Beyond the Psychoanalytic Legend*. Cambridge, Mass.: Harvard University Press, 1992.

Sutherland, John. *Fairbairn's Journey into the Interior*. London: Free Association Books, 1989.

Swales, Peter J. *Freud, Cocaine, and Sexual Chemistry: The role of cocaine in Freud's Conception of the Libido*. Privately printed, 1983a.

———. *Freud, Fliess, and Fratricide: The Role of Fliess in Freud's Conception of Paranoia*. Privately printed, 1982a.

———. *Freud, Martha Bernays, and the Language of Flowers: Masturbation, Cocaine, and the Inflation of Fantasy*. Privately printed, 1983b.

———. "Freud, Minna Bernays and the Conquest of Rome: New Light on the Origins of Psychoanalysis." *New American Review* (Spring/Summer 1982b):1–23.

Szaluta, Jacques. "Freud's Biblical Ego Ideals." *Psychohistory Review* 23, no. 1 (Fall 1994):17–46.

Tedlock, Barbara. *Dream, Myth, and Change*. Unpublished manuscript, 1993.

———, ed. *Dreaming: Anthropological and Psychological Interpretations*. New York: Cambridge University Press, 1987.

———. "Languages of Dreaming: Anthropological Approaches to the Study of Dreaming in Other Cultures." Pages 203–24 in *Dream Images: A Call to Mental Arms*, ed. Jayne Gackenbach and Anees A. Sheikh. Amityville, N.Y.: Baywood, 1991.

Thigpen, Corbett H., and Hervey M. Cleckley. *The Three Faces of Eve.* New York: McGraw-Hill, 1957.

Todes, Samuel J. "Knowledge and the Ego." In *Kant: A Collection of Critical Essays,* ed. R. P. Wolff. New York: Anchor, 1967.

Turner, Edith. *Experiencing Ritual: A New Interpretation of African Healing.* Philadelphia: University of Pennsylvania Press, 1992.

———. *The Spirit and the Drum.* Tucson: University of Arizona Press, 1987.

Turner, Victor. *Blazing the Trail: Way Marks in the Explanation of Symbols.* Ed. Edith Turner. Tucson: University of Arizona Press, 1992.

———. *The Drums of Affliction: A Study of Religious Processes among the Ndembu of Zambia.* Oxford: Oxford University Press, 1968.

———. "Encounter with Freud: The Making of a Comparative Cultural Symbologist. Pages 3–28 in *Blazing the Trail: Way Marks in the Explanation of Symbols,* ed. Edith Turner. Tucson: University of Arizona Press, 1992.

The Forest of Symbols: Aspects of Ndembu Ritual. Ithaca: Cornell University Press, 1967.

———. "Muchona the Hornet: Interpreter of Religion." Pages 131–50 in *The Forest of Symbols.* Ithaca, N.Y.: Cornell University Press, 1967. (Originally published 1959)

———. *The Ritual Process: Structure and Anti-Structure.* Ithaca: Cornell University Press, 1969.

———. "Symbols in Ndembu Culture." Pages 19–47 in *The Forest of Symbols.* Ithaca, N.Y.: Cornell University Press, 1967. (Originally published 1964)

van de Castle, Robert L. *Our Dreaming Mind.* New York; Ballantine, 1994.

van der Hart, Otto, Ruth Lierens, and Jean Goodwin. "A Sixteenth Century Case of Dissociative Identity Disorder." *Journal of Psychohistory* 24, no. 1 (Summer 1996):18–35.

von Grunebaum, G. E. "Introduction: The Cultural Function of the Dream as Illustrated by Classical Islam." Pages 3–22 in *The Dream and Human Societies,* ed. G. E. von Grunebaum and Roger Caillois. Berkeley: University of California Press, 1966.

von Grunebaum, G. E., and Roger Caillois, eds. *The Dream and Human Societies.* Berkeley: University of California Press, 1966.

Wallace, Anthony F. C. *The Death and Rebirth of the Seneca.* New York: Vintage, 1969.

———. "Dreams and the Wishes of the Soul: A Type of Psychoanalytic Theory among the Seventeenth Century Iroquois." *American Anthropologist* 60, no. 2 (April 1958), part 1:234–48.

Wautischer, Helmut, ed. "Dreaming and the Cognitive Revolution." Special issue of *Anthropology of Consciousness* 5, no. 3 (September 1994).

Wax, Murray L. "How Oedipus Falsifies Popper: Psychoanalysis as Normative Science." *Psychiatry* 46 (May 1983):95–105.

———. "How Secure Are Grünbaum's *Foundations?*" *International Journal of Psycho-Analysis* 76 (1995):547–56.

———. "Malinowski, Freud, and Oedipus." *International Review of Psycho-Analysis* 17 (1990):47–60.

———. "Method as Madness: Science, Hermeneutics and Art in Psychoanalysis." *Journal of the American Academy of Psychoanalysis* 23, no. 4 (1996):525–43.

————. "The Notions of Nature, Man, and Time of a Hunting People." *Southern Folklore Quarterly* 26, no. 3 (September 1962):175–86.

————. "On Dancing at Two Weddings: Should Psychoanalysis Espouse a Biomedical or Hermeneutic Paradigm?" *Child Analysis* 8 (June 1997):150–76.

Wax, Murray L., Rosalie H. Wax, and Robert V. Dumont, Jr. *Formal Education in an American Indian Community: Peer Society and the Failure of Minority Education.* Prospect Heights, Ill.: Waveland, 1989. (Originally published 1964)

Weber, Max. From *Max Weber: Essays in Sociology,* trans. and ed. H. H. Gerth and C. Wright Mills. New York: Oxford University Press, 1946.

Wilson, Diana de Armas. "Cervantes and the Night Visitors: Dream Work in the Cave of Montesinos." Pages 59–80 in *Quixotic Desire: Psychoanalytic Perspectives on Cervantes,* ed. Ruth Anthony El Saffar and Diana de Armas Wilson. Ithaca, N.Y.: Cornell University Press, 1993.

Winnicott, D. W. "C. G. Jung: Review of *Memories, Dreams, Reflections.*" In *Psychoanalytic Explorations.* Cambridge, Mass.: Harvard University Press, 1989. (Originally published 1964)

Woods, Ralph L., and Herbert B. Greenhouse, eds. *The New World of Dreaming.* New York: Macmillan, 1974.

Wright, Peggy A. "History of Dissociation in Western Psychology." Pages 41–60 in *Broken Images, Broken Selves: Dissociative Narratives in Clinical Practice,* ed. Stanley Krippner and Susan Marie Powers. New York: Brunner/Mazel, 1997.

Yeats, W. B. "He Wishes for the Cloths of Heaven." Pages 53–74 in *The Collected Poems of W. B. Yeats.* New York: Collier, 1989.

————. "Responsibilities." In *The Collected Poems of W. B. Yeats,* ed. Richard J. Finneran. New York: Collier, 1989.

Yerushalmi, Yosef Hayim. *Freud's Moses: Judaism Terminable and Interminable.* New Haven, Conn.: Yale University Press, 1991.

Young, Allan. *The Harmony of Illusions: Inventing Post-Traumatic Stress Disorder.* Princeton, N.J.: Princeton University Press, 1995.

Young-Bruehl, Elisabeth. *Anna Freud: A Biography.* New York: Summit, 1988.

Index

About the Author

Murray L. Wax has done anthropological fieldwork among the Oglala Sioux of Pine Ridge, South Dakota, the Cherokee of eastern Oklahoma, and other Native American peoples. He has published over a hundred essays in professional journals and a half dozen books or edited volumes on such topics as the schooling of Indian children; religion, magic, and worldview; the ethics of social research; and the epistemological foundations of psychoanalysis.

Wax's university training was interdisciplinary: Ph.D in sociology and anthropology, University of Chicago; M.A. in philosophy and linguistic analysis, University of Pennsylvania; B.S. in mathematics and physics, University of Chicago. He retired as a professor from Washington University, St. Louis. He has also served on the faculties of the Universities of Chicago; Illinois (Chicago); Kansas (Lawrence); Pennsylvania; St. Thomas (St. Paul, Minn.); Emory; and has taught at the St. Louis Psychoanalytic Institute.

From his early mathematical training, Wax's research instinct is to locate implicit axioms and to inquire about the consequences of replacing them with alternatives. In this book, the axiom of Western thought is that a dream is the private production of a neurologically based self, and thus it is to be understood via bioenergetics. The inquiry generates new perspectives not only on dreaming but also on the self and human group life.